INTEGRITY MATTERS

MEN OF HONOUR IN THE PUBLIC SQUARE
2ND EDITION

CEPHAS T. A. TUSHIMA

FOREWORD BY
YUSUFU TURAKI

INTEGRITY MATTERS: MEN OF HONOUR IN THE PUBLIC SQUARE, 2nd Edition

Copyright © 2017, 2013 Cephas T. A. Tushima. All rights reserved. Except for brief quotations in critical publications or reviews, no part of this book may be reproduced in any manner without prior written permission from the publisher.

Tushima, Cephas T. A.; Yusufu Turaki

Integrity Matters: Men of Honour in the Public Square / Cephas T. A. Tushima.

300p.

ISBN: 978-1-63360-066-9

1. Ethics. 2. Integrity. 3. Biographies 4. Christianity 5. Nigeria 6. America

Urban Press
P.O. Box 8882
Pittsburgh, PA 15221-0882

TO

My father Tushima John Anju, from whom I imbibed the sense of justice and equity.

ABOUT THE BOOK

Integrity Matters: Men of Honour in the Public Square contains short biographies of Christian men who have lived visibly public lives, and thus approaches ethical issues from a concrete (not theoretical) standpoint. These include the life stories of Engr. Rumberger, whose invention of the *Flex Ring* made the V-22 Osprey (a plane that takes off and lands as a helicopter but flies with the speed of a turboprop aircraft) possible; Dr. Dunn, who gives life to countless children through organ transplantation; Hon. Justice Ogebe, whose landmark judgments helped steer Nigeria's nascent democracy off the path of dictatorship and anarchy at the turn of the new millennium; Gen. Agwai, who defied all odds, not the least being falsely accused of coup plotting, to rise to the pinnacle of the Nigerian military and beyond; and Dr. Kolade, whose wise decision helped *Cadbury* Nigeria avert a dangerous World Bank debt trap in the dark days of the late 1980s.

The book has brought to the fore, among many other issues, the unparalleled significance of the family and good upbringing as prime factors for building virtuous societies. Similarly, the book has brought to light the often unnoticed impact of a truly Christian education on character formation.

The thrust of the book, as narrative, lies in "showing" how genuinely ethical lives are lived and how the life of virtue and integrity is still possible, even in the increasingly murky waters of public life. It likewise demonstrates the joys, satisfaction, and rewards that come with living with integrity in the public/market square, the challenges notwithstanding. While this book has popular readership in view, it will be a very good source for case studies in ethics classes.

ABOUT THE AUTHOR

Dr. Cephas T. A. Tushima studied at various times in University of Jos; Federal School of Surveying, Oyo; Jos ECWA Theological Seminary (JETS), Jos, Jerusalem University College (Jerusalem), and Westminster Theological Seminary (Philadelphia), where he obtained his PhD in Hermeneutics and Biblical Interpretation.

His ministry experience of over twenty-five years includes youth and student ministries, church planting, children's pastor, parish pastor, evangelistic campaigns, and Bible expositor and conference speaker (locally and internationally). He is a member of many professional associations, and has served on the executive of several of them at different times. He is currently the president of the Association of Theological Institutions of Nigeria (ATIN) and the President of the non-profit corporation, Hesed Resource and Development Foundation.

Dr. Tushima is an Associate Professor of Biblical Studies and currently serves the Academic Dean of JETS. He served as an adjunct professor at Eastern University, St. Davids, USA (2009-2015). Presently, he is a Research Fellow at University of South Africa, Pretoria and Research Associate at Stellenbosch University, South Africa. Dr. Tushima is also a Langham Scholar. His published works include *The Fate of Saul's Progeny in the Reign of David*; *Integrity Matters: Men of Honour in the Public Square*, and several articles in peer review journals. He is also a contributor to *Mission as Ministry of Reconciliation*, *Baker Illustrated Bible Dictionary*, and the *African Study Bible*. For the 2016/17 academic year, Dr. Tushima is a Fulbright Scholar-in-Residence at Geneva College, Beaver Falls, PA.

ENDORSEMENTS

Dr. Tushima has put together an excellent collection of essays from individual Christians, both in the United States and in Nigeria, who have sought to "live out" their Christian commitments in a variety of fields which are normally regarded as "secular." I commend this book to anyone interested in understanding how political and scientific and other leaders shaped their lives so as to testify to the grace of Jesus Christ.

—*Dr. Samuel Logan, International Director, The World Reformed Fellowship*

Dr. Tushima has taken us again to the Hebrew 11 country, this time from a different landscape and time scale. In a breathtaking style, he picks on names that we know so well, and takes us on a journey to their roots, and the fibre of their faith that we do not know as well. One thing stands out: heroes of faith do not emerge from battle-free zones, but have their fair share of the odds that are the native air of fallen humanity. What marks them out is how, by share tenacity of faith, they battled against the odds, standing firm where many have fallen, and ready to pay the high price of integrity. Humanity may put them in the docks - and they are men, not angels — but from these untold stories, heaven's label on most of them may well be "of whom the world was not worthy" (Heb 11:38). A huge depth of gratitude is due to Dr. Tushima for reminding us that integrity is still real and relevant for time and eternity. Disciples indeed!

—*Archbishop Emmanuel Egbunu, Lokoja Province, Church of Nigeria (Anglican Communion)*

Dr. Tushima's book is a timely call to arms against the perfidious moral degeneration that has gripped Nigeria and the World. We erroneously celebrate the notion that what benefits us or our society is ethically normal; an extreme form of cultural relativism where the dividing line between right and wrong has almost disappeared. The book provides a moral compass by seeking out islands of integrity in the sea of putrid corruption. Each of the role models exemplifies an exegesis of normal ordinary Christians making difficult moral choices in their leadership positions in the public sphere. Each of the icons is presented as a sensitive Christian acutely aware of the pull of Christianity to individual moral responsibility whether in the private or the public square. I strongly recommend this book to all those who have lost hope in our leaders, and are seeking new role models. The book is the affirmation that the Christian path leads to the emergence of leaders whom we can trust and who can be trusted to lead; leaders whose lives can bear close examination; and leaders who have mastered their inner impulses and freed themselves to committed public service.

—*Prof. (Amb.) Iyorwuese Hagher, Executive Director, African Leadership Institute and Pro-Chancellor Afe Babalola University*

TABLE OF CONTENTS

About the Book — iv
About the Author — v
Endorsements — vi

Table of Contents

Foreword — xi
A Word From My Publisher — xiii
Preface - Second Edition — xvii
Preface - First Edition — xix

Chapter 1   At Your Command: — 1
Gen. Martin Luther Agwai

Chapter 2   The Faithful Servant: — 30
Bulus Dogara Amishe

Chapter 3   Refined by the Refiner's Fire: — 45
Prof. Ishaya Audu

Chapter 4   The Teacher of Nations: — 63
Prof. Adamu Baike

Chapter 5   That They Might Live: — 86
Dr. Stephen Dunn

Chapter 6   A Prophet amongst Us: — 104
Evang. Paul Gindiri

Chapter 7   The Faithful Steward: — 126
Dr. David Tor Iordaah

Chapter 8   The Pacesetter: — 142
Engr. Dr. Ezekiel Izuogu

Chapter 9	The Leader's Sceptre Shall not Depart: Dr. Christopher Kolade	157
Chapter 10	The Prudent Manager: Mr. Jonathan Onigbinde	174
Chapter 11	On the Judgment Seat: Hon. Justice James O. Ogebe	188
Chapter 12	Giving Ideas Wings to Fly: Engr. William Rumberger	206
Chapter 13	Contending for the Faith: Engr. Samuel S. L. Salifu	226
Chapter 14	A Light for the Seas: Engr. John Ykema	248
Postscript	Unifying Themes and Motifs	265
Endnotes		275
Contact the Author		277

FOREWORD

Integrity Matters is an exciting, inspiring and a very simple book to read. I could hardly put it down; I read it through at two sittings. What is so interesting about this book that kept pushing me to read it all within a short time is that out of the 14 interviewed, 10 are people I know very well and have had intimate interactions with on serious Christian issues, life and ministry. Reading this book has helped me to appreciate their lives and commitment to Jesus Christ and the Word of God even more. Some of them were my spiritual mentors, and the others my fellow yoked-brothers in the service of Christ and the Church.

This book has great value especially for young people who want to develop a life of integrity, a disciplined life-style, a godly life and a formation of a spiritual and moral character and quality as these men did in their youthful days and have also withstood all odds by remaining steadfast and true to Jesus Christ and the Word of God. Secondly, this book has great value for Christian parents and Christian homes on how to raise Godly children who would grow up with Christ as the centre of their life as these men of God were raised up by their godly parents and in good Christian homes. Thirdly, the lives of these men of integrity are models of integrity for all Christian professionals to emulate. These lives represent a wide range of professions: the army, business, missions, academics, law, engineering, civil service, teaching and parenting. Because of their Christian up-bringing, commitment to Jesus Christ and the Word of God and a progressive cultivated and discipline Christian life-style, they became the examples and models of integrity.

Dr. Cephas T. A. Tushima has demonstrated his gift of drawing out of people their indwelling essential moral virtues that attest, promote and confirm the incomparable Christian virtue of integrity which is grossly lacking in our day. He could not have done better by elevating the central message of this book above all else in Christian life, that ***integrity matters*** most. On this note, I highly recommend this book as a text book for spiritual formation, character and spiritual development for young people, professionals and parents.

Yusufu Turaki, Ph.D.
Professor of Theology and Social Ethics
Director, Centre for the Study of Religion, Church and Society
Jos ECWA Theological Seminary, Jos, Nigeria

A WORD FROM MY PUBLISHER

I congratulate Dr. Cephas Tushima, my newest Nigerian friend and associate, on his work that chronicles practical examples from modern life of men who successfully meshed their faith and life purpose. The stories in this book are not just of men who believed the correct doctrine, they also found ways to apply that doctrine to everyday life. Their worldview was not one of escapism or isolation, but rather their vision was to serve their generation in practical ways, as it was said of King David: "Now when David had served God's purpose in his own generation, he fell asleep" (Acts 13:36).

The Church has engaged in a debate almost since its inception of how involved believers are to be in society at large. The monastic movement concluded that the best thing for some believers to do was withdraw to pray and perform acts of service far away from the eyes of the world. Then there were others who went in the opposite direction, becoming so involved in the world that they served its needs and eventually lost their distinctive identify, becoming like the salt that Jesus described: ""You are the salt of the earth. But if the salt loses its saltiness, how can it be made salty again? It is no longer good for anything, except to be thrown out and trampled underfoot" (Matthew 5:13).

It seems to me that there are two biblical models for those who fulfilled the prayer that Jesus prayed long before He prayed it in John 17:15-18: "My prayer is not that you take them out of the world but that you protect them from the evil one. They are not of the world, even as I am not of it. Sanctify them by the truth; your word is truth. As you sent me into the world, I have sent them into the world."

Those two men were Joseph and Daniel. Joseph served Pharaoh with distinction and Daniel served generations of Babylonian leaders. Both men faced their trials and temptations, and both men distinguished themselves not only through admirable public service, but almost superhuman integrity. It was written of Daniel, "At this, the administrators and the satraps tried to find grounds for charges against Daniel in his conduct of government affairs, but they were unable to do so. They could find no corruption in him, because he was trustworthy and neither corrupt nor negligent" (Daniel 6:4).

It seems that the men described in this book have followed in the traditions of Joseph and Daniel. These modern Daniels and Josephs were and are an answer to Jesus' prayer, and they are a testimony to us that excellence in public life and integrity in our walk with the Lord are possible. Their salt remained salty and their witness was not tarnished by tawdry behavior. If they did it, so can we and all the generations that are to follow.

Therefore, I urge you to read this book with one idea in mind, and that is to have your name included in subsequent books that describe men (and women) of excellence, purpose, and virtue. Read not just to be entertained or to learn, but read and be challenged to follow in the footsteps of the giants whose storied are told in Integrity Matters. The world needs to hear the gospel preached, but they also need to see models of what is being preached. The world needs to see that Christianity has ideals along with men (and women) who believe those ideals are possible to live out, by God's grace, in every area of God's creation. Thank you again, Dr. Tushima, for collecting stories and testimonies that will help us find the way as we attempt to walk the path of faith and purpose, and find an expression of both in the work that God has assigned us to do.

>Dr. John W. Stanko
>Publisher, Urban Press
>Pittsburgh, Pennsylvania USA

PREFACE TO THE SECOND EDITION

This second edition is, first of all, a response to the need to make this book available to a wider readership. The first edition was more of self-printed work than an actual publication. Thus, it was limited in circulation (mostly in Nigeria). Secondly, as with any publication, there were typos and glaring mistakes in the first edition. So , when the opportunity came to re-issue the book, it became pertinent to make corrections as needed. Thirdly, there are occasional significant changes in the life or work situations of a couple of the people featured in the book (e.g., John Ykema and Stephen Dunn). These needed additions have been captured in the present edition.

Aside from the above issues, the material is largely the same. The cover page has been redesigned, in response to feedback received on the previous cover page. The goal of the book remains the same, primarily to provide examples of people striving to maintain ethical standards in their daily life as responsible citizens and ambassadors of Christ. In other words, the book approaches ethics from a concrete standpoint rather than a theoretical one.

There are two major things I would like the reader to keep in mind. First, our world has changed considerably within the last quarter century. Questions are being raised as to the validity of any universal ethical discussions. This is not the right forum to engage in dialogue about the relativity or absolutism of ethical requirements. I wish to merely state here that this book assumes the validity of ethical universals in the mode of Kantian categorical imperatives, but with the biblical text as its derivative source. Second, notwithstanding the above assumption, I acknowledge that the understanding and implementation of ethical requirements are influenced by contextual factors. Thus, readers will do well to keep both of these factors in good tension as they read the book.

Furthermore, I have tried to eliminate the footnoting systemto avoid distractions and the make the reading smoother. Many of the footnotes have been converted into parenthetical notes in the main text. A few have been retained as endnotes.

As indicated in the preface to the first edition, this book has a popular audience in view. However, its depth of coverage will make it a good source for case studies in ethical discussions (or even courses) in such areas as cultural studies, international business, and human right and justice studies.

All the former acknowledgements and attributions in the first edition are hereby fully adopted. I wish to express my gratitude to the Bureau of Educational and Cultural Affairs of the US States Department, the Council for International Exchange of Scholars, and Geneva College for the opportunity accorded me to be a Fulbright scholar this year, which made the revision of this book possible. I am also additionally thankful to my sister, Sandy Ykema, for helping with some of the proofreading. I am also indebted to my publisher, John Stanko, for his assistance, creativity, and hard work, without which this second edition would not have been possible.

    Cephas T. A. Tushima, Ph. D.
    Geneva College
    Beaver Falls, PA, USA
    May 2017

PREFACE TO THE FIRST EDITION

When I returned to Nigeria after eight-and-half years of sojourn in the United States of America, I was shocked at the level of moral and ethical decay in our society. Perhaps the many years of being away had pulled off (even if partially) the native lenses through which I perceived the world around me, so that I was now looking at things with the detachment of a semi-outsider and was, therefore, seeing things the way I may not have seen otherwise. It is also possible that with a sensitive conscience, I would still have been scandalized even if I had not lived overseas. However, the re-entry reverse culture shock I was experiencing had accentuated the moral revulsion I was experiencing towards the ethical degeneracy of our national polity.

One thing that I noticed immediately was the unprecedented number of public office holders who were professing to be Christians (even born again, many claiming to be Spirit-filled, with the accompanying evidence of speaking in tongues; and not a few were deacons, elders, or even pastors in their churches). What was equally manifest was the palpable want of correspondence between their talk and their walks. As I pondered this emergent neo-Christianity, my mind could not help but go back to yesteryears, when there were fewer people professing to be believers in Christ in the public arena. Though small in number, the impact of the lives of these saints was so visible that they truly were the biblical city on a hill that could not be hidden. The inspirational aftereffect of their lives was that they became role models for the teeming generations of younger Christians, many of whom did not know these older publicly visible Christians at the personal level. It is in the light of this that I became troubled at the emergent face of the new Christianity in the land, which portends a bleak future if things should continue on the same trajectory.

My aspiration to raise a ray of hope for the future birthed the project that has resulted in the present book, *Integrity Matters: Men of Honour in the Public Square*. My desire was to capture the life stories of some of these remarkable Christians who live or lived visibly public lives with integrity, and bequeath them in a fixed form as a legacy to present and future generations of Christians, both within and outside Nigeria, as patterns for Christian living and engagement with society. I therefore crisscrossed Nigeria interviewing these people or, in the cases of those who have been called to glory, those who knew them well. From these interviews, I have crafted the public biographies of these great Christian gentlemen. Those whose testimonies have been included in this volume are Gen. Martin Luther Agwai, Mr. Bulus Dogara Amise, Prof. Ishaya Audu, Prof. Adamu Baike, Evang. Paul Gindiri, Dr. David Tor Iordaah, Engr. Ezekiel Izuogu, Dr. Christopher Kolade, Mr. Jonathan Onigbinde, Hon. Justice James O. Ogebe, and Engr. Samuel S. L. Salifu. The listing is alphabetical, ordered by surname.

In view of the universal nature of the body of Christ, I also requested a few Christians of high repute in the United States to contribute their stories to this volume. Three of these, namely, Dr. Stephen Dunn, Engr. William Rumberger, and Engr. John Ykema, obliged me. Their testimonies, which they wrote in their own words, are herein included.

In our contemporary sensitivity for gender inclusiveness, I am not unaware that not a few people will be alarmed that the book has focused exclusively on men. This is not an oversight. My initial intention was for it to consist of the testimonies of both men and women. However, it was neither easy to gain access to women of high status nor to get them to tell their stories. I realized that just as courtship in the past consisted in a delicate art of wooing, it would take a longer time to woo the women of "timber and calibre" (to borrow from Chief Mbadiwe's phrase that has become a Nigeria catch phrase for people of substance and high status in society) to open up and share their stories. I then decided not to delay the release of the present volume. However, as it goes out, work on its sequel, *Women of Honour in the Public Square*, will commence immediately. It is my sincere hope that through this volume, and its anticipated sequel, we shall be addressing our ethical quandary in concrete forms, not just in abstract theories. Enjoy the reading.

I am deeply indebted to the men of honour, whose stories are featured in this book. Most of them did not know me previously, but were willing to take me into confidence and open up their homes and lives to me. Without their cooperation, this project would not have been possible. I am equally thankful to my American friends, who also contributed their testimonies to this volume. I know it was quite a strain on their already busy schedules, but I am glad they did. I must mention my friend of nearly three decades, the Reverend Gideon Para-Mallam, the African Regional Secretary of the **International Fellowship of Evangelical Students (IFES)**, who linked me up with a number of these men. My appreciation also goes to my team of research assistants, Mrs. Uwani Ulegede, Pastor Ahywani Akanet, Ngutor Anga, and Sesugh Guusu, who worked hard in transcribing these stories from audio to written form to make it easier for me to turn the interviews into written stories. I wish to also express my gratitude to my proofreader, Henry Whitney, and my editor, Dr.

Paul Todd, for their thorough work and support. While I appreciate their contributions, I am solely responsible for any errors that may still exist in the book. This appreciation would not be complete without the mention of my family (my wife Nguhemen, and my daughters Salome and Deborah) for their love, encouragement, and support.

    Cephas T. A. Tushima, Ph.D.
    Jos, Nigeria
    May 2013

CHAPTER ONE

AT YOUR COMMAND

GEN. MARTIN LUTHER AGWAI

THE EARLY YEARS

In his childhood, Martin Luther Agwai used to think his name was rather strange. When he was growing up in the village in those days, it was more common than not to find children having Jaba and Hausa names, even if they were biblical ones such as Iliya (Elijah) and Bulus (Paul). Nobody had completely foreign names, like he did, and at one point he contemplated changing his name. He summoned up courage one day and asked his parents why he had been given such strange names. In response, his father explained that the young Martin Luther had been born during the former's student days at the Kagoro Teachers' College (an SIM[1] school), at the particular time they were studying the life of Martin Luther, the reformer, and in November, the month in which the reformer had been born; he had therefore decided to name him after the reformer. This simple explanation satisfied the curiosity of the youngster. Martin Luther was further delighted as he grew up and read about Martin Luther King, Jr., and his work in the civil rights movement in the United States, and that others who had borne this name have had a great impact on their societies. From this time on, he not only accepted his name but also took pride in it.

Martin's earlier life was characterized by frequent relocation of his family, which adversely affected his early education. He was born on November 8, 1948, to Mallam Agwai Anji and Mallama Shera Kyau Agwai, who both hail from Gidan Mana village in Jabaland, Kaduna State. His father had trained at Kagoro to be a teacher, and was initially employed to teach at the SIM primary school, Kurmin Musa. He worked there briefly before deciding to join the police force. After his police training, he was posted to Jos, and he moved his wife, and his children, which included Martin (who was four years old at the time) to Jos. While in Jos, Martin's father brought him to be enrolled in the Native Authority (N. A.) Primary School, which is near the local government office complex that is close to the palace of the paramount ruler of Jos, the Gbom Gwong Jos. In those days, for children to be enrolled in a primary school, they had to place their right hands over their heads and be able to touch their left ears. That is possible for a child who is around eight years of age. Even though Martin Luther's right hand could not touch his left ear, he was allowed to start school in 1955.

The general recalls that at that time only two of the pupils in his class were Christians; the rest of the students were Muslims, as the school was located by a Muslim quarter. During the Islamic and Arabic studies class period, the teacher would always say something like, "Christians *baya*" (roughly translated "Christians go to the back"). The two of them would leave their seats and move to the back of the class. They were allowed to be present in the class, but were not compelled to participate in the Koranic recitations or any of the rituals, and they were also never asked any questions. However, being allowed to stay in the class helped him, as a person, to have an understanding of the basic tenets of Islam, which in years to come helped him forge good relations with Muslims, even though he is a committed Christian.

By August of 1955, Martin Luther's father was transferred to Kafanchan. Because in those days the school year ran from January to December, Martin had not yet completed primary one when the family had to move again. At Kafanchan, there was no room for him to continue with school, and since it was in the middle of the school year he spent the rest of 1955 at home and was enrolled in primary one again in 1956. Then in October 1956, his father was transferred back to Jos, and the family had to move once more. Thus, again he could not complete primary one. When the family went home to Jabaland for the Christmas Holiday of 1956, his father decided that it was better for Martin to stay home with the latter's grandmother so he would be able to go to school.

The nearest school to his village was a Native Authority (N. A., which is the equivalence of what is nowadays called Local Government Authority, L.G.A.).) school at Jaban Kogo. That was where Martin did his primary two. He never liked the school, however, so he appealed to his father to take him to the SIM school, the school at which his father had taught briefly before joining the police force. His father obliged him. Even back then, mission schools were known to have higher academic standards than the N. A. schools. Thus, it was common that someone transferring from an N. A. school to a mission school would at best be asked to repeat the class he had completed at his previous school. However, because the school knew his father, Martin was allowed to enter the SIM school at primary three. The first term examination provided him with the opportunity to prove his mettle, and he did not disappoint the school headmaster, who had admitted him to primary three against conventional wisdom—he took third position in his class, to the delight of his father also.

The SIM school at Kurmin Musa, as at that time, was a transfer school; which means that it was a junior primary school; at the end of primary four, the pupils had to take an entrance examination to transfer to a senior primary school. Martin's class was the one with which a full-fledged primary school would be started at Kurmin Musa. Since there were other transfer schools whose pupils were also seeking admission into the senior primary school, admission was not automatic, even for those who were already at Kurmin Musa. Martin, along with his mates, took the entrance examination into the new senior primary school at the SIM primary school in Kurmin Musa. He was one of the fortunate ones who passed the examinations and secured admission. Thus, he proceeded to primary five and completed his primary education at the end of 1962.

Upon the completion of his primary school education, he went on to the then Provincial Secondary School, Zaria (it is now called Alhudahuda College) in 1963, and graduated from there in 1967. The future before him at this point was bright: he had many job opportunities. He decided to pick up a job with the state Lands and Survey Department. He, in company of three other colleagues from Kaduna State (the old North Central State), was then sent in 1968 to the Federal School of Surveying, Oyo, for the basic course in land surveying. He completed his course in land surveying, returned, and resumed work in Kaduna in 1969.

Providence has its way of keeping its appointment with one, no matter how long the intervening time period may take. General Agwai recalls that in his younger years, when he used to spend his holidays from school with his parents (who were living in the police barracks at the time), he and his peers would always speak of pursuing careers in the uniformed forces. Initially they all thought they would become policemen, largely because there used to be football matches between the police and the prison wardens, which the police always won. This made them think that policemen were superior to prison wardens. The Nigerian Army was not deployed in the Jos area but used to come to Bukuru, near Jos, for their annual bush camp. When it did so, Martin Luther and his peers again watched the football matches that took place between the army and the police. This time it was the army that would defeat the police in football contests, and their interest accordingly shifted from the police force to the army.

As Martin was completing his secondary school education, he applied to sit for the entrance examination into the Nigeria Defence Academy (NDA), hoping to join the army. However, he had by then taken the survey job and left for survey school, so he did not receive the notice of the time and place of the NDA examination. Several reasons accounted for this. Firstly, by this time, the Nigerian Civil War had broken out, and his mother, like many mothers at the time, did not want her son to die in the war, so she made sure he was not informed of the scheduled NDA examination. Secondly, communication back then was very tortuous.

After he graduated from survey school, most of his survey job assignments were in mining surveys, which were often in the wild countryside. One fateful day, as they were returning from one of such assignments, they were waylaid by a horde of baboons. The thought came to him that had he been in the uniformed forces, he would have had a gun with which to defend himself. Upon his return from this trip, he wrote a letter to the One Mechanized Division of the Army, Kaduna, indicating his interest in the Army and giving his academic qualifications. The Army One Division replied to his letter, pointing out that with his qualifications, he should not enlist into the Army as a recruit, but he should instead go through the Nigeria Defence Academy (NDA), in order to come into the force as an officer. They also sent him an NDA form. He promptly completed and returned it and eventually took the examination for admission into the NDA.

Meanwhile, recruitment into the police was going on at the time. Martin went for the interview and was enlisted. He quit his survey job, believing that that was not the place he would want to spend the rest of his life, and if that were the case, the sooner he left the better: he knew that the longer he lingered in the job, the harder it would be for him to leave. He moved to the Police College, Kaduna for his training. At their recruitment, they were told that they would be sent to the Cadet Inspectors' Course in Lagos, but after one month had passed they were still in Kaduna. It was while they lingered in Kaduna that news filtered to him that he had passed the entrance examination into NDA, which he had written before coming to the Police College, and that the weeklong interview was to be held the following week. After pondering the issue, he went to the Police College commandant to request that he be given one week leave to enable him to attend the NDA interview. The response from the commandant was predictable: the police would not play second fiddle, and he had to choose either to stay or to quit the police and go for the NDA interview. Martin Luther wasted no time in writing his resignation letter, which he turned in on a Friday and left the college to get ready for the interview on the following Monday.

When he got to his cousin's house in town, he had the opportunity to take a look at the *New Nigeria* newspaper, in which the list of those who had passed the examinations had been published. He got to know that about 400 of them had been invited for the interview but only sixty would be admitted into the NDA. At this, fear gripped him hard. He considered the odds: if he were not successful, what would become of him? For a moment he considered going back to the Police College with his tail between his legs to beg to be taken back. He is not certain whether it was because he was too proud to eat humble pie or due to sheer guts, but he chose to damn the consequences and plunge ahead with the pursuit of the passion of his life—becoming a soldier. He trotted fearlessly into the unknown.

At the end of the weeklong interview, they were required to submit a contact address. Recalling what had happened to the notice from the NDA a couple of years earlier, Martin was not going to allow history to repeat itself—he would not give his parents' address. Before heading home to his parents in Jos, he gave the address of his spiritual mother, Ms Vera Batke, who was at this time at the SIM headquarters in Jos. It was Ms Batke who had earlier on led Martin Luther to a personal saving faith in Christ Jesus. Ms Batke later married Rev. Crouch, who had been at one time the SIM—Nigeria director. One day, while Martin was not at home, Ms Batke came looking for him in the police barracks in Jos, where he lived with his parents. She left a message that he should come to see her whenever he returned home. Upon getting the message, he quickly rushed to see her. When he arrived at her office at the SIM headquarters, she handed him a telegram that had come in for him. Upon opening it, he discovered to his delight that he had been admitted into the NDA. The telegram gave all the details of when they were to report and how to obtain a travel pass at the railway station.

Martin Luther was now set to go to the NDA. His parents could not stop him now. They were at a dead end, so to speak: he had left surveying; he had also left the police college, and he had just been sitting at home. As they would rather have him do something than nothing, they had to let him go. That was in 1970. Promptly, this wannabe soldier left Jos and headed to Kaduna at the appointed time. Fifty-nine other young men had also undertaken their several journeys to report for training at the NDA. The training at the NDA was designed at the time to last for three years. However, because of the civil war, it was shortened to two-and-half years. All the cadets were together for eighteen months for the combined military training for all the services (Army, Navy and Air Force), at the end of which each of the cadets left for their service specific training for the remaining year. Martin performed credibly well during both segments of the training programme at the NDA. We will return to this theme later.

NOTABLE INFLUENCES UPON HIS LIFE

God in his providence had placed different people in the life path of the general to bring the right influences to bear on his formation. First and foremost were his parents. His father, being both a teacher and a policeman, had instilled in him the scruples of discipline, honesty, and hard work. From his mother, he had imbibed the virtues of love and respect for others, regardless of who they were. These lessons were well taught because along the way, Martin's father had backslidden in his Christian commitment and had taken a second wife, who was about the same age as his first two daughters from his first wife. Thus, these daughters used to consider themselves equals with their step-mother and would not give her the respect due a step-mother, but their mother would have none of that. Her reasoning was that the age of their father's new wife notwithstanding, she was their father's wife, and the way they treated her reflected on how they esteemed their father. Their acceptance of their mother's instruction brought such harmony in the family that, to this day, there is no division between Martin's six siblings from his mother and the three from his step-mother.

Besides, when he was in secondary school in Zaria, Martin served twice in the executive committee of the Fellowship of Christian Students (FCS): First as the general secretary when he was in form four, and, secondly, as the president in his final year in the school. These positions offered opportunities to be trained and to meet older Christian people (like Mr. Reuben Ariko, who at the time was the FCS traveling secretary, and later became the General Secretary of the FCS), whose lives had great influence on his character formation. Additionally, the committee training programmes and other conferences organized by the FCS provided avenues of meeting with Christian peers from other schools. Many of these people have been lifelong friends. All these godly influences helped galvanize in him the thought of striving constantly to be Christ's true ambassador at all times and wherever he may find himself.

The power of vivid life examples cannot be overstated. The prophet Samuel at the end of his life had placed his life for public scrutiny before the Israelites. The dialogue between him and the Israelites went thus: "Here I am; testify against me before the LORD and before his anointed. Whose ox have I taken? Or whose donkey have I taken? Or whom have I defrauded? Whom have I oppressed? Or from whose hand have I taken a bribe to blind my eyes with it? Testify against me and I will restore it to you." They said, "You have not defrauded us or oppressed us or taken anything from any man's hand" (1Sam 12:3 ESV). When such an exemplar is placed before a young mind, there is a greater chance that it will be indelibly inscribed with such good virtues as it has seen. General Agwai testifies to this end. He recalls that growing up as child he saw his father neither smoke nor drink alcohol at any time. That example oriented his life in the same direction. He was coming of age in the late 1960s, when it was fashionable to drink, smoke, be promiscuous, and do like things to prove one's liberation. Yet, with his Christian background, he was set on living as Christ's ambassador. So by the time he was going to the NDA, he had not taken to any of these vices. People thought it was a matter of time, and that once he was there he would be "liberated."

The young Army cadet knew that Christ had already liberated him; he needed no vice to help him feel liberated. Gen Agwai remembers that only two of them out of the sixty cadets in his course in NDA did not drink alcohol. Even there, people had said that once they became officers, they would join the bandwagon. Well, to cut to the chase, Gen Agwai says, *"I became an officer and have left the Army till today; I have never taken alcohol or anything of the sort."* He is grateful to those in the Army who were his superior officers when he was a young officer. He said they did encourage social drinking, but there was no compulsion in it. Even for toasts, officers were allowed to use non-alcoholic beverages or even water for the sake of their consciences.

Gen Agwai remembers another worthy influence in his life, this time from his adulthood. When he went to the United States for his graduate studies at the National Defense University (NDU), Washington, D.C., they had a Christian fellowship there. Specifically, he was undertaking his studies leading to the master of science degree in National Resource Strategy in the Industrial College of the Armed Forces (ICAF), one of the four faculties of the NDU. The Commandant of ICAF was a two-star general in the Air Force, a devout Christian and an active member of the Christian fellowship on the NDU campus. He was always present at the Wednesday morning prayer fellowship, where he was wont to encourage the Christian students toward steadfastness in the faith. In one of such exhortations, Gen Agwai recalls him saying that he believed that it was God's grace that had taken him thus far in his career in the military. Gen Agwai was pleasantly surprised by this man's life. He was deeply encouraged that even in America, with all of its technological advances, with much affluence and every convenience of life, with high secularism and atheists in no short supply, and with the strongest military on earth, there were people in the top echelons of the military who still not only believed in God but were actively seeking to walk with him daily. So when Gen Agwai found himself in the position of the Chief of Army Staff of Nigeria, the thought of this Air Force Major General at NDU came to his mind, and he told himself, *"If that Major General was so strong in his faith and commitment to the Lord, even in his high rank in the military, how could I be anything less?"* Thoughts like these spurred him to greater commitment and faithfulness.

CAREER DEVELOPMENT AND ACHIEVEMENTS

Commissioned in the Army to the rank of second lieutenant in 1972, Martin had a meteoric rise in the military and occupied several strategic positions. Many of the higher-level positions include (but are not limited to) the following: Chief of Training, Operations and Plans of the Nigerian Armed Forces; Director of Military Training at the Nigerian Defence Academy, Kaduna; Directing Staff and Chief Instructor at the Command and Staff College Jaji–Kaduna; Military Adviser at the Nigerian High Commission in Harare, Zimbabwe (where his range of duty covered all Southern African countries); Deputy Force Commander (DFC) of the UN Peacekeeping Mission in Sierra Leone; Deputy Military Adviser at United Nations Headquarters, New York; Chief of Army Staff (COAS); Chief of Defence Staff (CDS) of the Nigerian Armed Forces. His last post of duty was as Force Commander (FC) of the African Union, United Nations Hybrid Operation in Darfur (UNAMID), Sudan, which was one of the largest peacekeeping operations in the world, having approximately 20,000 troops and 6,000 police under his command.

When Martin enlisted in the Nigerian Army, one thing was paramount on his mind: serve his fatherland as a loyal and faithful soldier. It never crossed his mind, in his wildest of dreams that he would one day serve as the Chief of Army Staff (COAS). Yet he can look back with satisfaction and gratitude that he has been one of the longest serving Chiefs of Army Staff, having served in that capacity for three years. It is likewise a unique privilege and honor for him to have crossed over to the highest position in all of the Nigerian military services to have become the CDS of the Nigeria Armed Forces. Born to be a trailblazer, Gen Agwai was the first Nigerian soldier to leave the Nigerian military, not to head home but to a higher call of duty. When he was to leave the position of the CDS, the UN requested that he go and serve as the last Force Commander of the African Union Mission in Sudan (AMIS) in Darfur, Sudan. The AMIS was at the time transitioning into the first-ever hybrid force made up of UN and regional forces, which is the UN–African Union Mission in Darfur, (UNAMID). Thus, he became the first FC, UNAMID. At the end of his tenure in Darfur, UN officials invited him back to New York for debriefing so they could absorb the lessons learned from this first-ever UN-cum-regional forces in a joint peacekeeping operation.

God had cut Gen Agwai out for excellence right from the beginning. As a young secondary school boy, being a member of the Boy Scouts, he rose to the elite rank of Eagle Scout. In 1966 he was chosen to represent the whole of northern Nigeria in Scotland at the International Boy Scout Jamboree. At the beginning of his career in the military, during his training at NDA, he won the Silver Medal in the combined training of Regular Course 8 for being the overall best Army cadet. After the combined training, Regular Course 8 was separated according to their services (of Army, Navy and Air Force), he won the Gold Medal for being the first Army cadet in the order of merit and the Sword of Honour for being the best-all-round cadet during the passing out. For one individual to win both awards was and still remains a rare feat in military training. This successful beginning became a big challenge to him; he had to work hard to maintain the expectation that his initial success had generated; and he kept the faith. For instance, at the end of his graduate studies in NDU in Washington, D.C., he also won the Ambassador's Award for excellence in research and writing. In a training programme that had both American nationals and other international military officers, he was the first foreigner ever to have won this award. His pursuit of excellence was not limited to the classroom only, but it now became his default mode of operating. For someone who had very humble beginnings, as Gen Agwai is quick to point out, it was this orientation to virtue and excellence, with providence on his side, that propelled him to the highest heights of service to the very end of his long military career.

Having completed his debriefing at the UN to document the lessons learned in Darfur, Gen Agwai returned from the UN in December 2009, and had his ceremonial pull out of the Armed Forces on December 18, 2009. At that ceremony, the then Federal Minister for Defence, Major Gen Abbey, who represented the then president, Dr. Umaru Yar'Adua, had this to say of Gen Agwai:

> *The magnificent parade accorded Agwai is an indication that the nation is happy.... The country is proud to produce a fine officer and a gentleman who gave a good account of himself. I am expressing the Commander-in-Chief's pleasure ... for the service he had rendered to his country and beyond, and that is what an officer should be.*

SUSTAINED BY FAITH AND PRAYER

Faith and prayer have been the trademarks of the life and times of Gen Martin Luther Agwai. He knows from personal experience that with every privilege come challenges. In his earlier years in the military, he worked directly with many very influential military personages. At sundry times, he worked for such Nigerian military giants as Gen. Wushishi—a onetime Chief of Army Staff—as his military assistant; Gen. Babangida, as a General Staff Officer II; Air Marshal Daggash, who became Chief of Defence Staff; and General Salihu Ibrahim, who became Chief of Army Staff. In all those positions and their concomitant high levels of risk, Gen. Agwai found God's grace to be his sufficiency, even in such stressful times as seasons of coup. Never did his God allow him to be enmeshed in trouble.

In every situation and place, it is not hard to spot someone who has an appointment with destiny, and often such people are persecuted for no just cause. The biblical story of Joseph is a case in point. Gen Agwai did not have it differently. He faced many persecutions and much intimidation in the military. Yet, in all these, he was unwavering in his trust in God. He recalls how some people had sought to implicate him in the aborted Major Gideon Orkar Coup of 1990. He was even invited for questioning, at which point he remembers telling a group of friends, *"God knows that I know nothing about it, and it doesn't matter what human beings can do. If God destines that I should one day become the Chief of Army Staff, nothing will stop it; it shall surely come to pass."* Indeed, when his self-made prophecy came to fulfillment, and he became the Chief of Army Staff, some of those people reminded him of those very words, which words he himself had never forgotten. God vindicated him, and after a thorough interview, he was declared innocent of complicity in the Orkar coup. However, the experience had embittered him so much so that he even told his commanding general officer (the then General Officer Commanding [GOC] of the 3rd Armoured Division), Gen D. O. Diya, that he wanted to resign his commission from the Nigerian Army. What he found so upsetting was that when signals concerning the coup had been sent out, he had to take his own personal money to fuel military vehicles that were detailed to go round Bauchi for strategic coverage. He did this because the brigade headquarters was cash strapped at the time. For him to have done all that and yet have someone turned round to accuse him of complicity in the coup was like a stab in the back, and it hurt badly. God never abandons his own people. It was not long after he was cleared of this accusation that he was sent as a defence attaché to the Nigerian High Commission in Zimbabwe, with his duties covering all of the Southern African sub-region. During his tour of duty, the then Chief of Defence Staff, the late Gen. Abacha, wrote him an official letter of commendation for his meritorious service there. The general says that he owes a debt of gratitude to the late Gen. Sani Abacha, with whose help he was able to acquire his family house in Jos.

His faith has been tested even with regard to service to God. As it is common with many Christians to return to their roots at Christmas, Gen. Agwai and his siblings were home in their village, Gidan Mana, Kaduna State, at Christmas in 1990. Because the whole family was there with their friends, the little village church could not contain everyone. The pastor then appealed to the home folks to leave the church for the guests. A couple of weeks later into the New Year, the pastor and all stakeholders were persuaded that they should embark on the construction of a new church building. The pastor felt led to appoint the general as the chairman of the building fund-raising committee. Having seen the need himself, he did not hesitate to accept the challenge.

Martin Luther, still at the 3rd Armoured Divisional Headquarters in Jos, set to work inviting friends to the fundraiser. The committee had opened an account for the project and invited their bankers to be at the fundraiser to take the money with them. The two bank staffers, who came to the fundraiser, just strolled in with nothing in which to put the money. When he asked them why they did not bring a safe for conveying the money that would be raised, their response was that no fundraiser in the area had ever gotten more than ₦5,000, so they could conveniently pocket the amount that would be raised and go back to the bank. The general laughed. He knew that though many of his invitees were not going to come to the function, many had given their contributions, and he already had about ₦150,000 cash from such friends, in addition to cheques. At the end of the day, nearly half a million Naira was raised. (This was back in 1991 when the Naira was stronger than it is today.) The same bank staffers came back requesting him to give them a military escort.

With this success came a new challenge. The villagers, upon hearing that about half a million had been raised, came to the Martin Luther to request that the initial plan for a smaller church be set aside and a more auspicious building be constructed. He obliged them and got a friend of his, the late Arc G. E. Goyit, to make a new design, which ended up with a seating capacity of 1200. Unfortunately, inflation rose that year to previously unknown proportions. The cost of iron rods, which they needed in plentiful supply, skyrocketed. The half a million Naira could raise only the superstructure of the building and no more. This was in spite of the immense contributions of the villagers in terms of labour: they did the excavation for the foundation, carrying block, fetching water and the like. It was really a community effort. Completing the project became an uphill task. Gen Agwai confesses that he was ready to give up on the project.

While he contemplated abandoning the project, his father called him one day and asked him, "Son, are you in the military?" He replied in the affirmative. Then his father continued,

"In the military, if you are given a task to accomplish

and you do not complete it, will it be seen as failure?"

"Yes," was his reply once more.

His father again queried for the last time, "Is failure a desirable thing in the military?"

To this question, his reply was a resounding "No."

His father then continued, "You were made the chairman of the fundraising committee of this church. If you wash your hands off it, as many people are doing, it will remain uncompleted, but you will be the one that will bear the shame forever. People will say you were given this task for your village, but you couldn't do it."

The sting of those simple but candid words sent the soldier into frenzied action like a hornet that has been stirred. He could see the sentiments in the village. People no longer saw the church as an ECWA church; it had become more or less Martin's church because it was appearing to be a failure.

Martin now took the church project on like a crucifix that people wear on their necks. He took pictures of the church and carried them with him everywhere he went. He showed it to people he knew and asked them to support the project. Even when he went to Harare as a military attaché, he took the church pictures with him. At every opportunity he talked to people about it. One thing he learned about fundraising during that time was never to consider any amount too small. From the five, ten, twenty, fifty, or hundred Naira or dollars that he gathered over the years the church work was revived. He says that the lesson he learned about fundraising in the process was that if one needs to raise a million Naira, it will be easier to get half a million people to give two Naira each than to get two people to give half a million each. The construction continued ever so slowly but steadily until it was completed and dedicated by the ECWA president, Rev. Dr. Olowola, in 2004, thirteen years after the work had first begun.

Because the Gidan Mana Church was completed and dedicated when Gen. Agwai had been serving as the Chief of Army Staff for about a year, many people concluded he had used his position to rake money to build his village church. Aware of these stories that people were peddling around, he got someone to piece together a fifteen-minute PowerPoint presentation that chronicled the journey through the thirteen years of the church building project. The pictures, many of which were old, had in them some of the people who had by this time died; they also showed every stage of the work through the years. This presentation did a lot to disabuse the minds of many from the misconceptions they had of when the project was started and how it was financed.

During the dedication service of the church, Gen. Agwai placed a challenge before those who were present at the occasion. He told them that he would not like to see a situation in which, because the church was so nice and the parsonage so old and in such a state of squalor, the pastor would move his family to live in the church. He called upon the audience to give so the parsonage would be renovated. On getting back to the office, he got a letter from one of his officers, who confessed to the general that he was one of the skeptics who had believed that the general had used his position to misappropriate Army funds for his village church. Attending the programme had changed his mind, and he had decided that he would labour to make sure that the church also had a befitting parsonage. This officer drafted a letter that he would send to all those who attended the programme, believing that if everyone there were to give even ₦500, the amount needed for the parsonage would the realized. The fellow began by attaching a personal donation of ₦5000 to his draft letter. To cut the long story short, through this effort not only was the old parsonage renovated, but a brand new one was constructed, and both buildings were furnished before being handed over to the church.

Meanwhile, before he even became the Chief of Army Staff, Gen Agwai had been appointed by ECWA to serve on the governing council of its newly established Bingham University. He served on that council throughout his time in the military, even when he was posted to Sudan, and when he requested to be replaced, ECWA refused. Now, when he became the Chief of Defence Staff, the ECWA President invited him to a thanksgiving service they wanted to hold in his honour. He promptly turned down the request. He had held a thanksgiving service when he was appointed Chief of Army Staff, which also coincided with his silver wedding anniversary. After that he and his wife had agreed that they would not host any other thanksgiving services until the day he put down his uniform. ECWA then sent a message to him through its then general secretary, Rev. Ezekiel Dadang, saying, *"We are not asking you to come and host your thanksgiving service. Rather, we, as ECWA, are organizing a thanksgiving service in your honour; and all we require of you is that you bring your family and friends so that we can together thank God that one of us found favour in his sight to become a four star general, and to be made the head of the Nigerian Armed Forces."* Gen. Agwai was humbled by this statement. He had never seen his attainment in that light and the implication it held to the larger Christian community. He then accepted the invitation to the thanksgiving service.

Having decided to attend the thanksgiving service, he got to work inviting his friends. Seeing that ECWA was footing all the bills for the function, when he arrived at his house in Jos the night before the event, he kept asking himself, *"God, what will I do to show ECWA my gratitude for this honour that is being done for me?"* Then he remembered that Bingham University was squatting on the campus of Jos ECWA Theological Seminary (JETS) and that his alma mater, the NDA, had operated for over thirty years on a temporary campus until his own tenure as CDS, when it had moved to its permanent site in 2006. He then thought,

> "ECWA, in establishing Bingham, has started it on a temporary site, in JETS campus; if we are not careful, one day JETS and Bingham will fight over space and facilities. Since Bingham has land near Abuja, we must do something by pulling and pushing ECWA to get Bingham to go to its permanent site."

Being a Bingham council member, he was aware of the proposed projects. As he contemplated taking the lighter project, he providentially read in his devotional that day about how as humans we are prone to taking the easy way out and sticking to our comfort zones. It could not have been coincidental; the message was clear to him: He must go out on the limb and stretch his faith to do something great for the Lord. In faith, he followed the counsel of the great missionary statesman of the nineteenth century, William Carey, who said, *"Attempt great things for God; expect great things from God."* He settled it that night. He would pledge that he and his friends would raise the ₦23 million needed for a hostel project as part of the effort to move Bingham University to its permanent site. That night he drafted a pledge form and in the morning got it all typed and mass produced. In the church, he challenged all those present to not only pledge for themselves, but take copies of the pledge forms to their friends and have them make pledges also. He pressed his experience with fundraising for his village church project into service, aiming at getting as many donors as possible rather than aiming for the big-time donors. By the end of the service, ₦5 million had been realized. In the following weeks more money came in, the total rose to ₦8 million.

His faith was put to the test further. The ECWA general secretary came to him with the ₦8 million that had been collected and with a message from the ECWA board of trustees stating that they wanted not money but a completely built hostel complex on Bingham University's permanent site instead. God had prepared the answer to this challenge in the person of a Muslim officer under the general's command. The officer on his own accord had already set up a fundraising steering committee, comprised mostly of civilians but also including military and police officers. He came to the general with the draft of a letter that he desired the general to sign so the committee could begin to raise funds. The officer said, as he heard the general make the pledge at the church, it gripped his heart that it was not just the name of the general that was at stake but the reputation of the entire Nigerian military: if the general failed, then the military would be seen as failing. With his nod, the committee swung into action.

As the committee reviewed the architectural drawings, they came to the conclusion that the structure was not meant for a twenty-first-century school. It had no kitchen, no common room, and no space for the physically challenged. They set it aside and mandated a member, who happened to be an architect, to come up with a new design. The building changed from being a one-storey building to a two-storey one; and the cost went up as well, from ₦23 million to ₦40 million. This committee combed for money through the length and breadth of this country and came up with the needed funds so that not only was the building completed, but it was fully furnished, making it the first building on the permanent site of Bingham. In appreciation, ECWA gave him the prerogative to name the building, and after due discussion, he and his wife decided that it would be a befitting honour to name it after his own mother, that it is why it is named Shera Agwai Hall.

As a man of faith, Gen. Agwai is not a person who would be oblivious to God's manifold graces. Instead, seeing the goodness of God, he strives to remain loyal to him as a faithful ambassador. Thus, he always maintains a personal daily devotional life of Bible reading and prayer. He recalls that when he was going to New York to serve as the Deputy Military Adviser, he thought that would be his last military assignment. In fact, he had even given out all his uniforms, except the ceremonial one. Thus, seven months later, when he was appointed as the Chief of Army Staff, he had to borrow the uniform he wore for his decoration ceremony. The awareness that this appointment was an act of divine grace could not escape him. God had also gone ahead of him to provide for his spiritual sustenance. A friend had just given him a devotional guide by Maxwell. Its focus was on leadership. In God's providence, the Bible passages selected for each day's devotion and the comments made on them seemed to have been tailored for his daily need. Very often, the wisdom of the devotions would relate to issues he was dealing with at that moment, and as he then prayed and went forth, God would give him the confidence and the gumption to act with circumspection in every situation.

The following year, his elder sister gave him another devotional guide, *Faith to Faith*. This proved equally timely and helpful. It was as if God were telling him that having taught him about leadership, he wanted him to move on to a stronger faith commitment. To Gen Agwai, all these proved crucial because when he came into office he discovered how lonely such offices could make one. Unfortunately, his abiding source of companionship and encouragement, his wife, had remained behind in New York. They had just moved to New York in the preceding seven months with their youngest daughter, who was fourteen years of age at the time, and his return to Nigeria was in the middle of the school year. At that tender age, they could not leave her there alone, so his wife stayed behind with their daughter and he returned to Nigeria alone. Thus, ever more than before, God and his word became his greatest companion. This was what would then sustain him in the midst of the myriads of pressures he faced daily.

Additionally, Christian music has a great place in Gen Agwai's life. One of his favorite hymns is *"What a Friend We Have in Jesus."* This hymn is a constant reminder to him that there is no friend as faithful as Jesus, who will never abandon his people through thick or thin. In the most challenging of times, when he sings this song, it reminds him of the promises of Jesus, that he will never leave nor forsake him. It reminds him that there is no burden too heavy for Jesus to carry (1 Pet 5:7; cf. Ps 55:22). If Jesus is going to carry his burdens for him, he asks, *"Why do I get worried when there is somebody who will carry my burden?"* This has taught him over the years always to fall on his knees and cry out to the Lord in times of distress, knowing that God will surely come to his rescue, not because of his own merit but out of God's mercy and grace; and the Lord has never failed him.

A good example, amongst many others, of how singing reinforces prayer and faith in Gen Agwai's life is the experience he had at sea while returning from Scotland after attending the International Boy Scouts Jamboree in 1966. They made that journey by ship, as was common then. On the homeward voyage, around the Bay of Biscay, their ship ran into turbulent waves: For days they were tempest tossed. It was a frightening sight, merely beholding the other troubled ships in the bay as they uneasily swayed, waddled, and rocked back and forth with the rising and falling of the raging waves. Inside their ship, no one dared to venture out on the deck lest he be flung off into the churning waters. Even in their rooms, they had to fasten themselves to their beds with cords lest they be heaved off their beds to the floor. In this situation, he remembered Jesus as the friend who could calm the sea. Mary A. Baker's hymn *"Master, the Tempest Is Raging,"* was his theme song during that period. The words of the refrain of the song were more than comforting. Faith rose with fervent prayer in his young heart to the throne of grace for deliverance, as he sang the words of the refrain of the song over and over again:

> *The winds and the waves shall obey Thy will,*
> *Peace, be still!*
> *Whether the wrath of the storm-tossed sea,*
> *Or demons or men, or whatever it be*
> *No waters can swallow the ship where lies*
> *The Master of ocean, and earth, and skies*
> *They all shall sweetly obey Thy will,*
> *Peace, be still! Peace, be still!*
> *They all shall sweetly obey Thy will,*
> *Peace, be still! Peace, be still!*

Truly the Master of the ocean and seas came to the rescue and calmed the furious waters.

FAMILY LIFE

Martin married his dear wife Ruth (who hails from Mangu-Halle, Plateau State) on December 23, 1978, at ECWA Church, Gwari Road, Kaduna. They were joined by the late Rev. Tachio of blessed memory, a martyr of one of the several religious uprisings in Kaduna City. Their marriage has been blessed with three beautiful daughters, all of whom are adults now. Their first daughter, Rebecca, has been happily married since 2010. While she did her graduate studies in international development, she developed an interest in jewelry design and went ahead to train in it; that is the work she does now. Their second daughter, Abigail, is undertaking doctoral studies and lecturing in mechanical engineering in the United States (this was in 2011, when the interview for this book was conducted); and their third daughter, Miriam, who studied film and video, is working in the film industry in the United States.

Having love for God and His word as the anchor of

family life was what the general learned from his parents. Both his mother and father had impressed on him very early in life the biblical truth: *"The fear of the LORD is the beginning of knowledge; fools despise wisdom and instruction"* (Proverbs 1:7; ESV). Indeed, the first Bible verse that he ever knew (John 3:16) was taught to him by his parents. He will never forget the pious life and prayers of his mother and the godly counsel of his father. He remembers vividly how his father told him time and time again, *"In whatever you do, let the fear of God be your guiding light, for if you don't fear God, you will never amount to anything."* This is the legacy that he and his wife Ruth have sought to pass on to their daughters. For instance, even though he has occupied high offices, he has not gone in the way of corruption to enrich himself in order to leave fat bank accounts for their children. He is not afraid to state this publicly:

> *I know that the temptations are great. I have been in public offices and I know how much the pressures are in those offices. Nevertheless, I personally want to state that at no time throughout my public service did I ever sit down to work out with any person(s) any deal that this contract is worth X millions or Y billions and you will give me Z% or you will bring this or that to me, before the signing or after the signing of contract. I never did it.*

That is not to say the general has never accepted appreciation from people he has helped along the way. What he objects to is mortgaging one's conscience by collecting gifts from clients before they even do their job:

> *How can I in good conscience criticize a person's performance or hold him to the established standards for the job, if I have already taken part of the money for the job from him? I cannot. I won't have the guts to*

> hold you accountable even if you are not doing a good job. I don't have the temerity to live that kind of life; by His grace, throughout my life, I never did it and I will never do it.

Nonetheless, he readily points to a Mercedes car he bought in 1985, with the money someone he had helped earlier on gave to him. While he worked with Gen Babangida, there was an American who had some business interests with the government with whom he had interacted. For Martin, he had no idea that government officials were collecting money from people for doing the job for which government was already paying them. He simply did his job: if there was a letter to write, he wrote and dispatched it; he even took letters to some people to their homes. This American businessman was one of those he had dealt with in this fashion. While Martin was attending a course in the United Kingdom in 1985, this man called him to thank him for helping him back in Nigeria:

> I never knew there were clean Nigerians. Your assistance was instrumental in my getting the job, and you never asked me for anything, unlike most of your other colleagues, who requested money for literally everything they did for me.

The general's response was, "I did nothing extraordinary. I only did my job; that's all." Well, to show his gratitude, this man sent the general a gift of $5,000. In response to this gesture, the general recalls,

> When I collected this money, I told my wife, "I will want to buy something that will remain a constant reminder to me that it pays to be honest."

That was why he bought this 1983 Mercedes, and this is why he has kept it all these years.

Their daughters have learned their lessons well.

From very early, they taught their children the virtues of hard work and industry. He shared with them how as a young man his greatest ambition was to buy a bicycle; and the joy he had when he bought one in 1968 has not been equalled by the delight from the purchase of any other vehicle he has owned subsequently. Now, when he was serving as the Chief of Army Staff, a long-time friend of his—a state governor at the time—gave him the gift of a brand new car. One of his daughters, Rebecca had just returned home for national service. After completing her college education overseas, her father prevailed on her to come back home and do national service, so she was home. When he got this gift, he called her and told her that he had a car for her. The young woman's reply was,

> "Dad, remember what you have taught us. I have just graduated; I am only a youth corper. Besides, I have determined in my heart that I'll buy the first car that I'll own in this world by myself and it's not going to be as a gift from anybody—not even you."

The general had to give that car to his younger brother.

Another case in point is that even though as senior military officer he always had many people in the house to help with chores, he and his wife insisted that by the age of ten their daughters wash their own clothes and iron them, and then they would learn to cook and do other housekeeping chores. By age eighteen, when they were still at home, they would run the kitchen. Being all girls, when they were all at home, they took turns, month by month, of being in charge of the kitchen; and a healthy competition often ensued as to who would be the thriftiest and most innovative in managing family resources. Of course initially, the children had resented having to do the house chores, but later they were thankful for it. When his eldest daughter went to school in United Kingdom and found out that some of her mates from Nigeria did not even know how to plug in a kettle to boil water, to say nothing of making a meal, she felt proud of herself and thankful to her parents.

Openness and intimacy is a hallmark of his family. After being married for some time and keeping his income secret, the general re-thought this. One day, after dinner, he said to his wife,

> *I owe you an explanation. I have been working and, as my wife, you don't know how much I earn; so sometimes you are either underestimating what you want to ask from me or sometimes you over estimate my capability.*

So he brought all his pay slips and put them on the table for his wife. Not having been used to that, his wife was initially enraged, but after a good explanation, she was bought over. Subsequently, once his pay slip came, he would present it to the whole family at the dinner table. This openness strengthened the intimacy of the family, such that even though all his children are girls they remain very open to their parents. As the girls are now grown and away from home, they all strive to remain vitally in touch and connected with each other in the family through phone calls, emails, and social networking media like Facebook.

CONCLUDING THOUGHTS

In view of the acrimonious religious tensions in the country, the general calls for tolerance and understanding. In his personal life he has related with Muslims from his earliest years and has maintained his friendships with a number of his Muslim childhood friends through the years. For example, when ECWA hosted the thanksgiving service in his honour (as the CDS), the Emir of Birnin Gwari, Mal. Zubairu Jibril Mai Gwari II, a friend from their secondary school days in Zaria, was in attendance, along with many other Muslim friends and colleagues. Learning to build bridges across religious, ethnic, and regional divides is what will keep this country united in pursuing our commonweal.

Gen Agwai cautions against the present emphasis on measuring success solely by material possessions. He reiterates the need to stress ethical values in our society. For example, he points out that once people are perceived as having money, they are invited to fundraisers left and right, with no one asking questions as to how they came by their wealth. In his view, there is too much talk about religion, morality, and standards, but little action in the direction of maintaining integrity in our national and private lives. Christians especially have to remember, he insists, that they are called to be Christ's ambassadors in society. To him, this is a high calling that every Christian should take with all seriousness. He counsels that while it is important to aspire to better one's economic and social status, we all need patience and faith—trusting that God will provide the right doors for us at the right time, while we do our best without cutting corners.

Finally, Gen. Agwai believes that if we have been blessed by God, we should think of giving back to society. Just like God promised to bless Abraham, so that through him all nations of the world will be blessed (Genesis 12:3), when God blesses us, he expects that the blessing will be shared with others who are less fortunate than we are. Wealth and position for their own sakes are meaningless; it is only as they are used to make a difference for others that they create true meaning for life for those who are blessed with such possessions.

CHAPTER TWO

THE FAITHFUL SERVANT

BULUS DOGARA AMISHE

BIRTHED OUT OF AFFLICTION

Bulus Dogara is the eleventh and only surviving child of his father, the others having passed on before he was born. His early years were spent in his native village of Dogon Kurmi, in which there was no school at the time. Losing one child after another made the life of Bulus's father, Mr. Dogara Amishe, very difficult and filled with pain and disappointment. During those years of living a death-plagued life in his native village of Dogon Kurmi (also called Unner) in Kagarko Local Government Council of Kaduna State, Nigeria, Dogara was gravely misunderstood, as most people thought of him as a wicked person, whose woes were nothing other than retributive justice catching up with him. Deep down in his heart, however, he knew he had done nothing wrong, at least nothing other than the usual sins every other person commits. Fate itself had treated him unkindly, looking at the way in which he lost his children in succession. Bulus's birth came after a spectacular event occurred in Dogara's life—accepting Christ into his life as his Lord and Saviour. When he yielded his life to God, Dogara declared, *"If I have a child it's OK, but even if I don't, as a believer in the Lord*

God, I am still a child of the living God!" It was after Dogara made this declaration that Bulus was born. Bulus was raised in an environment saturated with faith in God.

When Bulus was born in March 1949, his father had no doubts in his mind that this was a divine visitation. Right from birth, Dogara turned over this child of his love to the Lord, saying half in faith and half in resignation, *"If he lives, he lives, but if he dies, he dies."* He had resolved in his mind not to go to the kind of lengths he had gone to previously trying hard, albeit to no avail, to save his other children. One day Bulus took ill so seriously that everyone thought he would go the way of the other children. Surprisingly, at that very moment, a Fulani cattle herder happened to have come around Dogara's home, and when he sighted the lad in this pitiful condition, he promised to return the next day with an amulet that could be tied around the boy's waist to secure him from all ills. Bulus's father wasted no time in telling the man not to bother; he had already determined that this child would never be made to partake in any fetishism. In his response to the unsolicited offer, he instantly recalled the pledge he had made before God at the birth of the child, as he retorted, *"If he lives, he lives; if he dies, he dies. I am never going to allow that happen."*

Since his experience of the new birth, Bulus's father's perspective on life had changed, so also his philosophy of life. He now believed that God is the one who gives life and he has the sole power to take it as well. Thus, as far as his son was concerned, only God could keep him alive. If the worst were to happen, he would take comfort that his son would be with God. God honoured his faith— his son did not die, neither did Dogara have to resort to medicine men or to any other method of traditional spiritism to save his son. His newly found faith had given him inner strength as well as meaning in life, and he could not sacrifice it for anything else; after all, he had tried the other things before, and they were of no help to him then, so they could not be of any help now. This is the legacy that Mr. Dogara Amishe passed on to his son, Bulus. Once the latter reached the age of discretion, these facts were firmly impressed on his mind.

CONTINUING THE LEGACY OF FAITH

On his part, Bulus came to faith in Christ at the early age of about eight years sometime in 1957. He recalls that joyous morning, as he sat in Sunday school with his peers, listening to one of his uncles speaking to them about Jesus. While he no longer remembers much of what his uncle said, he remembers vividly that he was one of the children that stood up at the end of the discourse to ask Jesus to come into their lives. At the time, he had no idea what a monumental change that simple step of faith would bring to the course of his life. He certainly cannot forget the joyful and happy feeling he had as he walked him home at the end of Sunday school that day. That experience subsequently made him see himself as a good person. As he grew up, however, it became clearer to him, from reading the Scriptures and listening to sermons, that the step he took as an eight-year-old boy was the right one, and that he was saved by grace, and not by his own goodness. He therefore rededicated his life to God and since then he has had no regrets whatsoever.

One of the many blessings that Bulus counts and is thankful for is the kind of father he had. For one thing, his father was good at providing him with necessary information but leaving the choices to him. This helped Bulus greatly because at the end of the day, he never saw his father as imposing anything on him. Taking his faith as an example, he proudly points out that while his father had introduced him to the faith, the church, and the Scriptures, the rest was his own choice. Because of this, unlike other people, who tend to rebel against God when they grow up because they have been compelled by their parents to perform religious "duties," Bulus, as he grew up, had and continues to have, only gratitude for God's goodness in his life. All through his life, he has never had a moment of regret for following Christ. For him, life is meaningless without Christ, notwithstanding one's education, possessions, positions, or status in society. His loyalty to Christ is without compromise, whether in good or bad times:

> *When the times are good, God is there; and when the times are bad, God is there; and when the times are neither good nor bad, God is still there. Thus the situation is inconsequential; it is one's trust and faith in the living God that keeps life going on—this I have seen very, very clearly in my personal life.*

THE FOUNDATIONAL YEARS

In the earlier years of missionary endeavours in Nigeria, denominational divides were much sharper then than they are today. More often than not such divisions, deriving from the proselytizing zeal of the adherents and agents of the various mission agencies, tended to have far-reaching implications. They had no less profound implications for the young Bulus. He had started elementary school in 1958 at a Roman Catholic Mission (RCM) School in his village. However, his teacher had insisted that he convert to Roman Catholicism if he were to remain in the class. It was a grave test of his faith. Even at that tender age, his father allowed him to make the choice. He opted out of the school rather than become a Catholic. The following year, the SIM started an elementary school in his village, in which he enrolled immediately, but his joy was short lived as the school shut down after only three months. As a result, he had to go to school in the next village, which was about 10–12 miles (i.e., 16–19 KM) away from his own village. This was a transfer school, so he had his elementary schooling up to primary four. Thereafter, he transferred to a senior primary school in a village about 23 miles (36.8 Km) away from home. It was there that he completed his primary seven in 1965.

Bulus's schooling went rather rapidly. After completing primary school, he immediately secured admission to the prestigious Government College, Kaduna, where he had his secondary education during the Nigerian Civil War years, from 1966 to 1970. Being successful in his West African School Certificate (WASC, this is the equivalent of the London General Certificate of Education (G.C.E.), Ordinary Level, or the American General Education Diploma, GED), he continued his education at the same school for his High School Certificate (HSC, was the post-secondary but pre-degree programme students undertook before proceeding to the university prior to the 1980s. HSC candidates usually took the London G.C.E. (A/Levels) in three subjects and English Language) from 1971–72. After his HSC, Bulus had a stint with teaching, while he waited for admission to the University. By the beginning of the new academic year in 1973, he enrolled for his B. Sc. Economics degree in Ahmadu Bello University, where he graduated in 1976. He did his National Youth Service in Akure, Ondo State (July 1976 to July 1977). Subsequently, he undertook a post graduate diploma in Manpower Planning at the University of Lagos (1978/79). He proceeded to the Institute of Social Studies in The Hague, Holland for his master's degree in Development Planning (1983/1984).

RAISING A FAMILY

Raising a family was a challenge to Mr. Amishe, though not of the same magnitude as the one his own parents had faced. He and his wife Esther were married on December 23, 1976. As with any African couple, they expected to have children, but that was not to be for a long while. The first six years of their marriage were very trying years, as his wife had several miscarriages. Relatives were also worried and would have loved to find out where the problem lay by consulting fortune tellers, diviners, or spiritists. Both Mr. Amishe and his wife were also concerned, but in the African context, pressure is usually mounted more upon the woman than the man, so naturally she was worried and would often cry. But Mr. Amishe stood by his wife, to comfort and encourage her. As he recalls, one day he sat his wife down and told her, *"I don't know when a child is coming; I don't know how a child is coming; all I know is that I will not see the grave until I have seen my child."* While this did not stop her from crying, his faith did not waver. Another time he told his wife in faith, *"Look, one day you will tell yourself that there is a need for you to start family planning."* This time around, he managed to squeeze a smile out of her, but true to his faith, that was the story of their life.

God honoured Mr. Amishe's faith and eventually gave them children until they themselves decided they had had enough. He recalls that before they had their first child, a doctor had told him that his wife might not be able to have any children:

> *"One day, a doctor invited me alone to his consulting room after he had examined my wife and said, 'Gentleman, we've examined your wife. The possibility that she will have a child is non-existent, but we're trying the best we know how.'"*

Notwithstanding, he never divulged this information to anyone, not his parents, nor even his wife. Rather, he took it to the Lord in prayer, and the Lord answered his prayers, and his wife conceived after six years of marriage. Even then the struggles weren't over yet. By the second month of Esther's pregnancy, she had to be placed on bed rest till she delivered. This time, another doctor told him there was no chance that his wife would have another child after this one, but he knew where to go with such information: just like, King Hezekiah, who took the threatening letter of King Sennachireb of Assyria to temple and spread it before the Lord (2 Kings 19:14), Mr. Amishe, also took his burdens to the Lord in prayer. After their first child, no other child came until the twelfth year of their marriage, but his faith was unwavering still. Indeed, he says, through all this, their faith in the Lord had been built up. After their second child, however, the other children came in rapid succession. They have five children of their own. Besides these, they have raised four other children, who are to them just like their biological children. Thus they proudly say the Lord has blessed them with nine children.

The Lord truly *"confirms the word of his servant and fulfills the counsel of his messengers"* (Isa. 44:26 ESV). Mr. Amishe had told his wife that there would come a time when she would desire to have children no more, and that moment surely came after the birth of their fifth child. Since it was the Lord who had given them their children, it was again to him that they turned when they thought they had had enough. They prayed and told God so, and the children ceased from coming—they did not have to take a single pill: the God who had been giving them children also caused them to stop coming.

The enemy is never tired of trying to frustrate God's children, but those who hold fast onto the Lord always triumph because in Christ they are more than conquerors. When the Devil could not stop the Amishes from having children, he made plans to scuttle their joy by attacking or even taking the lives of their children in other ways. But these attacks also became instruments in the hands of the Lord for building up the faith of his servants. Two examples will suffice to illustrate this.

In the first instance, their first son at a point took so ill that they thought he would not survive. Mr. Amishe remembers how he and his wife stood in the hospital over their baby for over 23 hours. At the end of it all, God triumphed and the baby lived. Second, about four months after the birth of their last child, armed robbers visited their home. Amidst their threats, one of them grabbed their four-month-old son and lifted him high in the air. Bulus and Esther knew the ruthlessness of these agents of evil so it was obvious to them that unless the Lord intervened, the criminal would dash this innocent child against the wall at any moment. Yet grace triumphed in the end: in accordance with the Scriptures, God kept all the baby's bones and not one of them was broken (Ps. 34:20). The similarity of Bulus's experiences with those of his father are striking, and just like his father, he also worked hard to transfer the legacy of faith to his family, sharing all these experiences with his children as they grew older, and it has pleased the Lord to open their eyes to the truth as well so that all of them are walking in the Way.

God's work in his life helped him to be a vessel in the Lord's hands. As a young man, just beginning his career in the civil service, he was chosen by his church to help nurture the establishment of the English-speaking section out of a Hausa-speaking congregation. The church he helped to plant is what is today known as ECWA Goodnews Church, High Cost, Narayi, Kaduna. He helped to run this church on a part time basis from 1978 to 1992; after this it began to have resident pastors consistently. One thing that Mr. Amishe is thankful for is the way God taught him, through this experience, to maintain good interpersonal relations with other people. Being aware of the frosty, often belligerent, relationships that exist between Hausa and English sections of ECWA churches, he worked assiduously to ensure that such an ugly situation never reared its head at Goodnews, Narayi, and the Lord granted his desires. What is more, combing a busy full-time career in the civil service and a busy church ministry (with several young people of marriageable age, whom he needed to be counseling on finding a spouse, courtship, and starting a home) coupled with family his own life was a daunting challenge. He can hardly imagine how he did it all:

> Let me be honest with you, I can now clearly see, with the benefit of hindsight, that God was surely in control; otherwise I can't see how I could have coped with all that: managing my large family, managing a very busy office, and at the same time also managing a very busy English Section ECWA Church. ... By his grace, I managed to keep all those schedules going, and to his glory, fairly well too.

CAREER IN THE STATE CIVIL SERVICE

In terms of his career life, except for the one year of national service, which he did in Ondo State, Mr. Amishe has given his life in the service of his state. After the year of national service, he returned to Kaduna to pick up an appointment with the state civil service as a planning officer II in 1977. From an early stage, his job required him to coordinate development planning for the state. He worked his way through the ranks, first, to the position of state director of planning (1992–98). In God's perfect timing, the year he became state director of planning was the year his church also began to have resident pastors. While he was doing pretty much the same job, with the title of director now, much more was expected of him than ever before. As director of planning, he had to interact with fellow directors, permanent secretaries, and commissioners of all the state ministries, and he often also had to meet with the state governor both in council and in person as well as liaising with the National Planning Commission (or ministry) on the behalf of the state. It was certainly a busy and involving office. He eventually became a permanent secretary in the ministry of finance (where he had the responsibility of managing the finances of the state government) in 1998 and served in that capacity until his retirement from active service in 2009. He also served, in his post-retirement days as a special advisor to the state governor.

Throughout his working career, Mr. Amishe worked in very sensitive offices that involved money and contracts and the like. These are places of power and influence, with temptation also lurking in the corners. Yet his commitment to God had clearly defined ethical standards for him:

> *I, early in my career, set my code of conduct for operating in my office, namely, 'Don't ever sit on somebody's papers when it is not necessary.' Here 'when it is not necessary' means that when jobs have been fully executed, it is my responsibility, whether asked or not asked, to process all papers and pass them out whether the individual concerned is there or not there. I trained myself, by the grace of God, to respect that position and throughout my working life that was my practice up till the time I left the civil service.*

As always happens in the civil service, even when the boss does not demand bribes from clients, subordinates would do that behind him. For Mr. Amishe, if at any time it came to his knowledge that anyone's papers were being withheld unjustly, he would immediately bring the weight of his influence to bear on whoever was carrying out such nefarious acts so that the client received his entitlement without delay.

Having come into the service at the time he did always privileged him to be the head of his unit. Thus, as virtue, morality, and integrity were vanishing in the public sector, he still was constantly in the place, more often than not, to dictate to others instead of others dictating to him. Having determined also not to soil himself, he never allowed his subordinates to be in a place where they could pressure him into doing anything against his conscience. He came to see that even his superiors, once they knew who he was and what he stood for, never really sought to make him go against his conscience. Thus he counsels that it is important for one to take a stand for the right thing and be public about it. More importantly, he identified his close walk with God as the saving grace:

> *Honestly, I can only say that whatever I did was by God's grace. It had always been God strengthening me—him working ahead of me. Thus all expected pressures just seemed to have always fizzled out of my way like dew before the rising sun. But truly, when I look back, I can only say it is the Lord's doing, and it is marvelous in my sight. He led the way, I only followed along.*

By the late 1980s and the 1990s, when the Nigerian economy nosedived into decline and earnings of public servants could no longer meet their needs (as aptly captured by the cliché of labour leaders in those terrible years, *"My take-home pay cannot take me home"*) and many public servants were being swept along in the torrent of corruption that was gushing through the land, Mr. Amishe was still able to hold his head high. A number of factors served him in this regard. First, his service in church (as a non-ordained pastor) was a check on his conduct in the office. He determined not to do anything in his office that would damage the image of the Lord and his church. Second, he found enormous support from his parents-in-law, who helped provide for some of their needs. Third, he remembered the motto of the NYSC: *Dignity in Labour*. With this in mind, he took to farming as a way of supplementing his income, and all the members of his family (including his own children, as they grew older) joined in the farming activities so as to produce most of the food they needed, allowing his salary to be used for other family needs. Fourth, led by the example he and his wife set, their family learned to be content, and as such they never pressured him or aspired to things they could not afford.

Even at the workplace, there were tough times through which the Lord took him. As Robert Schuller says, *"Tough times don't last, but tough people do."* That was Mr. Amishe's experience. One of many examples he could give illustrates the point, Mr. Amishe remembers a period of three or four months during which his salary was stopped. No one told him why: He himself was not sure of what was going on, but he asked questions of no one. He also did not share this with anyone, except his wife. Yet, without him petitioning anyone, his salary was restored as quietly as it had been stopped, and all the arrears were paid.

POST-RETIREMENT LIFE

After retirement in 2009, Mr. Amishe returned to farming and church work. Occasionally he is invited to deliver papers at public functions. In 2010, however, when Mr. Patrick Yakowa became the substantive governor of Kaduna State, Mr. Amishe was invited to serve as the Governor's Special Advisor on Economic and Budget Affairs (there has been two different administrations since them). In his new capacity as an advisor to the governor, he had to become involved in politics directly or indirectly. His greatest challenge was that the way politicians do things is different from what he was used to as a career civil servant, and he was still on the learning curve in the school of political life. He could already see problems with politicians' ingenuity with dishonesty and craftiness in their dealings with the public they are supposed to serve, all that in the name of politics. He was similarly befuddled by the same people's creativity in manufacturing falsehood to serve political ends. He was taking these challenges as they came, trusting the God of all grace who had led him in the past, to guide him through his journey in the wilderness of public service in a political milieu also.

CONCLUSION

On the whole, Mr. Amishe considers the exemplary life he lived as a civil servant as one of his greatest achievements. He worked as hard and as honestly as he could to ensure that the interest of the general public was served in the way and manner in which public works and contracts were executed. But he also sought to protect the interests of those who did business with government, so that they would not be unduly harassed and exploited by pen-robbers (a Nigerian term that refers to prominent figures, either in the public or market sector, who use the pen, in their offices, to loot public or company funds). He eschewed all forms of injustice and victimization, such as staff hiding people's files as a way of arm-twisting them in order to extort money out of them. He is known to have worked hard to ensure that contracts were properly executed as a way of protecting the interest of the state and the general public, but he also sought to ensure that those who invested in working for the state were paid promptly, as funds were made available. Similarly, it was his desire, and he worked hard, to ensure that he treated everyone with whom he had to deal equally without undue favoritism given to any. Certainly, his exemplary public service is worthy of emulation.

Another major achievement is his life of Christian service. His work as a tent-making urban church planter should make ECWA and other denominations like ECWA consider opening up the pastoral ministry to part-timers. He nurtured the church he had helped to plant from a membership of only about fifty people (including children) to a thriving congregation of over 2000. It is heartwarming to know that today, this congregation has also birthed two other churches. He is full of joy and gratitude to God for giving him the privilege of serving and bringing His work full circle. He considers this as a blessing because he is aware of the nature of crises that usually rock most churches, especially congregations with English and Hausa sections, but up till the time the section he led became an autonomous Local Church Board, there was no major crisis that warranted the mediation of third parties.

In the final analysis, Mr. Amishe counsels that people should first of all always,

> *...remember that life is a privilege. Secondly, they should also remember that in life, whatever you have is transient, and as such will vanish someday. Whether you gather or you don't gather, a time is coming when you will bow and take your exit out of this world. At your exit out of this world, you will take nothing with you, except your faith in the Lord God. That being the case, you need to constantly ask yourself, 'Why am I here on earth?' My belief is that God wants you to represent him wherever you find yourself—you are to be a witness of the living God.*

To Mr. Amishe, the task of being a witness to God's grace and faithfulness is a solemn and noble responsibility that knows no bounds: the home, church, market place, work place, and public square are all places in which one can bear witness to God's redemptive grace by one's life first and foremost, knowing that God himself is in every place.

To those who might feel that they would be cheated out of the "good things of life" if they were faithful in obedience to God, Mr. Amishe says,

> *I have personally carefully considered all these and have come to see that if God says, for*

instance, 'Don't defraud anyone,' this command is not meant to cheat you out of the proceeds of a fraudulent lifestyle; there is no need for you to begrudge God and be wishing you could be a fraudster like every other person on the street or in an exalted office. No! God doesn't want you engage in fraudulent activities because it is good—it is the right thing to do. When he says, 'Work hard,' it is not meant to cheat you, but to make you a better person so you can also help to make the society a better place for everyone. And when society is better, whether you like it or not, you too are better off for it. This is our calling as Christians.

CHAPTER THREE

REFINED BY THE REFINER'S FIRE

PROF. ISHAYA AUDU

THE BULUS AUDU FAMILY

The story of the late Prof. Ishaya Audu is told from the perspective of his beloved wife, Rev. (Mrs.) Victoria Abosede Ishaya Audu. Mrs. Audu met her husband in 1956, when he was a house officer at the University College Hospital (UCH), Ibadan, where she was a nurse at the time. They were married in 1958. While she never met her husband's mother because she had died in 1947, she knew his father, Pa Bulus Audu (Pa is a short form for Papa, which means father), whose life story is inextricably bound with that of Prof. Ishaya Audu.

A man of great intellect, Pa. Bulus Audu had been a Quranic teacher before he came to faith in Jesus Christ. He had learned the Quran by heart when he was a Muslim, and upon becoming a Christian, he similarly learned most of the Bible by heart. He and his family had lived in his ancestral home of Kano City, where he and several Hausa Muslims earlier on, based on their readings of the Quran, had become followers of Anebi Isa (the Prophet Jesus). Because of this, he, his family, and other followers of Anebi Isa faced persecution, so they had to relocate from Kano to Rafin Tabo, the hometown of his wife. At Rafin

Tabo they experienced a plague of sleeping sickness that nearly wiped them out, so they moved and settled at Anchau, where Pa Audu became a very prosperous sugar cane farmer, producing brown sugar for sale.

Pa Audu was ever so slowly being drawn closer to Jesus. While he was still a Muslim follower of Jesus, he had a glorious vision of the risen Lord. After this vision, he came to Zaria, where a Western missionary explained the gospel to him more perfectly, and he professed faith in Jesus Christ as his Saviour and Lord. He thereafter moved and settled in the Tudun Wada area of Zaria. In time, after proper discipleship, he became a skilled evangelist, able to share his faith effectively with Muslims using both the Quran and the Bible. Mrs. Audu recalls that by the time she met her father-in-law, he was already over 70 years of age, and he was called to glory when her husband was still the Vice-Chancellor of Ahmadu Bello University.

Prior to becoming a Christian Pa Bulus Audu had four wives. On becoming a Christian, as it was (and, unfortunately, still is) customary with mission church adherents, he kept his first wife, but sent away the other three. In the providence of God, his first wife died, so he brought back his second wife. When she also died in an epidemic, he brought back his third wife, who similarly died in the same epidemic. Finally, he brought back his fourth wife, who later became the mother of Prof. Ishaya Audu. Mrs. Audu does not know how many children her father-in-law had altogether, but she remembers that at the time she married into the family, eight of his children were still alive. Of these eight, three (a brother and two sisters) were siblings of Prof. Audu, from his own mother. Of Pa Audu's children, only one daughter (quite advanced in age herself) was still alive at the time of our interview in 2011. Mrs. Audu, however, acknowledges that her father-in-law has left quite a clan behind—his family meets once a year; and at the last meeting, where Mrs. Audu was present, there were over 180 descendants of Pa Bulus Audu in attendance, but that was not all of them.

PROF. ISHAYA AUDU'S CAREER PATH

By the time Ishaya Audu was born, his parents were already Christians, so he grew up in a Christian home, and by the time he met his wife, Ishaya was already a born-again Christian. Indeed, he was the president of the Scripture Union of UCH at the time. From Tudun Wada, the Audu family used to walk all the way to Wusasa to attend church activities at the Anglican Church. He attended elementary school at St. Bartholomew Anglican School. For both his O- and A-Level education, Ishaya attended Lagos Grammar School, from where he went to the University of Ibadan briefly before receiving a scholarship to study medicine at King's College, London. After qualifying as a medical doctor, Ishaya returned to Nigeria to do his housemanship at UCH. At the end of his housemanship, he again received another scholarship to return to the United Kingdom for his residency and post-graduate studies in pediatrics. He also obtained a diploma in public health while there.

When Dr. Ishaya Audu returned after the completion of his graduate studies, UCH did not have a place for him, so he moved north to Kano, working with the government of Northern Nigeria as the personal physician of the then Premier of the region, Sir Ahmadu Bello, the Sardauna of Sokoto. Dr. Audu was later transferred to Kaduna, as the Sardauna stayed more at the regional headquarters of the north. The Lagos University Teaching Hospital (LUTH) was established around the time he relocated to Kaduna, and with the nationalism of the post-independence era, there was a desire to make it truly national in outlook. Thus Dr. Audu and others were recruited from around the country as its founding faculty. He was still with LUTH when the first coup d'etat took place in Nigeria—the coup that swept away key leaders from the northern and western regions of Nigeria. This event would eventually lead to the thirty-month Nigerian Civil War. The ensuing violent conflict caused the then British vice-chancellor of Ahmadu Bello University (ABU) to flee the country in the latter part of 1966, in response to which the emergent head of state, Gen. Yakubu Gowon, appointed Dr. Ishaya Audu (at the time an associate professor of medicine) to be the first indigenous vice-chancellor of ABU. He was subsequently promoted to full professorship in ABU.

Prof. Ishaya Audu served as the VC of ABU for about nine-and-half years. It was the changes that accompanied the ascension of Gen. Murtala Mohammed to power that swept him out of office in 1975. At the time of the change, Prof. Audu, accompanied by his wife, had gone to Russia to attend a conference of university Vice Chancellors. On his way back, he stopped in Poland for recruitment purposes. In their first night in Poland, Prof. Audu's wife had a dream in which someone woke her up and told her to read Psalm 37. She asked, as she woke up, still half asleep, almost to herself,

"Why should I read Psalm 37?"

She then woke her husband up, his eyes were barely opening when she inquired of him, "Did you tell me to read Psalm 37?"

His tender response was, "My dear, you just woke me up, and are you asking me if I told you to read a Bible passage?"

Still perplexed and curious to know what was in that text of the Bible, she further inquired of her husband, "What is in Psalm 37?"

Desirous of resting from the weariness of the conference and travel, he gently replied her "Well, you can read it in the morning."

Presently, the phone rang. Local time at the moment was 4:00am. The call was from a staff member at the Nigerian embassy in Warsaw, who told Prof. Audu that a new Vice Chancellor had just been announced for ABU back home. The puzzled professor asked his informant what was supposed to happen to him. The voice on the other end of the line simply said, "Well, there was no mention of you"— and the phone went dead.

After that night's phone call, the reading of the psalm could no longer be postponed till the break of day, so Prof. Audu prodded his wife, *"Why don't we read Psalm 37 now?"* After that reading, he said to her, *"The Lord is talking to us through Psalm 37."* In their reading of Psalm 37, it was verse 25 that stood out for Prof. Audu: *"I have been young, and now am old, yet I have not seen the righteous forsaken or his children begging for bread"* (Psalm 37:25 ESV). The verse was the word of promise that the Lord gave to them that he was going to take care of them. On this word they hung as a drowning person would on a lifeline thrown out to him. As she looked over the ensuing times, Rev. (Mrs.) Audu recalls, *"Those were traumatic days, but thank God, my husband knew God; he knew God. So he was like the rock for the family."* What preoccupied Mrs. Audu for the moment was the trouble of having to pack out of the house in which they had been living for nearly ten years; this had to be done in just three weeks.

Prof. Audu was later informed by the ABU London office that the university authorities back home had approved for him to proceed on his sabbatical leave, and he could stay in the UK for that purpose. Prof. & Mrs. Audu had to first of all return to Nigeria to pack out of their official residence, to make room for the new Vice Chancellor. It was after this that they returned to London, as a family, for the professor's well deserved sabbatical leave. His entitlements from ABU as a professor on sabbatical were never paid, however, so life was hard. He had a job, but his wife also augmented their income by continuing her business in distributive trade. To make matters worse, the one-year Sabbatical extended to three years, and by 1978 the beckoning of home was too much for Prof. Audu. He could no longer continue to sojourn in a foreign land. He told his wife, who would have preferred to stay in London, to consider the long commute across town he had to make to work every day, and how nasty it got in the winters.

At that time, Ashaka Cement advertised the position of chief medical officer, and Prof. Audu applied. Initially, he was interviewed and offered the job, but later on, the Ashaka people told him that they did not plan on having a Nigerian for that position; they were, however, willing to take him on as deputy chief medical officer. This was rather an unpleasant development, but since Prof. Audu's mind was turned homeward, he decided to take the job anyway. He subsequently resigned his appointment in London and returned to Nigeria at the approach of winter in 1978. Because that was in the middle of the school year, Mrs. Audu stayed with the children until the end of the school year.

After having been home for some time, Prof. Audu called his wife and told her that old friends of his, like Chief Dr. Solomon Lar, were asking him to run for the governorship of the now defunct North Central State on the ticket of the Nigerian People's Party (NPP). This was in the early stages of the process that led to the return to civil rule in 1979. Prof. Audu's consideration of politics was a big surprise to his wife, as she never envisioned him as a politician. Her husband told her he was still praying about it, and the idea of being the governor's wife was attractive to her, so she never objected. After some time of prayer, he felt persuaded to veer off into politics. Later on, she learned that her husband had been tipped to be the running mate to the NPP's presidential candidate, the Rt. Hon. Dr. Nnamdi Azikiwe, the Owelle of Onitsha. Prof. Audu resigned his job at Ashaka and took up a part-time appointment with a clinic in Wusasa, where he was given accommodation. Mrs. Audu also eventually returned to Nigeria and joined him on the campaign trail. On the side, she ran a restaurant in Samaru called Ace of Heart. The restaurant was convenient for her because her husband and other politicians would return from their busy schedules around midnight wanting food to eat, so she did a brisk business serving them.

Maintaining integrity is usually not a path to wealth. It is inconceivable in today's Nigeria that a man who had been the personal physician of the powerful premier of Northern Nigeria and had served as vice-chancellor of a premier Nigerian university for nine good years would find himself without a car. But that was the Audus' story: Prof. Audu, as a presidential running mate, had no car. People kept telling him to buy a car, but his simple response to them was that he did not have the money to do so; and that was the truth. During his tenure as vice-chancellor, his wife used to be vexed with him because she saw people in similar positions stealing public funds, and she could not understand why he would not also steal. His abiding response was that people shall stand alone before God as individuals on the judgment day to render account of their stewardship of the trust God gave them. So if his wife made him steal, she would not be there to defend him; he alone would be accountable for what he had done. Now they were out of office and had to begin again from scratch, and Mrs. Audu did not find it funny.

FAMILY LIFE

At the time of his call to glory, Prof. and Mrs. Audu had been married for forty-seven years. Together, they had seven biological children and a few adopted ones, and by 2011 they had nineteen grandchildren and were expecting many more, since their youngest son had just gotten married a couple of years earlier. The late Prof. Audu was a family man per excellence and was very fond of his family. He cared deeply about the welfare of members of his family, even though he did not have much in the way of material goods. As a vice-chancellor, once he got his salary, he would give three-quarters of it to his wife for the upkeep of the family. Of the remaining one-quarter, he would tithe to his church and fulfill his obligations to extended family members. At the end of the day, his personal pocket money was never more than 5% of his total pay. Even though his wife was not yet a believer in the true sense of the word, the way he cared for the family ensured that there was harmony in the home. In sum, Mrs. Audu remembers her husband as a loving husband and a caring father. She, on her part, to augment the family income, did work some of the time that they were married, but she loved business more, and always found things to sell.

Mrs. Audu recalls that faithfulness to the Lord was very central to her husband's life, and that he taught this to the family as well. Prof. Audu always wanted the best for his children, so he taught them that the fear of the Lord was the foundation of a truly satisfying life. He taught them to pray. The early morning family altar was always very important to him. He lived by example, and the children grew up knowing that integrity and hard work were important virtues. Mrs. Audu recalls that after she challenged one of her daughters to hard work, the daughter made her promise to buy a car for her if she became a doctor before her twenty-first birthday. Nobody thought it was possible, but the daughter worked hard and made it, and so she got her car.

TRIUMPHING IN
THE VAGARIES OF LIFE

Not only is life not a bed of roses, even rose flowers come with thorns. In God's providence, the Audus have had rosy moments in their lives, but with those roses have come thorns. Mrs. Audu recalls that a Christian lady in

ABU taught her a song with lyrics that say, *"After the sun comes the rain, after the rain the sun."* That is the way their life had been. After the hard time of his campaigning without a car and her running a restaurant to make ends meet, her husband's party (the NPP) did not win the elections, but it entered into an accord with the winning party, the National Party of Nigeria (NPN), and as a fallout from the deal, Prof. Audu became the Minister of Foreign Affairs and for the next four years, they were comfortable financially. Midway through Alh. Shehu Shagari's first tenure as president, however, the NPN-NPP accord broke down, and Prof. Audu changed party membership to the NPN so that he could remain in the government. By the end of Shagari's first tenure, however, Prof. Audu was not keen on continuing as minister, so he was sent to New York as Nigeria's ambassador and permanent representative at the United Nations (UN). It was while he was there that the military coup of December 1983 took place.

Meanwhile the Lord had been working with Mrs. Audu by revealing future major events to her via dreams. Thus, barely one year into Alh. Shagari's tenure as president, while her husband was serving as minister, she dreamt that there was a coup at the end of that first tenure and that they were imprisoned. In that dream, Mrs. Audu and the children escaped through the Republic of Niger to the United Kingdom. She therefore urged her husband to go warn the president, but her husband gave her a typical macho response: *"Do you mean I should go to the President, and tell him my wife had a dream that there will be a coup in four years' time and we will be imprisoned? He will think you and I are lunatics."*

Mrs. Audu implored her husband with much entreaty: *"No, remember the 1966 coup. I also had a dream about that, even though I didn't understand it and I didn't know how to pray, but I knew a great commotion was coming,"* she reminded him. The former dream had been of a coming commotion, and after she shared that with Prof. Audu, he had driven through the night from Lagos to Kaduna to see the Sardauna and warn him. He had just arrived at the Sardauna's house in Kaduna when all of a sudden they began to hear gunshots. He had arrived too late to warn the Sardauna of the imminent danger, and the Sardauna had died in the coup. But time had passed, and Prof. Audu had forgotten the incident.

The 1983 elections had come and gone. Prof. Audu was now in New York. The then Secretary General of the UN was to visit Nigeria early in the New Year, and as Nigerian's ambassador to the UN, Prof. Audu was supposed to go ahead and prepare the way for a proper reception for the August visitor. As he prepared for that journey in late December 1983, his wife had completely forgotten about the dream she had had four years earlier. However, as soon as Prof. Audu's plane took off, the memory of that dream returned to her mind like flash photography. She became frantic, wanting to get in touch with her husband. She waited for him to get to London because he was to change planes in London. She kept on calling the Heathrow Airport VIP lounge and nobody was answering her calls. Finally, after several hours, a protocol officer at the lounge answered her. She heard what she didn't want to hear: for the first time in many years Nigerian Airways (the now defunct Nigerian national carrier) plane had operated punctually and they had taken off. Mrs. Audu began to cry; she cried all that night. Then in the morning she phoned the Ministry of Foreign Affairs, and they told her they had not seen her husband.

"What! You've not seen him?" She asked anxiously.

"No," came the answer from the other side of the Atlantic.

Determined to know the whereabouts of her husband, she called her late uncle, who was then a police commissioner in Lagos State. She described her desperate, fruitless attempts to get in touch with her husband and ended with this passionate plea:

"This is what happened, please, look for my husband."

He did the necessary checks and confirmed her fears by evening. "I am sorry, he's in Kirikiri," he told her.

The anguish in Mrs. Audu's was telling, as she could barely manage to get her question out, "He is in Kirikiri? For what offence"? She was told that, just as she had dreamt, the military had taken over power in a coup, and all prominent political figures, especially those in the ruling party, were being herded to Kirikiri Maximum Prison.

After several months of unjust incarceration, no charges were pressed against them. Mrs. Audu had hired a lawyer to defend her husband, but they were told that though he had not done anything wrong, he and the other political prisoners had to be kept in prison so that the new military regime could secure their hold on power. The months turned into years, while Prof. Audu and other political prisoners languished in prison, until another coup occurred in 1985. Gen. I. B. Babangida engineered another coup, and his way of securing his hold to power was to ingratiate himself with the people by freeing all political prisoners, Prof. Audu inclusive.

While in prison, Prof. Audu received a call to the gospel ministry. He devoted his time to reading the Bible and the Quran, the only books they were allowed to read. Before his release from prison, he had read the Bible through three or four times, and he began preaching to his fellow inmates. He would pray for those who were sick, and many of them received healing. He also devoted a good amount of time to praying for his family, and it was during this time that his wife came to the saving knowledge of the Lord Jesus Christ. Meanwhile, his family had initially moved to London, where his wife started attending a Bible school. When Prof. Audu was released from prison, some of his children returned to join him in Zaria, while his wife completed ministerial training.

Life after imprisonment was a new experience entirely. By the time he was released from Kirikiri, Prof. Audu did not even have the money to return to Zaria. An old friend of his, the late Mr. Sunday Dankaro provided money for him to fly to Kaduna, take a taxi to Zaria, and keep body and soul together for some time. Upon his return to Zaria, he was engaged by Anakitch Hospital as a doctor. Along the way, the Lord impressed upon him the need to be independent so he would be able to do the things he was called to do. In response to this, he took a bank loan to start the Savannah Polyclinic, which became his operational base for ministry as well.

THE AUDUS AND MINISTRY

Prof. Audu knew that he was not meant to be dealing solely with people's bodily ailments but their soul sicknesses as well. Having never traveled on that route before, he was unsure how to begin. By now his children, who had returned from overseas to join him, were also on fire for the Lord, though his wife was still in mission school. Together with his children, they started the Savannah Fellowship. They did not know much, but what they knew, they taught others; and people started coming. They soon found friends from ABU (like Rev. Boye Alonge, who now ministers in Abuja), who were further along the way in the knowledge of the Scriptures, to help with the teaching ministry. In time, his wife also returned and joined the fellowship, which consisted mostly of youths. Prof. Audu felt that they needed to turn the fellowship into a full-fledged church. He called on everyone to fast and pray. They fasted for thirty days, and at the end of the fasting period, the Lord confirmed to them in a dream that the fellowship was to become a church. Some of the members of the fellowship did not like the idea and left, but the Audus continued.

Savannah Polyclinic on its part was doing very well. It became the major source of support for the family, the fellowship, and the rural outreaches in which they were actively engaged. The success story of the hospital, according to Mrs. Audu, is largely attributable to the diagnostic capacities of her husband: *"I remember an American professor of medicine saying that my husband is one of the best diagnosticians in Africa south of the Sahara."* She views her husband's diagnostic acuity as a divine endowment. He was so good at diagnosis that whatever he thought was the matter with a patient would invariably turn out to be the case no matter the number of tests that were performed. Notwithstanding, he always ordered tests to get the needed confirmation for the right course of treatment.

Prof. Audu did not reserve his medical skills for paying patients only. He also cared for those who could not pay, viewing it as part of his ministry calling. It was also not uncommon for him to receive payment in kind from those who did not have the cash to pay for services rendered. An example of this would be a Fulani cattle herder, paying for a hernia surgery with a sheep or a goat.

The work of the ministry was focused on the many villages around Zaria. They were reaching out to the Fulani people, who are usually bypassed by Christian outreaches. Prof. Audu also became concerned about the fate of the children in the villages where they were ministering; they were not going to school at all. So they would also have an opportunity for an education, he started a school. The children who attended the school needed to live in the town, so the Audus took them into their home, providing housing, clothing, food, medical care, and all of their other needs. The girls lived in the family house with the Audus while the boys stayed in another building. The number of the children brought over from the villages kept increasing until it reached thirty-two, and still more needed to come. At that point, the Audus expanded the house, but eventually they had to build a separate house for the children. Today a full-fledged hostel has been built that accommodates about a hundred children, thanks to the generous bequest of Gen. T. Y. Danjuma. From its humble beginning, that school has grown today to consist of nursery, primary, and secondary schools for both paying and sponsored students. Because the people they were ministering to consisted largely of students and villagers, the demands for funds for ministry support was huge. Much of this cost was defrayed from the professor's medical practice. However, they also had two friends from Canada who regularly sent support for the work. Their own children, who were now living overseas also became financial supporters of the ministry. They also received support from other friends from the United States and the United Kingdom.

Upon the death of Prof. Ishaya Audu in 2005, his wife considered how to sustain his legacy. She therefore launched the Prof. Ishaya Audu Foundation, which received generous gifts from friends, not least Gen. T. Y. Danjuma. The foundation now runs the schools, the churches around Zaria, and the extension of the work to several villages in Niger. It supports the pastors who are serving in rural Niger, and it brings their children and sponsors them in the schools in Zaria so they will not be deprived of good education because their parents are serving the Lord. The foundation also carries out yearly short-term missions in the villages of Niger, where it provides free medical services to the indigent people there.

EXCURSUS ON MRS. VICTORIA AUDU'S JOURNEY OF FAITH

Though married to a born-again Christian for 25 years, Mrs. Victoria Ishaya remained a nominal Christian.

It took the catastrophic impact of the 1983 coup to shake her to her foundations so she could hear God. For a while after the coup occurred and her husband was imprisoned, she did nothing but sit in her apartment in New York and watch TV. One day she stumbled on a Christian channel and heard the preaching of Dr. Fredrick Price. What he was saying sounded so outlandish to her that she wondered about the kind of Bible he was reading. Then she reached for her Bible, opened it, and started reading the passages he was reading. To her surprise, she was reading the same words he was. She was sold in, and she listened to the end. After him, came Dr. Kenneth E. Hagin, and then others. That was how God started breaking up the fallow ground of her heart. She eventually left New York and joined her children in London, where they were attending secondary school.

Though God had already begun to draw her to himself in New York, it was in London that she made a complete turnaround. One day, a niece of hers, whose husband was a diplomat in Russia at the time, was visiting; and she asked Mrs. Audu if she were born again. That question stirred up rage in her, and she replied feistily, *"Please, don't talk to me about **born again**; don't talk to me about God. Where was God when all these things were happening?"* Knowing better than to argue with someone in that state, her neice just handed her a little booklet, *Plead your Case with God,* by Kenneth E. Hagin. Mrs. Audu started to read the booklet and was immediately drawn into it. She read it through, then she read it through again, and then she read it one more time. Then she began to cry. As St. Augustine of Hippo said, human souls are restless until they find their rest in Christ, Mrs. Audu's soul was at last finding its rest in Christ alone by grace alone through faith alone. At the end of that booklet was the sinner's prayer. She prayed that prayer and invited Jesus into her life. She would never be the same again.

The following Sunday, her niece came and took her to church—a Pentecostal church, not the Anglican Church she had been attending. Once the preacher mounted the pulpit, it was as if her niece had gone to tell the man about her life. She was deeply offended, and turned to her niece and queried her why she had gone to discuss her life with the preacher. Her niece denied even knowing who the preacher was, let alone having met with him. Well, the power of the message was so strong that Mrs. Audu could not resist it. The sermon was followed by an altar call, and she knew deep down within her heart that she could ill afford to miss this opportunity to have a new beginning with God. She stepped forward and answered the altar call. She was counseled by a lady pastor at the church by the name of Jane, who instantly took to liking Mrs. Audu. She regularly visited her at home, studied the Bible with her and her children, and prayed with them

Mrs. Audu's heart was now aflame for God. She wanted to know more about faith—how faith works in daily life, and how it is that nothing is impossible with God. Her hunger and thirst for God's word was insatiable. She decided to attend Bible school so she could learn more. At the end of her training in Bible school, she was unsure what to do with herself, but at that crucial time, an American preacher visited her church in London. The man called her and told her that God was going to bring beauty to her ministry, and that worship and prayer would be the strength of her ministry. He also told her that affliction would not arise for her a second time, that the days of her affliction were over, and that her husband was going to be out of prison soon.

None of these made sense to her. What ministry was he talking about, and where? In Nigeria? No, not her. She would never return to Nigeria again. Then the visiting preacher invited her to attend a mission school in Tulsa, Oklahoma, in the United States. She asked him how about the children—how would they be provided for? They were at that time in one of the most expensive secondary schools in London. His reply was that God would take care of them.

Mrs. Audu took up the invitation and went to the mission school in Tulsa. But before committing herself to the school, she visited the area to attend a conference there. While she was gone, the late Chief M. K. O. Abiola, a friend of the Audu family, came to visit. When he arrived, he was told that she had gone to a Bible convention in America. He replied that he thought the Audus had no money. The relative who was watching over the children told him that truly they didn't have money, but that Mrs. Audu had *"gone crazy about God, and she keeps saying that God will provide everything they need."* Chief Abiola's response was, *"Well, I am not God, but I came. Take this cheque and give to her, when she returns."* The cheque was in the amount of £70,000, which provided for the children's school fees and more. Through this, Mrs. Audu continued to learn by experience the faithfulness of God, and they continued living by faith, believing God for what they needed. Her belief is that God's principles for the physical earth apply in spiritual things as well. After the flood, God told Noah, *"While the earth remains, seedtime and harvest, cold and heat, summer and winter, day and night, shall not cease"* (Genesis 8:22 ESV). So, for her in terms of giving, there is always seedtime and harvest. God will never fail his people.

Now, everything was set for her to go for her training in the mission school, so she finally left for the United States. The training went by quickly, and the time for their practicum came. They were to go to Guatemala. They had a three-week crash programme in the Spanish language, and they were flown to Guatemala. In Guatemala, they went to market squares to share their faith with the people there. They also went to a village and helped a local pastor build a church. Having completed their time there, they returned to the States, where she finished her mission training programme and returned to the UK. By this time, her husband had sent word that they could all return to Nigeria now. All of their children, except the youngest one, had finished their A-levels and were ready for the university when they returned to Nigeria. The youngest one got a placement at the United Gospel Faith Tabernacle Secondary School, Jarawan Kogi. So all the family was together once again.

LAST WORDS

As Mrs. Audu muses about their lives, she recalls two fundamental biblical truths that undergirded the life philosophy of her late husband. They are, first, *"The fear of the LORD is the beginning of knowledge"* (Proverbs. 1:7 ESV), and second, *"For we must all appear before the judgment seat of Christ, so that each one may receive what is due for what he has done in the body, whether good or evil"* (2 Corinthians 5:10 ESV). He was guided by the desire to honour God in all his ways, and he at the same time lived with the consciousness that he will one day stand before God to render account of his life. Mrs. Audu believes that this stood her husband in good stead. She is happy that, guided by these truths, he refused to yield to her urgings (when she was still a nominal Christian) to enrich himself corruptly via the public offices he held. Through the years they came to enjoy God's faithfulness to his word and to his people. His word says, *"Seek first the kingdom of God and his righteousness, and all these things will be added to you"* (Matthew 6:33 ESV). This has been the story of their lives. She notes that they may not have been millionaires or billionaires, but they have never lacked anything that they needed, God's hand always provided, for which they remain eternally thankful. This is the kind of life she recommends to other believers as well.

CHAPTER FOUR

THE TEACHER OF NATIONS

PROF. ADAMU BAIKE

FAMILY BACKGROUND

The city of Kano, prior to British colonial rule, was a well-known centre of Islamic civilization and a major hub in the trans-Saharan trade. The articles for which it was reputed include hides and skins, and woven and dyed cloth. During the British colonial administration, especially after the railroad reached it, Kano became the commodities hub for northern Nigeria. The rising groundnut pyramids that came to define its horizon were a testament to its rise as the commercial capital of the north, just as Kaduna was the north's political capital. It was in this city that Adamu Baike was born to the family of Jacob and Rebecca Baike on October 2, 1931. At his birth, his father named him after their ancestral village, Dumo. The family name of Mr. Jacob Baike, of Shuwa Arab origin, was Abdallah. Mr. Abdallah, who like his wife (of Fulani extraction), was a Muslim from birth, became a Christian through the ministry of a missionary of the Christian Missionary Society (CMS), Rev. Baike. It was this missionary's family name that Jacob adopted on his day of baptism.

Jacob Baike's conversion to Christianity was a life-transforming experience. Under the mentorship of Rev. Baike, he trained as an evangelist and teacher in all of the training programmes that were available at the time. He used those skills in his service as a missionary in the CMS until his retirement in 1921. Upon his retirement from CMS, Jacob worked with the Nigerian Railway Corporation as a clerk until 1932, when he entered the service of the Kano Native Authority. In the Native Authority offices, Jacob's proficiency as a clerk earned him the privilege of working with the Madaki, and eventually he was moved to the office of the Galadima of Kano, where he work as the chief scribe until his final retirement in 1949.

Jacob Baike learned how to navigate his challenging working environment as he strove to maintain loyalty to his employers while retaining unflinching faithfulness to his faith. In the entire period of his work in the colonial Kano Native Authority, Mr. Baike was the only Christian. In those days, Sharia law was the norm in Kano; Fridays were work-free days, while Sunday was a regular working day. For much of his days in the NA employment, Mr. Baike had to be content with attending only evening services on Sunday. One interesting thing Prof. Adamu Baike recalls about this period is that even though his father was such an insignificant minority, there was no pressure on him to revert to Islam: bigotry was not part of the way Sharia law was implemented in those days.

The two faiths co-existed and tolerated each other so well in those days that though Mr. Baike had become a Christian, when he sought to marry Rebecca, who was still then a Muslim, her parents raised no objection. For the first thirty years of their marriage, Mrs. Baike remained a Muslim. Indeed, all her eight children were born and raised while she retained her Islamic faith. Ever so slowly, however, Mrs. Baike began to warm up to the faith of her husband and children. She occasionally attended Sunday services, but she never professed faith in Christ, though over time she learned the Lord's Prayer, and how to say grace. Finally, in 1948, her family enjoyed the thrill and exhilaration of seeing her declare her faith in Jesus Christ as her Lord and Saviour. No words could express the joy of her children and husband when they saw her take her stand for Christ. It was only then that it dawned on them how much they had desired and longed for this glorious day. Mama Baike was promptly baptized, on which occasion her husband gave her the biblical name of Rebecca.

The advent of Western education placed severe financial strain on large people who wanted their children to be educated, and the Baikes had eight children. While the mission schools offered the best education in those days, they were expensive. An evangelist, however, would never think of having his children attend a public school, so because Mr. Baike's meagre wage as a clerk could not adequately cater to the needs of such a big family, Mrs. Baike also had to take up menial jobs in order to supplement his income. As hard as they worked, they rarely had enough money for either their children's tuition fees or their uniforms. Adamu's mentors at St. Peter's College often stepped in to pay his tuition fees, which made it possible for him to complete his secondary education.

The peaceful ambience of the Jacob and Rebecca Baike's home, in spite of their difficult circumstances, was a strong witness to Christ's grace to their Muslim neighbours. In spite of their hardships they remained radiant. Though Rebecca had to work as hard as her husband, she never nagged him about it. The Baike family never despaired nor complained about their challenges, but always bore them gracefully. Unbeknownst to them, the peaceful demeanour of their family dynamic attracted much attention, and through their virtuous exhibition of the Christian family life, they bore eloquent testimony to the transforming grace of God to the Muslim community, and earned its respect.

Being one of the first to receive Western education in Kano, Mr. Baike never took it for granted. As an educated person of his day, he took a keen interest in his children's performance in school. At the end of each term, he would scrutinize their report cards so as to know how they were performing. He never paid attention to academics only; he paid equal, if not greater, attention to the report on their conduct. On this score, he would be as much irked with poor conduct as he would have been with poor academic grades. While he paid ardent attention to his children's performance, he never pressured them into pursuing any career path. He only spurred them on to be the best that they could be or desired to be. The opposite was the standard practice of his contemporaries, who tended to insist on their children entering elite careers in medicine or law. His approach helped his children to thrive in the areas of their interest and capabilities.

EDUCATION AND CAREER

Adamu, just like his siblings, attended CMS schools, beginning in a CMS preparatory school in Fege, Kano, where instruction was solely in the Hausa language. Later he attended the Holy Trinity School, Kano, which at the time was a transfer school. He eventually transferred to Holy Trinity School, Lokoja, where he completed his primary education. Upon his return from Lokoja, Adamu spent his next three years of schooling at the Wusasa Military School, which was then run by the CMS. For his secondary education, Adamu attended St. Peter's College for two years of middle school (1949–1950). As it was the custom then, his education was punctuated with a year's teaching service, which he did in Gusau. When he returned from Gusau, he along with other students, was admitted to be one of the pioneer students of the high school section of St. Peter's College, Samaru, whose campus was later taken over and turned into the Samaru Campus of Ahmadu Bello University.

When he completed his secondary education, Adamu went on to teach at the St. Peter's Practising School in 1955. After a stint with teaching, he proceeded to pursue his bachelor's degree at the then Nigerian College of Art and Technology, Zaria, which would later become the Ahmadu Bello University (ABU). After his graduation, Adamu was one of the first Nigerian nationals to be recruited into the faculty of ABU. He was employed as a graduate assistant in 1962 and immediately sent overseas for his master's degree, which he completed in 1964. After three years of service at ABU, Adamu went to the United States for his doctoral studies in education in 1967. In the record time of three years, Prof. Adamu Baike completed his Ph. D. in Education Technology (with a minor in Psychology), being the first Nigerian to have that specialty. He then returned and taught at ABU without interruption from 1970 to 1978, when he was appointed as the Vice Chancellor of the University of Benin.

Of the roughly four decades of his career in the ivory tower, Prof. David Adamu Baike spent nearly three in university administration. He served for eight years as the Vice Chancellor of the University of Benin, after which he proceeded on his sabbatical leave. After his return from sabbatical leave, he spent only one year at ABU, and in 1988 he was asked to serve as the Vice Chancellor of the National University of Lesotho, in southern Africa, where he served for two terms again. He returned to Nigeria in 1996. By 2001 he was once more appointed the pioneer Vice Chancellor of the newly established Nasarawa State University, Lafia, where he served out two full terms, and then voluntarily retired in 2009.

CHOOSING CHRIST

Though having a Muslim wife, Mr. Jacob Baike

faithfully raised his children in the Christian faith. They were usually introduced to the Saviour very early in their lives; and in the times in which "decisionism" had as yet to be the norm in Christian tradition, most young people who grew up in Christian families were not accustomed to speaking of a specific day on which they became Christians. Nevertheless, their experience of Christ's saving grace was never in doubt. Such was the experience of Adamu and his siblings. This is not to say that theirs was purely an inherited faith, but they made the faith of their father theirs very early in their lives.

Aside from the influence of his godly father, the benefits of an early Christian education in his life are incalculable. Adamu recalls that in those days, beginning in elementary school, instruction in the basics of the Christian faith and virtuous living were fused with all school activities. The first opening activity of every school day was a devotional time, and the first subject to be studied each day was Christian religious knowledge. Throughout the day, break times were heralded with the singing of spiritual songs, and the school day also ended with singing. In this way, the schools' atmosphere was permeated with thoughts of God and spiritual things. At the secondary education level, greater attention was paid to developing Christian discipleship and character. These experiences became the bedrock of Adamu's life orientation, and this is the legacy he endeavours to pass on not only to his own children but now also to his grandchildren.

FAMILY LIFE

Adamu Baike and his wife of over fifty years, Yarbaba Elizabeth Sa'adatu (née Usman), were married on July 1, 1961. Elizabeth came from a Muslim family. Her aunt, by whom she was raised, was the first in her family to become a Christian; and she, her Ghanian husband and their family attended the same church as the

Baikes. It was at this church that Adamu met Elizabeth and became interested in her. It happened that Adamu's mother and Elizabeth's mother were friends. All this made the courtship and marriage arrangements much smoother. Elizabeth was the second person in her family to become a Christian: her parents were still Muslims. Notwithstanding, there has always been a wonderful relationship between the two families. They have mutual respect for each other's faiths, and they support each other and exchange gifts during each other's great festivals such as Christmas and Salah. Not only so, in the typical African tradition, the Baikes trained several of Elizabeth's relatives up to university education level. The gracious demonstration of Christian love by the Baikes to their in-laws has borne such strong witness that a couple of them have elected to be followers of the Messiah.

The Baikes have followed in the footsteps of Adamu's godly father in raising their children with the fear of the Lord. His goal when they were raising their children, like that of his father, was that he and his wife would exemplify the precepts they were teaching their children. According to the grace provided by the Lord, this they did to the best of their ability. The Lord blessed their hearts' desire in bringing all their children to the knowledge of the truth. Even as grown men and women, they are not just Christians but are also actively involved in the ministries of the churches where they attend: two of them are even deacons in their respective churches.

Though raised in his native city of Kano, Adamu had earlier on adopted Zaria as his domicile. They make trips to Kano from time to time to visit extended family members, but for them Zaria is home. Both in their growing up years and adult lives, they have always lived as a Christian minority in Muslim majority neighbourhoods. They have learned not only to maintain good neighbourliness, but more so to be Christ's ambassadors and represent him well before their neighbours. By this, they have always had excellent relationships with their neighbours, even though they are of a different faith, and by extension they have become Christ's open letters to their neighbours.

A FAITH TRIED AND TESTED

Prof. & Mrs. David Adamu Baike do not believe in bifurcating life into the sacred and secular, as is common these days. For them, life is one, and has to be lived in honour of the great King. Thus, in all of their vocational lives they always strive to be the best that they could ever be in those positions for the glory of God. Similarly, their strong faith in God keeps them from being intimidated by anyone or anything. A few examples will suffice here.

Coming from northern Nigeria, where fetishism is not universally an open affair, part of the culture shock Prof. Baike had to contend with when he moved to Benin City was the fetishism that is endemic in Benin life. He recalls that while in Benin, and working with people of divergent religious persuasions, he often got many unsolicited divinations from them. Counsel like this was not uncommon:[2]

"Oga sir, if dem bring kola for you, no chop am o. Bad bad dey inside."

"Even sef, make you no drink the palm wine wey dem go serve you there o."

In his characteristic manner, Prof. Baike would assure them he would follow their advice. However, when the moment came, he would do the opposite of their counsel. God protected him throughout these experiences. Prof. Baike recalls times when because of strife within the university community, people who thought they were doing him a favour would come to warn him not take particular roads, as his enemies were believed to have planted fetish articles to harm him. With faith in God, he would take the same routes and nothing happened to him, to the astonishment of those people. While Prof. Baike may not have thought of Mark 16:17–18, his testimonies are a manifestation of the perfect fulfillments of the promises that Christ had made to those who would believe in him.

His administrative philosophy was to place service above self, almost to a fault. Though he and his wife shared the same values, she would tease him for his Spartan-like austere lifestyle, calling him "the missionary Vice Chancellor." For example, throughout their eight years in Benin, he chose to retain the furniture his predecessor had used, even though he could have rightfully changed the furniture. Prof. Baike appreciates his wife, who, unlike many others of her contemporaries, was not given to ostentatious living, and as such never pressured him into any illegality. Together, they gave their children the same orientation, so that they never at any point sought to be "like the Joneses."

At the end of his tenure in Benin in 1986, he left the huge balance in the university coffers of ₦11 million.[3] One day during his last few days in Benin, he got what he thought was a routine call from the manager of the university's bankers. The voice at the end of the line, deep and hard at the same time, blurted out, "Good day, sir. This is the Manager of the UBA branch, sir."

"Hello, good day," Prof. Baike responded in his usual calm and calculated voice.

"Mr. Vice Chancellor, sir, there is, eh, this, eh, money in the University account," the bank manager mumbled, finally finding his voice.

"What money"? The professor asked, with a slight surprise in his voice.

Mustering some courage to continue the discussion, the bank manager said, "You have ₦11million and you are not doing anything about it."

"So what do you want me to do about it?" Prof. Baike's voice became impatient and stern.

A deafening silence fell at the other end of the line, and then came the click of a dropped phone line: end of discussion. Shaking his head, Prof. Baike hung up his phone receiver, but he couldn't help wondering whether this manner of solicitation was not becoming the norm since the military era of the mid to late 1980s.

Prof. Baike left Benin with nothing material, but to his delight his integrity was intact. As he prepared to leave, he realized that he didn't even have a car anymore. The car he had had as a professor in ABU eight years earlier had become too old and of little use. As he contemplated what to do, a friend of his, Senator Osakwe, a student of the university's faculty of law at the time, called and solicited his patronage. The senator owned a dealership of Peugeot cars, which were the reigning cars for people of moderate income in those days.

"I would like you to buy some cars from me before leaving, perhaps, one or two," said Senator Osakwe.

"But I don't have money to buy a car, much less two," was the professor's reply.

"Sir, you are my Vice Chancellor. Take as many as you want; pay me whenever you are able to pay."

This was a great offer coming from someone who was eager to repay a kind gesture, having obtained his admission into the university via the courtesy of the Vice Chancellor.

Prof. Baike weighed his options carefully, but concluded he was not in the position to take this offer: having not been materialistic previously, he couldn't afford to start now. "No, I can't," was his resolute, honest and straightforward answer. At that time a Peugeot 504 salon was going for ₦8,000, while the wagon sold at ₦4,000. Senator Osakwe, whether out of a desire to spawn a business for his company or to reciprocate a kind gesture or simply to assist a friend in need, was insistent. He also met with an adamant posture from his professor friend.

When his persistence failed to yield the desired result, he at long last decided to make a free gift, as the transportation need of his friend was obvious. The senator finally said, "Ok, just take one car."

Not wanting to appear too difficult, the professor agreed to take one. But Prof. Baike, not being accustomed to taking things he never paid for, was determined to pay for it. He obtained a ₦15,000 bank loan, with which he paid for the car. That car was the only car Prof. Baike had on leaving Benin, and it indeed became very useful in supplementing the family's income, as he had to give it to a driver to run on commercial basis.

Besides his faith and love for God, another ethical motivation for Prof. Baike was being the first northerner to be appointed to head a citadel of learning in southern Nigeria. In his thinking, in addition to being an ambassador for Christ, he was also an ambassador for the north. So he thought that it should not happen that other northerners would be denied the opportunity of serving in similar capacities in the south in the future because of a dismal performance on his part. Thus, besides personal integrity, he also adopted the committee style of governance in his administrations. This meant inclusiveness and transparency in all he did: All the major players in the university administration were involved in all major decision.

Doing the right thing does not make one immune from false accusation. In fact, in our contemporary world, standing for what is right could even earn one more enemies who would seek one's downfall for refusing to oblige them in their sinister schemes. Prof. Baike came to learn this from a personal experience. He at one time had gone to Lagos (the then seat of the federal government) to defend the budget on behalf of the university. While in Lagos, he was surprised with a visit from the University of Benin public relations officer (PRO).

"Wh...wh...what is the problem?" the professor

asked the PRO in surprise.

The PRO had an uneasy quiet about him, but he finally found the voice to utter, "The NSO are looking for you, sir; and I thought I should come and tell you. They've asked me to ask you to release your passport to them." Now, NSO stands for National Security Organization, an FBI type security apparatus that was the predecessor of the present Department of State Services, SSS).

"Do you have any idea what they want?" Prof. Baike queried.

"Well, they are accusing you of taking kickback from a contractor to whom you awarded a contract to the tune of 11 or 12 million Naira."

"Is that all?" The relieved Professor Baike inquired, to the PRO's surprise.

"Yes, sir." He replied.

"It's alright," Prof. Baike assured him. "It's late now. Go get a room in one of the hotels for the night. Tomorrow morning, when you get back to the office, open my top drawer, I never lock it, anyway; you will find my passport there, remove it and give it to them."

"But sir, in the event that they request to search the house, is there anything you would want us to remove from the house?" solicited the PRO.

"What do you mean?" Prof. Baike asked in astonishment.

"Just in case there is anything incriminating..." he started with trepidation.

"Just go and rest your mind." Professor Baike said casually. "There is nothing, absolutely nothing, to hide; just go and sleep."

"No, sir." He said. "We can't spend the night here, nobody knows we are here; and nobody must know we were here. I've to get back to Benin tonight."

Professor Baike was stunned at the level of sacrifice his PRO had gone to help him cover his tracks, when there was, indeed, no need for it: all this the PRO did notwithstanding the dangers that are associated with the Benin–Ore road.

Prof. Baike concluded the budget defense and flew back to Benin. No sooner had Prof. Baike reached his office after his arrival than an NSO operative who had been lying in wait for him introduced himself and announce his intention to interrogate the professor on the allegations leveled against him. Prof. Baike gladly obliged him. When the interview was under way, Prof. Baike began to hear noises coming from the security operative's pocket caused by one of the pocket-sized tape recorders that were used for covert operations in those days (digital recorders did not exist back then). Aware of what was going on, Prof. Baike said to the young officer, "Young man, remove what you are hiding in your pocket, put it on the table, I will gladly speak into it."

Befuddled by this bluntness, the embarrassed officer apologized. As he arose and headed out of the professor's office, he confessed to having been the professor's student in the past. Prof. Baike assured the young officer that he took no offence, as the latter was executing his duties; he then requested furthermore that the agent inform the state NSO director that he would be paying him a visit the next day.

When faced with this challenge, Prof. Baike fell back on the foundations on which he was raised. As he searched his soul, he never found anything that he had done wrong that would warrant a sleepless night of prayer vigil. Being a man given to neither dramatic nor hysterical display of his religion, after committing the situations in the Lord's hands, Prof. Baike went off to bed and slept like a baby, knowing fully well that grace for the circumstance had already been provided by the God of all grace, who needed no further prayer gymnastics to arm-twist him into releasing needed favors. God, in faithfulness to his promise (Philippians 4:7), gave his servant the peace of mind he needed.

It was in this state of peace that Prof. Baike strolled into the office of the state director of the NSO the next morning. In the characteristic uncouth manner of Nigerian security operatives, the NSO director, on sighting him, started to shout at him, but Prof. Baike gestured with his hand that he should hold his peace.

"Look here, mister, don't you shout at me. You've not found me guilty of any wrongdoing. So don't shout at me. Many of your bosses are my students, but I don't want to go into those details. Now, don't you shout at me. If you have any questions, ask me." (For sure the Scripture says that the righteous are as bold as lions; Proverbs 28:1.)

At this, the director calmed down and began asking him pertinent questions, to which Prof. Baike responded satisfactorily. Suddenly, the man picked up his phone and called Lagos and told his boss on the other end of the line, *"I have investigated Professor Baike, but I find nothing incriminating against him."* He then turned to an officer in the room and ordered him, *"Bring his passport and give it to him."* The professor stood up, shook his hand, and took his leave. That was the end of the story. It was much later that Prof. Baike got to know that his own children knew the NSO director's children, and that the latter, in fact, had attended the University of Benin. What is more, Prof. Baike had, indeed been instrumental to the admission of some of his children into the university.

As a African proverb goes, there can be no smoke without a fire. The story behind this NSO investigation is that the University of Benin, of which Prof. Baike was the VC at the time, had advertised for tenders for the award of contracts for certain jobs, and a contractor, a member of the then ruling political party, the National Party of Nigeria (NPN), had come to see the VC over some of the advertised contracts in which he had vested interest. He wanted the VC to influence the award of the contracts in his favor. Prof. Baike, however, took his papers and put them through the tenders board, along with all the other tenders. About a week later, the man came back to tell Prof. Baike that he had "seen" the quantity surveyor, and that together they had adjusted some figures to make sure everyone would smile at the end of the day. Little did he know that as far as Prof. Baike was concerned, with his corrupt antics, the contractor was taking himself out of consideration in the award of the contract.

"Is that right"? Prof. Baike inquired.

"Yes," he replied proudly.

"Very well," Prof. Baike said sarcastically. "Don't worry one whit. I'll make sure everything is fine and dandy."

As soon as the dubious contractor left his office, Prof. Baike directed the registrar to have the quantity surveyor's appointment terminated, since he was even on temporary appointment, and to ensure that due process was followed in the award of the contracts.

Trouble began to brew when the corrupt NPN contractor discovered that his gimmicks had no traction with the VC, and that he had lost out in the contract award. The contractor presumed that Prof. Baike was of similar corrupt disposition as himself, and as such must have given the contract to the contractor who had doled out the heftiest graft. He was gravely mistaken. In his ignorance, without checking the facts, and with rage, he hastily wrote a damning petition against the Vice Chancellor to the then president of the federation, Alhaji Shehu Shagari. The petition was passed down to the then vice president, Dr. Alex Ekwueme, for action. Upon reading the petition, Dr. Ekwueme summoned some Igbo lecturers from the University of Benin, with whom he was acquainted.

"You people keep talking about this Vice Chancellor of yours, what saintly a man he is. Here is a petition against him," Dr. Ekwueme teased them.

"Ah, no! This can't be our VC. He isn't one to do such a thing as this at all," was the immediate response of these Uni-Ben professors.

"Alright, then, I'll send the petition to the NSO. Let's see what happens," was Dr. Ekwueme's resolve.

That was the beginning of the NSO's investigation and interrogations. Prof. Baike got to know these facts long after the dust had settled. At stake here was not just his own integrity, but also the trust of so many of his protégées, which they had reposed in him and for which they were willing to vouch. In the end, however, no case of corrupt practice or impropriety could be established against him, and his protégées felt vindicated, not betrayed.

Although he was determined to live right, Prof. Baike discovered in his lifelong career of public service that there were always fifth columnists, who would ever so often work tooth and nail to ruin some honest person for no just cause. The manifold deliverances he experienced are testaments to the faithfulness of God, in whose character it is to work *"righteousness and justice for all who are oppressed"* (Psalm 103:6, ESV). Thus, the name of the Lord was a stronghold that sufficed for him, and as such he had no reason to wander from the God of his love. In the embers of trials, his faith in the unfailing God waxed stronger, even though he is of the sort who are not given to wearing their faith on their sleeves. The welfare of his constituents was always uppermost in his mind, and that is why, for instance, he used the same official car for seven good years in Benin. These principles were the trademarks of his work wherever he went.

When he was the Vice Chancellor of the National University of Lesotho, the government increased school fees without contacting the school authorities. When the students reacted with violent demonstrations and riots, Prof. Baike summoned a meeting of the university council, which agreed to shut down the university to avert further violence and possible destruction of life and property. This had never happened in Lesotho before, and many students were very angry, thinking, *"What has this Nigerian come here to show us? Who does he think he is?"* They then organized further demonstrations and subsequently took him to court.

Lesotho being a very small country, its people usually unite against foreigners. It was no surprise, therefore, that on the day the case was heard, Prof. Baike, was literally alone with his lawyer. Even people who ordinarily would have stood with him maintained their distance, being afraid of reprisals from the students (and, perhaps, the community) for showing any form of support or solidarity or sympathy for this foreigner. The court, was packed with students and the staff union members, who obviously were in solidarity with the students. The judge ruled in Prof. Baike's favor, exonerating him in every sense of the word and leaving him to determine whether or not to reopen the school. To everyone's surprise he ordered that the school be reopened for lectures to commence immediately. The students also lost their appeal, in which they alleged that the three South African judges who had sat on the case in the lower court were biased. The students' loss of the appeal brought the whole matter to a complete end. Here was professor Baike, all alone in a foreign land in the middle of all these crises, not even having his family with him. In spite of all that, he was never for one moment driven to despair or fear, but, having a strong faith and the assurance of God's abiding watchful presence as his solace, pushed ahead in his task. He constantly retired to his house in the evening for moments of quietness in meditation on the word of God and prayer. These kept him praising God in spite of the challenges he encountered.

At the beginning of this millennium, the government

of Nasarawa State, in central Nigeria, set out to establish a new university, and the then state governor invited Prof. Baike to be the pioneer Vice Chancellor of the university. When he was moving to Keffi, Nasarawa State, to take up the position of the Vice Chancellor, a friend wrote him a letter telling him that Keffi people hate to hear the truth and whoever stands for the truth stands the risk of getting into trouble. This did not deter him from sticking his neck out for the truth. At a point when the university was having some problems, one of the fellows instigating the problems had the temerity to write Prof. Baike, *"You came into Keffi with your front but you are going to go back with your back."* By this he meant that Prof. Baike came to Keffi alive, but was going to leave Keffi as a dead man. Prof. Baike also got text messages on his phone that issued assassination threats. None of these moved him, nor did he rush to seek police protection. He would normally drive around the town with just his driver, never bothering to carry along security details (whether from the police or the university security system) for protection. The Lord, in whom he trusted, protected him throughout his eight-year tenure in Keffi until he returned to his hometown of Zaria "with his front." Some of the ill-will against him manifested one time when he traveled for a medical checkup in South Africa; some malicious person churned out a rumour that he had died there. When he returned, people were trouping to his house to see him. When he got wind of the rumour, he was persuaded that a number of these supposed well-wishers were simply coming to assure themselves that he had actually come back alive. Through all these trials, God proved himself faithful. At the end of the day, it was clear to those who sought his harm that his God was greater than theirs, and they probably resolved that it would be better to leave him alone.

Another area in which the faith of Baike's has been tested relates to surviving as a Christian minority in a

Muslim majority society in northern Nigeria, in a polity of heightened religious polarization that was alien to the Kano of Prof. Baike's childhood. The challenges have become enormous. However, the Baike family has never wavered in their Christian faith. Their resolute commitment to their faith is also evident in their undaunted spirit, in spite of incredible denials of their fundamental human rights, such as the refusal of local authorities to issue certificates of state origin to their children unless they renounced their Christian faith (or camouflaged it by reverting to Muslim names). Similarly, Prof. Baike's Christian extended family members—who came from Muslim families, but became Christians during the years they lived with the Baikes—demonstrate much strength in the face of the marginalization and deprivations they experience in their workplaces in Kano. Yet the joy of the Lord continues to be their source of strength.

At a personal level Prof. Baike continues his father's legacy of maintaining cordial relationships with people of Muslim background, from whom he traces his ancestry. For example, he and the Emir of Kano, His Royal Highness Dr. Ado Bayero, remain close friends. He and his family visits the emir every now and then, sometimes at His Royal Highness's invitation. This relationship goes all the way back to when Prof. Baike's father, Mr. Jacob Baike, worked for the father of the present Emir of Kano. The emir and Prof. Baike happen to be age mates, and theirs has been a lifelong friendship. His Royal Highness regularly sends Sallah goodwill messages to Prof. Baike, and Prof. Baike in turn reciprocates in sending goodwill messages to the emir during Christian festivals like Christmas.

LOOKING BACK

Throughout his years of service from one place to another, Prof. Baike always made himself available to serve the Christian community. Though a Christian of the Anglican persuasion, he was willing to minister in all church denominations as the opportunity arose. In Benin, he was seen as an unusual person, being a Christian from the north. They wanted to be convinced that his faith was genuine. Barely seven days after his arrival in Benin, Prof. Baike was invited to preach in an interdenominational service in Ogbuwo. He also played an active part in the activities of the campus Christian Union (CU), the southern campus counterpart of the Fellowship of Christian Students (FCS) in the north. He was often invited to preach at their services, which were held in the university stadium. He still has texts of those sermons. He was similarly involved with the Christian communities of the other universities he headed both in Lesotho and Keffi. In Keffi, he had to bear in mind the contemporary polarized nature of our body polity along religious lines, having being appointed to the position of the Vice Chancellor by a Muslim governor. Nevertheless, he never shirked the responsibility of praying with and being an encouragement to the campus Christian body.

In all of Prof. Baike's years of service, he is grateful to God for the things He enabled him to achieve. Looking back he and members of his family have never ceased to marvel at the blessings of God, particularly that he never had to apply for any job but was always literally drafted from one job to another. Many times he had pondered and speculated about the human connections that had paved the way for his appointments, but he was left without any iota of doubt that they had come from the hand of Providence, working behind the scenes to bring to pass divine purposes. Since these are the gracious acts of God, only God knows why he has shown his servant these manifold graces. Each time Prof. Baike found himself working in a position that he never applied for, he always felt obliged to work for God's glory, taking his work as a university administrator as service to Christ and not just to human beings. Thus, he strove constantly to ensure that his work created a healthy environment for his subordinates to thrive and be the best that God intended them to be, realizing that he could not claim to be serving the God he cannot see, if he did not faithfully serve the human beings that he did see.

This approach to work has always ended up endearing him both to those he served and to his employers. A case in point occurred at his last point of employment, the Nasarawa State University. When he had a back problem that required surgery, he asked the then state governor to release him from his job as Vice Chancellor. Gov. Abubakar Adamu was unwilling to lose him, so after the surgery, the governor procured an automated bed that made it possible for Prof. Baike to continue working for the university from his living room. The governor jokingly told him, *"You are not going anywhere. Sleep and work from that place"* (he said this while pointing to the bed). At the height of his back problem and the subsequent surgery he underwent, all the Nasarawa State University council meetings, tenders board meetings, Finance and General Purpose committee meetings, as well as the Staff Appointments, Promotions and Disciplinary committee meetings were held in his living room because the members appreciated his service and desired to ensure that even with this challenge to his health, he was able to continue contributing to their deliberations. While Prof. Baike does not fail to acknowledge the magnanimity of the people he worked with at this institution, he also knows that but for God's favour that kind of understanding is very rare to come by.

Prof. Baike also considers his wife's support as his backbone through the years of trial. She contributed tremendously to his stability. She was never demanding, never given to any form of ostentation; in fact, she was hardly known in the university community as the Vice Chancellor's wife. It was at the end of her husband's tenure that she attended a function or two organized by the university. She had a calm disposition about her. You would never find her running around looking for her husband. On one occasion, when a student of Nasarawa State University was killed by a passing vehicle (as the school is located by a major highway), and the students were rioting, Prof. Baike asked his wife how she was able to maintain such poise. She simply shrugged her shoulders and said *"I know who you are and I know you are capable of handling things. Yes, I am worried for your safety, but I know you can handle this situation. You have already taught me how to accommodate situations like these by the way you do things, so I feel confident that you will be OK."* That is the nature of Mrs Baike: her faith and conviction coupled with her being a very prayerful person all added to make her husband's job easier. Metaphorically speaking, he said that he always puts a tube in her heart to connect to his own so he could be tapping into all of her prayers.

LOOKING FORWARD

Prof. Baike desires to see more of our young people learn to integrate their faith with their career lives. He agrees that the environment has changed drastically in Nigeria today and that it will take more than one approach to get the next generation on the right path. He insists that the effort has to begin from the home. He sees definite evidence that the young people are embracing religion in the frenzied way in which they participate in worship at church services or such other programmes. While this in itself is a good thing, he sees a lot of showmanship in the contemporary religiosity of the Nigerian church. He is of the view that much more than public display is needed. He, therefore, tasks parents to carry their children along in their journey of faith by exhibiting not only an open profession of faith but an inner conviction that undergirds their lives. This inner conviction, he believes, will condition them to face up in appropriate ways to life's challenges and all the distracting and disturbing circumstances they encounter from day to day.

Prof. Baike acknowledges that young people today are confronted with greater challenges than the ones he and his generation faced in their younger days. While they may have imbibed Christian virtues in the home and church, the materialistic world in which contemporary young people live pushes them to join the rat race for possessions or positions. Christian youth of today will have their convictions tested, just as Christians of any other era. They will necessarily come face to face with situations where they are cheated, or it seems to them as if nobody cares for them. The natural tendency is for them to feel the need to act the way every other person is acting. At such points, they are likely to respond according to their natural inclinations, not according to God's standards. But it is at such points, Prof. Baike insists, that we are tempted to ask where, then, is the value of faith?

Youths today, according Prof. Baike, face conflicts—conflicts of what their faith says vis-à-vis the realities they face in the world. They are working hard to walk the right path, but then they are confronted with these conflicts that tell them that their faith means nothing. This is the point where those who yield to the pressures of the world are drawn into walking according to the dictates of the world in order to also succeed in life. Young people today need inner convictions; these are ultimately vital and essential in helping them to refuse to be intimidated by others and to live out the true meaning of their lives joyfully, thereby fulfilling their God-ordained destinies.

CHAPTER FIVE

THAT THEY MIGHT LIVE

DR. STEPHEN DUNN

MY HERITAGE

Southern Indianan economy in the immediate years after the Second World War was dominated by farming. Most families lived in small towns or on farms. Electrification of farm homes was a new thing that was just beginning to catch on. Hand-pumped wells, outhouses and coal oil lamps were still common. Spending the evenings talking and watching the sunset was the most common form of entertainment. Churches were social gathering points in addition to their religious roles. Each community had several churches but congregation sizes were small. Families stayed in the same church communities for generations. Most people knew not only their neighbors but the neighbors' parents and grandparents. Schools were likewise small with many children of differing ages sharing a single classroom. High school graduating classes frequently had fewer than thirty students, all knowing each other very well.

It was within this cultural milieu that my parents first met at Indiana University in Bloomington, Indiana. My father had three siblings—all boys, who all attended college, which was not the norm back then. My mother had come from a family that never had a college graduate. They met at a Nazarene church near the college campus and they were married a year later; their first son (me) was born while my father was still a student at college. Mother stopped her education at that point and started working nights to help keep us going. My father joined the Reserve Officers Training Corps (ROTC), which provided financial support to students. With both of them coming from relatively poor families, times were hard. The first stories of family miracles date from this time. Food was provided in answer to prayer; payments from the ROTC came when they were most needed, and there were unexpected but much-needed gifts from friends. The provision of God for this small family was very real.

My father was a gifted musician and was studying music at college. My earliest memories are of his singing at church. The gospel songs of that time were simple, clear and heartfelt. I can still hear them in my head. One of the lyrics is as follows: *"I sing because I'm happy. I sing because I'm free. His eye is on the sparrow and I know he watches me."* I was raised watching faith and praise in action, aware nearly every day of the presence of a redeeming Lord.

My grandparents were important to our family. My mother's father was a farmer and a superior carpenter. He was a man of few words most times, but when he spoke everyone listened. He was revered in the community for his upright life. No one was trusted as much as he. His word and work were unfailing. His loyalty and friendship were unshakeable. He rose early to perform his duties and went to bed early at night to be ready for the next day. My brother and I were privileged to spend a few weeks in summer on the farm for several years. Life with my grandparents was sometimes boring but always good. My grandfather set an example of manliness that stood the test of time.

My paternal grandfather was a pastor and educator.

He had become a Christian college professor during my early childhood. Visits to his house were always a huge contrast to my other grandfather's house. They lived in a relatively modern house with modern plumbing and current decor. They had books and magazines, and they lived in a small college town. During my summer visits the college library became a second home. My grandfather had a wonderful laugh and loved to tell stories. He frequently quoted the Scriptures. His most violent epithet was "fiddlesticks." I don't ever remember a cross word toward anyone coming from his lips. When I think of what it is like to be a godly man, he is the one who first comes to mind.

Being a boy in my family was the norm. My father was one of four boys. I was one of three boys. This culture of boys is part of who we were. The only women we ever knew were mothers, grandmothers, and eventually wives and friends. The starting point for us was the things that interested boys. We loved the outdoors. My immediate younger brother and I would play so hard outside all day every day that our legs would literally ache at night. We played any game that had a ball or stick or required running and competition. We found ways to play team games with the minimum number of players. We made up games. We rarely saw the inside of a house unless we were asleep or eating. It was a great way to grow up.

Our local church in Valparaiso, Indiana, was where I heard the gospel clearly proclaimed. I was young when I felt the weight of my guilt and my need for salvation. I accepted Christ when I was seven and was baptized not long afterwards. The pastor's teaching about the Christian life had a heavy emphasis on sins that trouble the Christian. His teaching of Scripture was down to earth, and his examples were drawn from daily life experiences. One of the unintended results of this approach was that discipleship was not a focus for church members. Later, when the loss of a small community with close and enduring relationships became my life experience, the absence of understanding the need for personal accountability and a daily walk with the Lord would be a problem for me.

My father was called to active duty with the military when he graduated from college. After completing his duty, he took a position teaching music in a small town. After several years, he became the chair of the music department at a very large new high school in suburban Indianapolis. Moving to a large school with multiple classes for each grade was scary and challenging for me. Sports opened the door to new friendships and acceptance by my fellow students. My father became even busier than before with more jobs outside the home. He continued to serve in the Air Force Reserve. He directed our church choir, and also became director of a men's club choir. Furthermore, he studied and obtained a graduate degree in music education. In all these activities he sought to meet the financial needs of our family. He was frequently out of the house several nights per week. Life was comfortable, but none of the work provided excess finances. However, I learned that hard work was not something to gripe about and that you did what you needed to do to provide for your family.

School and athletic activities became the focus of most of my energies. The academic atmosphere became quite invigorating during middle school, and the sports teams more competitive. During these years I had the first realization that I would need to do something with my life. I am not sure why medicine came to my mind, but it was one of those times when I was sure this was what I should do. I was only in the seventh grade but I never doubted this goal after that time and directed my academic studies to be prepared for college and medical school. I had been exposed to missionary medicine at an early age. Stories of illness and injury in foreign lands caught my attention and strongly influenced me. I had a desire to help others, and the combination of faith and medicine was very satisfactory.

My local church became to me a routine of meetings. The content of church meetings was good, but very little focus was placed on young people. My father's involvement changed rather suddenly when a new choir director was appointed. Our family began a search for a new church, which lasted for some time. Eventually, we joined a wonderful congregation of believers with excellent biblical teaching and a large missionary program. We remained in this church for many years and benefited greatly from the pastor's teaching of the Scriptures and sound doctrine.

COLLEGE AND CAREER PATH

In the midst of everything else I began to experience the need to have money that was mine to spend. Following my father's example I searched for ways to make some money that I could use for discretionary spending. A local paper route became available and I started delivering papers early every morning. This would continue until I graduated from high school. The Lord used this activity in many ways. I learned the need to be reliable even at significant personal sacrifice. Winters in central Indiana were bitterly cold and wet. I learned to be careful and accountable for business matters. I had to collect payments from customers who were often grouchy or unable to pay. I had to deal with unruly dogs and the personal discipline of rising early. This in particular resonated with me later when rising early to begin the day as a resident in surgery. The Lord specifically directed me to a small college in St. Louis, Missouri, through one of the customers on my paper route. This woman asked where I would attend college and recommended Washington University. I had not known of this college and only later found out it was well known and obtaining admission into it was not easy. I applied there in ignorance and received an acceptance with a good scholarship and loan, allowing me to attend. This was another miracle to me and my family. The newspaper company for which I worked even granted me scholarship and loan support.

Shortly after starting college I found an Inter-Varsity Fellowship (IVF) group on my campus. Members of this group directed me to a local church that was filled with young seminarians and others who had studied with Francis Schaefer at L'ABri in Switzerland. The teaching and discipleship in this church placed my Christian life on a different level. Gone were the days of wandering mentally or spiritually. Christ was real in my life and I was living for him. My brother joined me at college and we established an apartment together. Our fellow students in IVF were frequent guests. Our church members lived nearby. This was a happy and challenging time as we worked out our faith and lives. One of the most important personal disciplines I learned at this time was the importance of a daily time alone with the Lord for Bible reading and prayer. This has been the keystone for maintaining my faith, and all my major decisions have been made through the filter of God's Word and led by His Spirit. Hopefully that is true of all the smaller decisions as well, but I am not claiming to have always understood God's leading correctly.

College began with a feeling of isolation and the extreme challenge of studying with intelligent classmates who were highly competitive. A dear family friend had recommended that I study chemistry, as he did prior to entering medical school. I took his advice only to find out that I had chosen one of the most difficult courses of study at a very good school. Only eleven students would graduate with me as chemistry majors four years later. The fiery furnace of serious academic work was refining my mind and challenging my heart. Often I despaired in the face of academic challenges only to see the Lord pull me through. During one of these crises I was able to spend time with other Christian students at a retreat weekend organized by the IVF. One night as I watched the stars, praying and meditating, I saw a falling star. To me it was not a coincidence. I had seen it because I needed to see the power and presence of God in my life, and this was his evidence to me that He was there. I asked the Lord to help me. I promised that in return for his help I would go where he wanted me to go and I would be what he wanted me to be. This covenant with the Lord became my defining commitment. He has not failed me and I have not forgotten my word to keep it and to act upon it.

In the first IVF meeting of my second year I met a freshman student, Karen Courtright. I was immediately attracted to her and began to spend as much time with her as I could. We worked together on IVF activities and studied together. We spent a lot of time later talking about many things, especially what our relationship was. Karen forced me to accept that friendship was all we could have till we were ready to make a commitment to marry. Eventually we were ready and we decided to marry. At that time we had both just left Washington University. I had been accepted to medical school in Indiana and she to nursing school in Kansas. We began our engagement with a two-year wait for her to finish nursing school. Again, this wait was very good for us. Our communication through letters made us speak about important things and focus on the Lord's will for our lives. Our earlier discussion had led us to conclude that a decision to marry must be based on the firm belief that two were better than one in the Lord's service and that we would be trusting the Lord to have that become true in our lives.

Medical School at Indiana University was as challenging as my undergraduate experience. The class size was one of the largest in the country, and most of us only became familiar with students in our own alphabet group or our cadaver dissection group. Studies were intense, but no more than they had been. I performed as well as most but did not distinguish myself in the first two years of study. The clinical years were more to my liking and it was good to be actively engaged with real patients and their problems. I was still overwhelmed by all that could go wrong with the human body and began to be discouraged about successfully learning enough to be a competent physician.

MARRIAGE, FAMILY, CAREER DEVELOPMENT, AND FAITH

Karen and I married after two years of medical school. My life suddenly became more stable and intensely fulfilling. I do not think I understood how lonely I had been until I was no longer alone. We were both involved with other Christian students in the Christian Medical-Dental Society and in a small-group Bible study that encouraged us to continue the habits of personal prayer and Bible reading that we had begun in college. We also learned to spend time as a couple praying about personal problems and decisions as well as praying for patients, our church and missionaries we were supporting.

We began to think about what we would do after medical school. I sought and was accepted for support from the United States government to pay my medical student tuition and provide a small stipend. Karen worked as a nurse at the local city hospital. Late in my third year of medical school I realized that surgery was the best fit for me, but this decision had several implications for me. First I had to redesign my senior year to provide more surgical exposure. Second, I had to find a residency program that would allow me to leave the training program and return after two years of payback service to the government for their support of my medical education. We also began to plan a medical missions experience to West Africa.

We left for Liberia in early 1978 for three months at the (SIM) ELWA Hospital, Monrovia, where we had many experiences that changed our lives. Nearly 40% of all children admitted to our hospital died. I went from a position of feeling overwhelmed by what there was to learn to being overwhelmed by what I did not know. I determined to learn enough to be of help to someone, for I realized at that time that I was of little help to most. The people I met were poor, which made me realize how much I had. Their poverty was cultural as well as material, and was probably made more severe by the movement of young people to the cities looking for work. The instability in the lives of these people and their government would later erupt into civil war and numerous crimes against their fellow citizens.

At the end of our three months in Liberia, we returned to the United States ready for more training. The surgery residency at Indiana University Medical Center was renowned for its difficulty. Twenty interns would start the first year in either one of four hospitals, with only six to be selected for the second year of training. I started knowing I was not one of those six, as I must begin my payback to the government at the end of the internship. Nevertheless, the need to learn enough to be of help spurred me on to greater effort and dedication. I enjoyed what we were learning and the opportunity to help others. The operating room became the playfield with intense concentration on the surgical procedure. I loved it and the long hours went by quickly. The chairman of surgery became aware of me, and he was able to allay my fears, telling me he would take me back after my government service. Again, the Lord provided help when I could not help myself.

The government service years loomed large ahead of us. I dearly wanted a surgical position but almost none were known to exist except in Alaska. I had been guided to an Indian Health Service (IHS) surgeon in Alaska by the surgeon at ELWA Hospital in Liberia (the term Indian as used here refers to Native Americans, in contemporary American common parlance.). On our last night in Liberia I had mentioned the problem of my two years of service to the government after internship, and he had given me the name of the Alaskan surgeon. I called him and he was able to arrange for me to attend a recruitment fair in the mid-west. They made a position for me at a small hospital in Bethel, Alaska for two years starting after my internship. Again, the Lord provided this place for me and took care of all the uncertainties that had beclouded my mind.

Karen and I learned that we would become parents of our first child during my internship year. Our son Mark was born while I was temporarily stationed in Anchorage on our way to our duty station in Bethel, and he was 6 days old when we arrived in Bethel. Our second son was born in Alaska one month prior to our return to Indiana. Family life in Alaska was wonderful. We had two good years of real time together with lots of things to do in a very interesting part of the world. We learned much about the native people of Alaska and saw the saving grace of God at work in the hearts of people who had the same needs we had for a Saviour. We also saw a culture with great pride and traditions of hard work and strong family values. This was a marked contrast to the unsettled people of Liberia. We reflected on God's work in the world and the redeeming power of the gospel.

Practicing medicine in Alaska was a great privilege and challenge. I was drawn to children and began to consider the possibility of pursuing pediatric surgery. I became quite busy serving as the only physician in a 250,000 Kilometre square area (slightly larger than either the United Kingdom or Uganda) without any surgical training. Major elective surgery was done in Anchorage.

Patients with appendicitis, lumps and bumps or surgical emergencies that rendered too unstable to travel became my responsibility. I also did Caesarean sections when necessary. It would be hard to imagine that this kind of practice would be allowed today, but all of our patients did well. I learned much about what could be done safely and the limits of my ability. These experiences shaped my opinion of what I could do as a surgeon, what was safe, and what was effective.

While I was in Alaska, the chairman who had promised me a position upon returning to Indiana University developed lung cancer, throwing my future into doubt, but he recovered and was able to make a place for me in the program. I returned and contacted the pediatric surgeon in chief at the Riley Children's Hospital in Indianapolis. Dr. Grosfeld agreed to mentor me and assist with my attempt to become a pediatric surgeon. He allowed me to work in his laboratory for one year and to author papers with him. His support allowed me to be selected for training in Philadelphia at St. Christopher's Hospital for Children at the end of my general surgery residency training. Only later did I realize that Dr. Grosfeld was one of the most recognized pediatric surgeons in the United States and his support was uniquely important. Again, whether by blessing me through the remission from lung cancer leading to my chairman's timely recovery or guiding me to train in a program with an important figure in pediatric surgery, the Good Shepherd was leading me in the path he had for me.

St. Christopher's Hospital was founded in north Philadelphia in the latter half of the nineteenth century and it continued to serve a population of children in north Philadelphia. It had become one of the premier pediatric training institutions under the leadership of Dr. Nelson. The fellowship in pediatric surgery had trained more pediatric surgeons than most of the other hospitals in the United States. The kidney transplant program was the only one in Philadelphia and one of the busiest in the country.

A program of liver transplantation was begun at St. Christopher's shortly before I arrived in 1985. A child with a transplanted liver was still in the hospital when I arrived to begin my fellowship. One weekend day, she became acutely ill and died while undergoing emergency surgery. I was frightened by this event and felt that while I loved renal transplantation, liver transplantation was difficult and would not be what I wanted to pursue. At the end of the first year of fellowship my mentor in renal transplantation left for a new position. I was asked to stay on and take on these duties after receiving additional training in renal transplantation at Thomas Jefferson Medical College in Philadelphia.

Simultaneous with this renal transplantation training, I also continued as a fellow in pediatric surgery. Later in the year the director of the liver transplant program fell ill and was unable to continue. I recognized that I would need to assume these duties also if the program were going to continue. My academic chief at Temple University Hospital with which St. Christopher's was affiliated, was able to arrange a month of training for me with Dr. Byers Shaw in Nebraska. What I saw there transformed my opinion of liver transplantation: I saw a well-conceived operation conducted by an expert surgeon, and I now understood that liver transplantation could be done successfully. My professional future had opened before me, and it would take the better part of my time and ability. Once again, the Lord had put me in the right place at the right time to do the right thing by supplying what I needed for what he wanted to do.

Family life for the Dunn's had moved along. Our third son was born while I was a resident at Indiana. Karen had decided to school our three boys at home so that I could have more time with them, and they were growing up active and happy. Having now moved to the Philadelphia Metropolitan area, we found a church home in the near northern suburbs of Philadelphia, Faith Community Church, Roslyn. Our pastor, Dr. Kreuger, was a gifted teacher and leader. Our family grew up in a good spiritual home and I will always be thankful for that influence on our children's lives. Sports became dominant in our young boys lives. They were all talented athletes, overcoming deficits with tenacity and hard work. We especially enjoyed the diversity of our community. Our children grew up with other children from different cultures and traditions. After our travels to Africa and Alaska we treasured the people from every nation and every language that we knew our Lord had commanded to follow Him.

Practicing medicine in Philadelphia in the 1990s was a difficult undertaking. There were literally too many hospitals and medical schools competing for the best-paying patients, while there were also too few and too poorly funded hospitals and medical schools caring for the poor. The economics were brutal. I remember one conversation with the chief financial officer at St. Christopher in which he told me we had lost money on every child to whom we had given medical assistance. Worse still, the care we gave to children from our city was frequently reported in the news to have been given by our better-funded and more widely known competing children's hospital. Furthermore, the practice of liver transplantation was in conflict: legal action over who would provide these services had gone all the way to the Pennsylvania State Supreme Court. One outcome of the legal process was that a court ordered me to oversee a liver transplant programme at a competing hospital, to help sustain the programme at that hospital. This was up close and personal conflict between highly trained professionals who had sworn to care for patients as their first and highest priority. My faith was strengthened time and again as I sought the Lord for the right actions and words to use. These tests and trials drove me to trust in the Lord as never before.

The crises in the practice of medicine in the city of Philadelphia did not affect my personal fortunes. The financially at-risk inner city hospitals were starting to crumble. New hospital systems saw their opportunity and began to buy up the distressed medical properties. At one time, St. Christopher's had been sold to a competing medical school, which was actively placing competing faculty within the building. There were not enough patients for the staff who had been present prior to this move. The only professional group that was thriving in these circumstances was the attorneys. Eventually the buyer of St. Christopher's declared bankruptcy. In the meantime, our liver transplant program had become very busy and successful: we were following over 200 children who needed or had had a liver transplant. We needed a stable environment. By the year 2000, it was time to move the program and our team.

I had worked with a gastroenterologist at Nemours/Alfred I. Dupont Hospital for Children and he had subsequently become the chief executive of their practice. I called him to see if we could move our program 30 miles south to state of Delaware. This would allow us to continue to care for our patients, and most of us would not have to move. Our offer to move was accepted and we completed the move in July of 2000. We quickly reestablished our clinical practice, giving our first organ transplant service to a child within weeks of our move. Our new home was slower paced but more financially stable. We were able to reorganize our group into a new structure that allowed us to have the services of all the experts we needed to run an excellent program.

At my first visit to discuss the move of our team to

Nemours/Alfred I. Dupont Children's Hospital, as I parked and left my car, the bell tower on the hospital campus was playing an old hymn: "Rock of ages cleft for me. Let me hide myself in thee." Only the Lord of the universe could so fittingly arrange background music for real people in real life addressing real circumstances. True to the lyrics of that old hymn, the Rock of ages provided the needed refuge for the children's transplantation programme I head at the Nemours/Alfred I. Dupont Children's Hospital.

Practice at DuPont has not always been easy. My responsibilities increased as I became the Chief of Pediatric Surgery. Earlier on we had recognized that we needed to grow our program and attract more patients, as well as increase our role in trauma care delivery in Delaware. Promoting this development was not easy and required new programs and staff. However, the trauma program has had more impact in attracting patients with more medical needs than any other program that has been developed at the hospital. More importantly, as an institution, we began to provide needed medical care to the children of our region. For me the lesson learned was to do what was right and trust the Lord for the result.

SERVICE IN THE LORD'S VINEYARD

Church leadership positions had become part of my life while in Philadelphia. I first began serving as an elder at Faith Community Church in Roslyn, while we lived in Pennsylvania. I was also elected to the elders board of Grace Evangelical Free Church in Wilmington, when we moved to Delaware.

I came to know that there are many challenges in church leadership. Faith Community Church had been a large church, but it was beginning to experience decline in membership and Sunday attendances. I had joined the leadership team of the church when it was in a period of budget cutting, going so far as to close the church's day school so the doors of the worship sanctuary could remain open. The church budget had to be cut to bring it in line with giving. Not all the work was financial and negative. Some of the positive ministry things we were involved in included starting small groups and increasing the number of missionaries that we were supporting. Later on, after my time of service on the board of elders had elapsed, Pastor Kreuger retired and a new minister was selected. Having by this time rejoined the elder board as its chairman, it fell to my lot to encourage the pastor to find a new church without letting this disagreement escalate into a church split. This was a difficult task, but it was accomplished nonetheless.

I had sensed the Lord's presence when the church elders laid hands on me to ordain me as an elder. I am sure the Lord needed to strengthen me for the challenges that would lie ahead. The letters of Paul became dear to me as I grew to understand the need for good leadership in my church. The Lord has given his instructions and we need to follow them.

We have been challenged throughout our life as a family with the stewardship of the Lord's resources. In the early years of our marriage we followed the principles of tithing that my parents had taught me. Karen had not grown up with this concept, but she had been introduced to it in our college years. It was never taught as an absolute requirement to tithe on gross rather than the net income, or even that tithing was strictly required, but after much prayer and discussion we settled on the principle that we have followed both in the lean years of medical school and training and in the improving years that have followed: We tithe to our church on the gross income, including any bonuses, tax returns, or miscellaneous income. The Lord tells us to give the first fruits and we make our first decisions about giving when income is received. Then we work with the rest. We give more, as we feel led, to other ministries. All I can say is, we have never yet been able to out-give the Lord.

Another part of stewardship involves our time. I am blessed to have a wife who has always seen her role as that of a partner in ministry, so during the times I have had to be away from the family she has taught our children to understand that their role in my ministry was to be cheerfully supportive. As a busy surgeon with the additional pressure of 24/7 responsibility of being on call for organ transplantation, answering the call to serve as an elder has often been a personal as well as a family sacrifice. In more recent years there have been opportunities to travel to both India and Bolivia to build programs in pediatric liver transplantation where none had existed before. This has involved giving up vacation time to work often harder than I have to work at home. The rewards, as always when following the Lord's call, have been great in relationships built, lives changed, and opportunities to share Christ and demonstrate His love.

MY DRIVING PASSION AND RECENT ADVANCES

I see life as a service. And the best service I can provide is to use the things I know to give children a second chance. Nothing is more rewarding than knowing we helped someone to have a normal childhood and grow up to live a happy, productive life as a result of our solid organ transplantation program.

I am passionate about taking solid organ transplant programs to the next level — introducing what we've learned to societies that have not been able to take advantage of these medical techniques before. So, I devote a lot of energy to discussing and critiquing work that is going on in transplantation programs for children around the world. I have also tried to use what I have learned to help children in need in other countries. The missionary physicians I had heard of when I was young inspired me to do something similar. I have set up viable solid organ transplant programs in Bolivia and India and established a live-donor liver transplant program in Philadelphia, PA, and later Wilmington, DE.

I really want to help heal children through my work. We have found a better way to treat a specific liver-related form of high blood pressure and I am working toward more children being treated using this technique.

CONCLUSION

This short history of what God has done in my life and in my family's life has been requested by Dr. Cephas T. A. Tushima. He and his family lived with my family for over a year, and we enjoyed having them with us. Sharing with him, I came to understand the problems facing Africa and to better understand the forces and difficulties for Christians there. It is my hope that the path through which the Good Shepherd has led this sheep will resonate with others. The Lord is faithful to his servants. We need to be faithful to him in every aspect of life. We are no longer our own. The sacrifice is but for a moment. The upward call of Christ must be answered, and it is also our hope. I pray that I and all my brothers and sisters will be found faithful and fruitful when the Master returns or calls us home.

TUSHIMA'S NOTE

Dr. Stephen P. Dunn chairs the Department of Surgery and doubles as the Chief of the Division of Solid Organ Transplantation at Nemours/Alfred I. Dupont Children's Hospital. He also serves a professor of Surgery and Pediatrics at Thomas Jefferson University. As an accomplished academic, Dr. Dunn has made presentations at countless international professional conferences, and has authored over 100 peer-review articles in journals, book chapters, and abstracts.

CHAPTER SIX

A PROPHET AMONGST US

EVANGELIST PAUL GINDIRI

HIS ROOTS

In the early 1800s, many residents of Gobir, one of the seven ancient original Hausa city-states (Hausa Bakwai), set forth from their ancestral domicile to flee the stern and scorched-earth military onslaught of the Usman Danfodio's jihad. While a major segment of these fleeing Gobir folks (including members of the ruling dynasty, whose leader, Sarkin Yunfa died in a massacre in 1808) moved north to settle in Tibiri (in present day Republic of Niger), a portion of them journeyed southeast toward Bauchi. Though they first settled in Bauchi, as the Danfodio jihadists advanced further southward, they continued their flight, in the process being dispersed in different directions. A group of the Gobir diaspora continued in their wandering away from the advancing forces of Danfodio, until they finally found refuge and shelter among the foothills of Pyemdere, in present-day Mangu Local Government Area of Plateau State. These foothills later proved to be conducive for farming purposes for these refugees from Gobir, who decided to settle in the area. A major town in the area today is Gindiri. It was from amongst this people group that, later on, a man and his wife, Gunen Saidu Sedet and Magajiya Naru, from Punbush Gindiri (in the present Pyem chiefdom) had a son on March 3, 1935. The child, named Gofo Gunen, was the second of fourteen children in the family. Gunen Saidu Sedet, Gofo's father, was from the royal family of Pyem and primarily a farmer, just like almost everyone else in Punbush, and was an adherent of African tradition religious practices. When Gofo became a Christian, he took on the name of the Apostle Paul and adopted the name of his village such that he came to be known as Paul Gofo Gunen Gindiri, simply shortened to Paul Gindiri.

A PASSION FOR LIFE

Paul Gindiri grew up at the time when the Sudan United Mission (SUM) had just established a mission station in Gindiri, and missionaries in the area were introducing Western education as part of their mission work. He witnessed these early missionaries moving from settlement to settlement, preaching the gospel of Christ. Although in his early years, he greatly admired the work of the missionaries, especially the lives of the first two converts to Christianity (Akila Wantu Nachunga and Mallam Tagwai, from whom he may have first heard the gospel), he personally as yet had had little contact with them. His father, being a farmer, had introduced him to farming, as the case was with most traditional African families at the time. For people like Paul's father, the certainty that farming provided for the subsistence of the family could not be traded for the uncertainty of Western education that they had not known previously. Thus, Paul learned the discipline of hard work from his father, a virtue that would become manifest in all of his later life and work.

Prior to his meeting with the missionaries, Paul Gindiri had had peculiar and somehow strange and mystical childhood experiences. He not only saw spirit beings waging attacks on him, he also had one experience of being mysteriously displaced from his house while he was sleeping. Anytime the spirits were chasing Gindiri in his dreams, however, he always acquired the ability to fly to the sky for safety. Bewildered by these dreams, he kept trudging along in life until he encountered the missionaries. However, these early experiences served as preparatory grounds for his later life of fervent and bold evangelistic and revivalist ministry. He had learned from his early life not to be terrified of anything but to march bravely on to his goal, believing that notwithstanding the fierceness of any threatening enemy, safety and deliverance were assured from a God who never fails.

As the young Paul was growing up in his home village of Punbush, he never lost sight of the activities of the early SUM missionaries, personal contact with whom had initiated his own journey of faith. His secret admiration of their lives and work was ever so slowly pulling him toward them. During his first major face-to-face contact with the missionaries, they presented the gospel message to Paul in its simplicity, which he received with joy. He decided to give his life to Christ. He thereafter became ever more eager to learn from the missionaries, and as such he and other young early converts to Christianity frequented the mission station at Gindiri so as to receive teachings from the Bible.

In the course of time, these newly converted young Christian enthusiasts were admitted into the SUM Junior Primary School in 1944. This school thing was one step Mallam Gunen Saidu Sedet, Paul's father, could not stomach. To him, Gofo was going too far in his involvement with the missionaries, and thereby getting distracted from the more serious business of farming, and so the natural concomitant response was to subject his son to intense persecution. Things got so bad that at a point, Mallam Sedet shot an arrow at Gofo as a way of dealing a final blow to the school madness that had come over his otherwise malleable son. It was at this turn of events that Paul's mother, Magajiya Naru, who all along had been at polar opposites with her husband over Paul's schooling but remained a submissive wife, jettisoned all restraint and intervened to rescue her son from imminent death at her husband's hands. His mother's intervention enabled Paul to complete his junior primary school (i.e., four years of schooling up to primary or grade 4). In spite of his father's intense persecution and opposition to his faith, Paul Gindiri had an overwhelming sense of God's presence that he would not trade for anything else; it was better for him to endure hardship as good soldier of Christ than to draw back.

Having tasted and experienced the benefits of education through the junior primary school for four years, Paul Gindiri desired to continue on to the senior primary school. However, without his father's support, he could not afford to pay the school fees, so he dropped out of school. In all the disappointments and uncertainties that surrounded his life, Paul, in later life, could attest to the hand of Providence working behind the scene to bring about the fulfillment of his destiny. His faith in Christ Jesus had enabled him to trust God absolutely with his life.

Forced out of school, Paul began thinking about what to do with his life. Though a youth at the time, he was clear headed and very focused. He decided to work as a casual labourer for the masons, who were at the time working on the various on-going building projects on the missionary compound at Gindiri. His goal was to save money, move to the city, learn a trade, get a good job, and live out a decent life. This plan he shared with his mother, who lent him her support and influenced her husband to give to Paul money received as the bride price for one of his younger sisters. It was only after Mallam Sedet had given Paul the money that he realized the real plan for its use, and predictably was adamantly opposed to losing an industrious and capable farm hand to the city. Nevertheless, the lure of the city for Paul was as unstoppable as the flood waters from a broken dam. He left the village in 1949.

THE WILDERNESS WANDERING YEARS

Paul, seeing no future for himself in the village, left the village in search of the good life. Though he had little education and no trade skills, he was ready to explore all the opportunities that the wider world offered him. He first came to Dorowa, in the present Barkin Ladi LGA, where tin mining activity was going on. He took a temporary job as a casual labourer with a mining corporation, the Amalgamated Tin Mines of Nigeria (ATMN). After a while, he quit the job and decided to explore apprenticeship in driving and auto-mechanics. As a hardworking young man, he was the favorite apprentice of his master. After two and a half years of training, he moved to Vom, where he secured his first job as a commercial bus driver and later a better job as a driver for the National Veterinary Research Institute (NVRI, Vom).

Because his job with the NVRI involved a lot of traveling across the country, Paul eventually gave it up, and moved to Barkin Ladi to take a job as a driver and mechanic for the Tin Mining Association. Though he was receiving a decent wage at this job, he was still restive, constantly desiring more money. After some time, he moved to Bukuru, where he reconnected with ATMN, for which he had worked in Dorowa. ATMN itself had grown over these years and become better at catering to the welfare of its staff, so Paul was earning a much higher income now than before.

Once the pursuit of the good life had become a driving passion in Paul's life, he was devoting more and more of his time to work and less and less time to the nurture of his soul. Consequently, just as a good crop in an unattended farm plot would soon be overrun by weeds, the seed of God's word sown in Paul's life was beginning to be choked by the cares of this life, such as lasciviousness, alcohol, partying, and women. Notwithstanding, God's love never let him alone. Every time he regained his sobriety after indulgence in such reveling, a strong sense of guilt would come over him. The perturbing question, *"Where will you spend eternity if you die?"* would keep ringing in his heart. Efforts to sedate his disquieted conscience by more gross indulgence in reveling and license proved futile.

In pursuit of the Golden Fleece, Paul once more left ATMN and took a job as a haulage truck driver. This once again involved long distance trips, crisscrossing the length and breadth of Nigeria. As is customary with most folks in this trade, he plunged deeper into profligacy, drunkenness, and smoking. Additionally, his travels brought him into contact with different people. He soon began to strike up close friendships with Muslim colleagues of his. Soon he began copying their customs and diction. Some of his Muslim friends even thought he was one of them by the way he so mastered their way of life and language.

Paul, being a vocationally very mobile person at the time, soon left his job as a truck driver and picked up a job with the Nigeria Railway Corporation in Jos, laying rail tracks from Jos to Maiduguri. When they had reached Maiduguri, Paul resigned his appointment with the Railway Corporation and took to driving once again. Rather than return to the Plateau, Paul decided to make Potiskum, in the now defunct Borno Province, his domicile. This was in 1958.

As far away as Paul had wandered from home, so far away had he also drifted from God. Drowning in his sinful lifestyle, he was finding neither job satisfaction nor the better life for which he had left the village in the first place. In spite of all these, God in his infinite mercy was preserving his life on account of the purpose for which he had prepared him.

When he moved to Borno Province, Paul encountered a different strand of Islam that was syncretistic in nature. In addition to his vile lifestyle, he was now wrapped up in Islamic mysticism. He delved deeply into the use of charms for protection and to fight all who stood in his way. He became strong in the powers of darkness and was dreaded by his foes and friends alike because of the things he could do with those charms. He had charms strapped to his body and loads of them in both his house and the truck he drove. He was able to do many extraordinary things like chewing bottles and yet remaining unharmed. He continued in his constant search for a better life, changing jobs as one changes clothes, and engaging in mystical schemes, yet without finding the fulfillment and satisfaction he so desperately desired. Life grew more miserable, even with the acquisition of more material things. In 1959, he moved back to Jos and was employed by the British Engineering West African Company (BEWAC) as a driver and salesman.

NEW LIFE FOR PAUL, NEW LIFE FOR ALL

A remarkable event happened in 1962 that brought about a turnaround in Paul Gindiri's life. He was away to Minna for an official assignment. And as usual, he and his colleagues were lodging in a hotel with the luxury of prostitutes, alcohol, and cigarettes. He had a clash with one of his colleagues over a prostitute, which led Paul to hit him on the head with a bottle, leaving the fellow unconscious. Paul was arrested, while the victim was rushed to the hospital. While in police custody, the now sober Paul began to mull over questions of eternal destiny. The ever-present nagging question that frequently tormented his soul in his sober moments returned: *"Where will you spend eternity, if you were to die today?"* He had no doubts in his mind that he was on the path of destruction. Yet he did not allow this to trouble him too much. He got out of the police cell by bribing the police to file a report in his favour.

Once out of police custody, he and his colleague were set to leave Minna to Gboko via Keffi. At a hotel in Keffi, Paul for the first time chose to be in his hotel room instead of being in the company of his friends reveling in the hotel bar. His friends were surprised at the sudden withdrawal and change. As he lay on his bed and closed his eyes to sleep, there came to him a man in white robes, who identified himself as Jesus Christ. Christ rebuked Paul for his evil ways and charged him to repent or else he would be destroyed at the next appearance Jesus would make to him. Consequent to this theophany, the Holy Spirit of God began to convict him of his sinful ways and to nudge him toward repentance.

Undoubtedly, the sanctifying work of God's Spirit began to take hold of Paul's life subsequent to Christ effectual call on his life. While in Gboko, he chose not to lodge in a hotel, a place he had come to associate with prostitutes, drinking, and smoking. Instead, he sought out an old acquaintance and stayed with him. There he decided to destroy his cigarettes, kola nuts, and match boxes. Unstoppable change had come over the life of Paul.

Upon his return to Jos, he told his wife of his new decision to stop drinking because he wanted to return to the Lord. For his wife, it was an answered prayer because she and others had been praying for him. She advised him to buy a Bible for himself and invited him to church the next Sunday, a place he had not visited for over a decade. The sermon that Sunday seemed to have been custom made in heaven for Paul's situation. The pastor's vivid portrayal of a perverse life that was doomed to an eternity of destruction corresponded so well with Paul's life that he suspected that one of his friends had come to tell his wife about his life, and she in turn had divulged the information to the pastor. His suspicion notwithstanding, he still went to church the following Sunday. There was yet another fiery message from the pastor. This time around, he responded to the altar call. Unabashedly, he walked down the aisle to the front of the church; there he surrendered his life to the lordship of Christ. True change had come to his life to stay. It felt as fresh as the commencement of the rainy season after the chilly, dusty spell of a wind-filled Harmattan[4] dry season. He felt totally clean as he was truly washed in the blood of the Lamb of God. Paul knew happiness once again—the happiness that had eluded him in all years he was pursuing it. He now came to know that true happiness can only be found in the new life that Jesus Christ the Saviour offers. He destroyed all his charms and the things he had acquired for protection: he needed them no longer, as he now knew that his true protection was in God alone. He who was once bound by the chains and drudgery of sin for so many years, was now experiencing true freedom that only the truth of God's word could bring. His joy knew no bounds.

With this new life that Paul received from Christ Jesus came a great burden and passion for ministry to Muslims. Sensing this burden Rev. and Mrs. Jacobson, missionaries with the SIM, took him under their wings and began instructing him in the basics of evangelism. Without wasting time, Paul launched into the ministry of street evangelism in Jos, taking after Dr. Andrew Stirrett (another SIM missionary), who had previously done street evangelism in Jos for about eighteen years. This was the beginning of Paul's evangelistic outreach to Muslims for which his prior years of association with them had prepared him. He was conversant with their language and customs, so he could adequately reach them. The joy of his experience of the new life in Christ created in him the strong passion to see all people receive it as well. Thus he poured himself wholeheartedly (his soul, his time, his resources, and his might) into New Life For All (NLFA, also known in Hausa as *Sabon Rai*), a ministry which had been started a few years earlier by Rev. Gerald Swank, another SIM missionary. Paul and New Life For All became great tools in the hands of the Lord, by which he brought about revivals throughout north-central Nigeria (with reverberative effects further north as well) from the 1960s to 1980s.

TOWARD ECONOMIC INDEPENDENCE

The Evangelist Paul Gindiri was ever more eager to spread the gospel of the Lord, who had rescued him from perilous eternal consequences. At the same time, he came to the stark reality that money is needed to spread the gospel. He was not one to sit back and complain of the challenges in his way. He would rather plunge right into the thick of things to find the solution to the problem he had encountered. With the need to raise funds to support the gospel, he decided to venture into the business world.

When he had first started his street evangelism ministry, Evang. Gindiri was still doing his job as a driver and demonstrator salesman for BEWAC. At some point, he got a contract with the same company to deliver trucks on its behalf from Lagos to Kano at the price of £50 per truck. This was good business in those days. He began to save a good portion of this money so as to be able eventually to start up his own business. Having been involved in long-distance trucking for a long time, he was naturally drawn to that. He had desired to purchase a lorry for his transport business.

Evang. Gindiri had made a couple of attempts at partnering with others in business. At first, he joined hands with some folks and started a bookstore in Jos. This venture did not last long, and he was unhappy with the way things were going, so rather than engage in quarrels, he just quietly withdrew from the venture. In his second attempt at partnership, he partnered with one of his brothers and purchased a haulage truck for a transport business. However, their truck was struck with mishap twice; it had major accidents on two different occasions, the second fatal to the driver. After this second accident, his brother washed his hands off the truck business.

With the withdrawal of his brother from the business, Evang. Gindiri now had to bear the burden of repairing the truck all alone. Fortunately, they had comprehensive insurance on the truck. However, getting the insurance company to live up to its obligations was quite an uphill task. After importunate visits to the offices of the insurance company, all the frustrations associated with those visits notwithstanding, the evangelist eventually got the payment from the insurers of his truck. With this payment, he decided to take up the repair of the truck himself, since he was a competent mechanic.

Once his truck was repaired, Evang. Gindiri decided it was time to devote more of his time to both his business and the gospel. Therefore, he quit his job with BEWAC, even though he was just a few months shy of the length of service needed to qualify him for the company's gratuity. During the weekdays, he would use the truck for business purposes, and on the weekends he would use it to convey NLFA gospel teams and their equipment to the places they were going for outreaches. Driving and maintaining the truck himself brought prosperity to his business. Before long, he had enough money to buy a second truck, which he committed to hauling smoked fish from the Lake Chad basin to Lagos. The returns on this route were greater than even the evangelist had anticipated.

Having gone into transport business with the sole aim of financing the gospel meant that a chunk of his profits were channeled into gospel endeavours. Even as his business continued to grow and prosper, Evang. Gindiri continued to be personally involved in street evangelism and open-air gospel campaigns throughout the emirates of northern Nigeria. He had the courage of a lion and the audacity of a prophet. He did what no other preacher had done before him, and I do not think any has done after him: he personally visited many (if not all) of the emirs in northern Nigeria to witness personally to them concerning the new life that is found in Christ alone.

Evang. Gindiri's business continued to grow and diversify. His earnestness, hard work, and dedication to his work as service to the Lord all combined to bring the desired results. His life and work also well demonstrated the biblical teaching on stewardship, faithfulness, and prosperity. The Bible teaches that more will be given to one who is faithful in little (cf. Matt 25:22; Luke 16:10–11; 19:12). Evang. Gindiri had discharged his stewardship faithfully and God also honoured his servant and prospered his business. He is the antithesis of those who nowadays acquire prosperity by sleazy means using the gospel as a cloak.

Evang. Gindiri had an eagle's eye for discerning the direction in which to invest his resources. In the post-civil war reconstruction phase of Nigeria, General Yakubu Gowon, the then head of state, came up with a small-scale industrial entrepreneurship loan scheme to spur development. In the defunct Benue-Plateau State, this was being implemented by the administration of J.D. Gomwalk, the state governor at the time. Sensing the number of road construction and other building projects that were being embarked upon, Evang. Gindiri had already started a stone-crushing enterprise in Jos. This was a line of business not many people thought much about at the time. Indeed, the only other person who was also invested in it for a while was Mr. Peter Gowon. Evang. Paul Gindiri saw this loan scheme as opportunity to grow his business and he cashed in on it. Within a short time, subsequent to availing himself of the loan opportunity and boasting his investment in the stone-crushing business, the business mushroomed like the rising ashes from a volcano; it raked in huge profits, sizeable portions of which were plowed into evangelistic endeavours and the support of many Christian missionaries and mission organizations.

Evang. Gindiri's rise from rags to riches is a true Cinderella story. Having started out as an ordinary driver with primary four education, he built a multi-million Naira business empire in the days when the Naira had real value, yet he was well ahead of his time in living out a mission strategy that is just beginning gain traction among missiologists and mission practitioners, namely, engaging in business or development as a mission strategy.

Evang. Gindiri was himself a gifted preacher, with evangelistic fervor, who usually held his audiences spellbound. But he knew too well that God's kingdom endeavours are not for lone rangers, and so he laboured hard to mobilize other likeminded individuals and churches to build the strong gospel coalition that was NLFA, which spread revival like wild Harmattan fires throughout northern Nigeria.

FAMILY LIFE

Paul Gindiri and his wife Lami (nee Daspan) were married in 1960. Lami, who was raised in a Christian home, had a firm Christian commitment. Upon moving to Jos with her husband, she soon realized that her husband was not a believer. She, therefore, committed herself to interceding fervently for him. To this end, she enlisted the prayer support of other members of her church, ECWA Bishara 1, Jos, which was close to their family residence. As shown above, Paul's passion for the good life had taken him far afield from a normal life. This invariably had adverse effects on his family life. He was scarcely at home, and more often than not when he returned home, he came in drunk. He thus never really had quality time with his wife. God, in his infinite mercy, gave Paul's wife, Lami, the grace to persevere as an intercessor for her husband. To her importunate prayers, the answer came in 1962, when the Lord of the universe, Jesus himself, had to come down and appear in person to Paul. It is significant that Paul's conversion took place just before his first son, Musa, was born the following year. The Lord blessed Paul and Lami with six other children, namely, Iliya, Dauda, Yakubu, Joshua, Victoria, and Wudeama. As committed Christians, Paul and Lami Gindiri made their home a sacred altar and raised their children in a godly environment.

The life-transforming appearance of Jesus to Evang. Gindiri on the road to Gboko (comparable to the Lord's appearance to Saul of Tarsus on the road to Damascus) had great ramifications for his family as well. As a changed man, Evang. Gindiri now truly loved and cared for his family: providing for its material and spiritual needs as well as being very protective of them. Through his business endeavours, he was able to provide his family's necessities of food, shelter, clothing, and a sense of security and dignity. His family always took priority over every other consideration. A case in point is the time thieves attached his house and made off with many valuable things. At that material time, he had withdrawn money from his savings for re-investment. Nonetheless, with the tragedy that struck the family, he had to divert a sizeable amount of the money for his wife to replace the things that the thieves had carted away. Not only that, he was desirous of seeing his children receive a decent education, an opportunity he never had himself. He therefore sent them to the good schools that were available in Jos at the time and taught them the virtue of hard work, again through personal example. In this regard, he introduced them to his stone-crushing business, and prepared them to eventually take over the running of the business from him. Spiritually, he assumed his role as the leader of the family, taking on the responsibility for the daily family altar. Through his personal example, he taught his children prayerfulness. He similarly taught them many spiritual songs. He was not content to teach his children only, but would also gather the neighbourhood children and instruct them in the way of the Lord. Because of all of this he was dearly loved by his family and was greatly missed each time he traveled out either for business or for his evangelistic mission trips. Yet the family was now fully behind him in all that he did and, indeed, was his first line of support; led by his wife they were the strong prayer team upholding him before the throne of grace as traveled on his business and evangelistic exploits.

Not only was Evang. Gindiri willing to share the gospel with others, he was also willing to reach out and bless others out of the abundance of God's blessing for his family. It was common to see many people, who were not members of his family, at their dinner table virtually at every meal of the day. He and his wife helped sponsor many poor children through school. They regularly provided support to poor families, especially widows and orphans. It was also not uncommon to find them paying hospital bills for those who could not afford to pay.

CHALLENGES AND STRENGTHS

The business world had intrigued and beckoned Evang. Gindiri into its orbit very early in his life. However, he went into it with warped motives, as we have seen. This drove him to the path of self-destruction, but once the grace of God had taken hold of him, his motivations were also re-birthed, and this set his life on the course of stellar accomplishments with eternal ramifications. This road was strewn with risks, dangers, and challenges, but his newly found faith provided a deep reservoir from which he drew upon an interminable source of strength.

Evang. Gindiri had come to learn that the critical issue in life is decision making. Intuitively, he came to know that timing and discerning the right opportunities that were coming one's way were the most critical ingredients in making wise choices in life; and he followed this keenly in his life. Examples of this include his choice to quit his job with BEWAC at a time that conventional wisdom would have considered inauspicious and downright foolish. He never ever once regretted that decision. Similarly, when he decided to take a loan for the stone-crushing business, he was treading in uncharted territory, but he followed his gumption and it set him on the course of unprecedented success in business. All these were undergirded by his faith in God, his strong passion to spread the new life he had found in Christ, and his belief that he needed financial muscle to accomplish his life calling and the mission of spreading the gospel. The Lord honoured the faith of his servant in all these. Similarly, his decision to concentrate his evangelistic outreaches in Muslim-dominated areas was no less strategic. All these decision were fraught with risks and dangers, but he was not afraid to take the dangers as they came, one at time, believing the Lord who called him was faithful and would watch over him through them all, even if it meant walking through the valley of the shadow of death.

Evang. Gindiri's career was twofold, business and evangelism. The two were so intertwined that it is futile to attempt to disentangle them. His passion for evangelism propelled him into business, yet he never got carried away with materialism after recording huge successes in business—he already knew the emptiness of a purely materialistic life from first-hand experience. Conversely, success in business furnished the resources for his evangelistic activities, primarily but not exclusively, through

NLFA. With these twin passions he could weather any storm that life (or even the devil) hurled at him.

We have already seen that branching off into business as an entrepreneur (not an employee) was not easy. There were several false starts, mishaps, and failures, but giving up was something Evang. Gindiri would not do. The first major temptation came to him in those early days. As he was making waves in street evangelism among Muslims in Jos, his entrepreneurial endeavours were faltering and he was at the same time experiencing disappointments with some Christians. It was then that a group of Muslims, who were alarmed at his evangelistic exploits, came to him with a proposal: if only he would convert to Islam, his life from then on would become *hakuna matata* (no more worries)—they would give him loads of money, take to Mecca, and bestow on him a harem also. This offer he flatly turned down without even thinking twice. He had chosen to move on with God to the Promised Land of Canaan, notwithstanding the challenges in the desert. He could no longer endure to linger behind to enjoy the pleasure of sin in Egypt.

Evang. Gindiri not only engaged in open air evangelistic campaigns and street evangelism, he also participated in apologetic debates with Muslims over what the true way of salvation is. These debates were a growing phenomenon in the 1980s and early 1990s in northern Nigeria, where well-rehearsed Muslim apologists were using these public challenges to mystify and discomfit ill-prepared pastors, as a way of undermining the faith of many young and naïve Christians. Evang. Gindiri's erudite performances at these debates further exposed him to militants, who were opposed to Christianity, who targeted him for assassination. It was not uncommon for him and his band of evangelists to be stoned during open air campaigns, one among many such instances occurring in Lafia in present day Nasarawa State. During one of his outreaches in Maiduguri, his life was so much at risk that he was housed in the home of the late military Head of State of Nigeria, Gen. Sani Abacha, who was a good friend of Paul. This protected him to some degree from physical attack, as the phenomenon of suicide bombing was then unknown in these shores.

Although his association with Gen. Abacha protected him from physical attack, it could never protect him from all dangers. There were some elements that were determined to eliminate him at all cost. Thus they succeeded in poisoning him through *kunu*, a local gruel made from millet or corn that he loved to drink, especially when he retired from his day's busy schedule. But what no human being could do, God did because of his faithfulness to his word. The Lord says that he watches over his word to perform it (Jer 1:12). When Jesus gave the command to his disciples to go into all the world and proclaim the good news of the new life found in his grace, he also left these promises to those who would go:

> *"And these signs will accompany those who believe: in my name they will cast out demons; they will speak in new tongues; they will pick up serpents with their hands; and **if they drink any deadly poison, it will not hurt them**; they will lay their hands on the sick, and they will recover" (Mark 16:17 ESV).*

This promise of protection from poison came alive to Evang. Gindiri. As he drank the *kunu* that was served him one evening, little did he know that it had been poisoned. It was only after he had drunk it and he began to experience severe stomach pains and vomited clouts of blood that it dawned on him that he was poisoned. Being a man of prayer, he brought that situation to the throne of grace and without fail, found the mercy needed for the moment. He went to bed and slept like a baby. The next day, while the perpetrators of the heinous act were waiting to hear of the demise of this troublesome evangelist, Evang. Gindiri awoke hale and hearty and went on to conclude his evangelistic campaign before returning to Jos.

One of the severe tests that Evang. Gindiri underwent was when he lost his daughter through an auto crash. She was part of the team he was leading on an outreach when the crash occurred. Grieved to no end as a father, Evang. Gindiri still felt it necessary that his daughter's sacrifice for the cause of the gospel should not be in vain. He got her body taken and preserved in a mortuary, while he continued with the team to execute the outreach as had been scheduled. What a bountiful harvest of souls, the Lord brought in on that tearful outreach!

Evang. Gindiri was not only an evangelist but he was also an advocate for the rights of the northern Christian community, which often lacks a voice. He often confronted governments both federal and, especially, northern state governments over their anti-Christian policies. A good example of this was the ban of open-air preaching during the military administrations of Gens Buhari and Babangida. That was one instance in which Evang. Gindiri was ready to engage in civil disobedience, because it went counter to the direct command from his high King. In his defiance, he was arrested and detained by the police several times, but God always brought him out. In all this, he was steadfast in faith, believing that the God who called and commissioned him to his task would always be there for him; and God never did disappoint him.

Toward the end of his life, the phenomenon of religious aggression and violence against Christians in northern Nigeria, which, beginning from 1984/85, attained monumental proportions hitherto unknown in the country, had become a recurring fact of life. The common feature in all of these was that whenever such violence broke out, very little was done by those who control the state apparatus to either nip the violence in the bud or to contain it. Such efforts invariably came too late, long after Christians had been annihilated or maimed, their churches ruined, and their property and businesses wasted. Evang. Gindiri was one of those who began to advocate for Christians to rise up to defend themselves, since the government that was supposed to defend them would not. Even though he had not studied philosophy, his proposal could be said to be in the sphere of the just war theory that is encapsulated in the cliché, *"If you want peace, prepare for war."* He was often amongst the first to visit Christians who were displaced by religious violence, often times he would be there before any government official; and naturally, he would bring relief materials for the victims as well.

CONCLUSION

The evangelist Paul Gofo Gunen Gindiri answered the homeward call to glory on April 8, 1996, at the age of sixty-one years. His death seemed rather untimely for many, but for God, his servant had accomplished his task on earth. It was time for him to enter his Sabbath. His mantle was left behind for others to take up. Perhaps, it was rather too heavy, and as such there does not seem to be anyone who has arisen to fill the void he left behind. It is rare to find in one saved sinner the qualities that were all present in Evang. Gindiri: love for God as a saint; a compassionate heart as a husband, father, and philanthropist; passion for souls as an evangelist; astuteness as a businessman, with the mettle and grit of a prophet.

Though he was a charismatic leader with a strong personality, Evang. Gindiri clearly understood the power of team spirit. He always sought to build vibrant coalitions and networks of Christians across denominational lines for common goals, as his work in New Life For All shows. He also was one of the founding fathers of the Christian Association of Nigeria (CAN) as well as a great mobilizer for CAN (through New Life For All), especially in northern Nigeria. He sought to strengthen the hand of CAN so it could stand up to defend the rights of northern Christians, who are more often than not treated as second—if not third-class—citizens of their fatherland (and on occasions worse than aliens). However, with his pre-Christian background, Evang. Gindiri was also a bridge builder. Thus, he was a strong supporter of the inter-faith dialogues initiated at the behest of the then Federal Military Government, when it established the National Council on Inter-religious Affairs.

The lessons that Evang. Gindiri's life has for us are numerous. Recapping just a few of these, we must first realize, as he did, the importance of cultivating and nurturing our relationship with the Lord. We live in a fallen world, in which nothing is exempt from the principle of degeneracy and decay that was introduced with the sin of our first parents (Adam and Eve). So even our relationship with the Lord, if not consciously maintained through a devotional meditation on his word and prayer, could ebb and wane. Second, true pursuit of happiness is found in the pursuit of God, his righteousness and kingdom, not in the pursuit of materialism. Jesus' statement in this regard has been proven to be so true times without number, namely, *"Seek first the kingdom of God and his righteousness, and all these things will be added to you"* (Matthew 6:33 ESV). Third, true wealth and prosperity are not gained through naming and claiming or extortion and exploitation of haplessly naïve religious ignoramuses. Rather, hard work, discerning the right opportunities for investment, and God's blessings are the keys to a prosperous life (cf. Proverbs 3:1–10; 10:4, 22; 12:24, 27; 22:29; Ecclesiastes 9:11; Deut 28:1–14). Fourth, the Christian life must be lived in service to others. God loved us and gave his one and only Son. Jesus loved us and gave his life in our stead. Thus, the Godhead has shown us the way of love—true love gives sacrificially for the good of others. Evang. Gindiri's love was great, and he gave of himself, his time, and his resources that so many who were dwelling in the shadow of death could see the light and come out of darkness into the marvelous light of the kingdom of God's beloved Son. Fifth, having a vision is what results in purposeful living. All Christians, who want their lives to count in life and eternity, must come to the point of agonizingly petitioning our heavenly Father, as the apostle Paul did, *"Lord what wilt Thou have me do?"* The clear understanding of the divine purpose for our lives brings zest and vigour for daily living. These were some of the things that defined Paul Gindiri's life after his encounter with the risen Lord on the Road to Gboko.

CHAPTER SEVEN

THE FAITHFUL STEWARD

DR. DAVID TOR IORDAAH

WHERE IT ALL BEGAN

David Tor Iordaah grew up in Zaki-Biam, Ukum Local Government Area of Benue State. His father, who was a trader and farmer, had moved from Shangev-Ya District of Kwande Local Government Area to Zaki-Biam because of the golden opportunities that the latter place offered for both farming and business interests. David was born in Shangev-Ya on July 23, 1950. His family migrated to Zaki-Biam when David was still a little boy, yet the memories of that journey are indelibly engrained on his mind. He recalls with picturesque vividness the bumpy ride they took on the haulage truck (the ubiquitous Mercedes 911 trucks) on those treacherous tracks that were the only means of moving people and goods in rural Nigeria in those days. For a young boy, who had never being in a motorized vehicle before, that journey was simply exhilarating, and for many years he remembered it with relish, as it stood him from his peers, whenever he told them about it, since they had never had such an experience previously. After more than half a century, it is rather a sad commentary on our national development that much has not changed for our rural folks.

Soon upon arrival in Zaki-Biam, a neighbour of the Iordaah's, one Mr. Wuave Malu (popularly called Ticha Wuave, Ticha being the way locals pronounce the English word, "Teacher"), who was a teacher at the local Dutch Reformed Church Mission (DRCM)[5] Primary School, took special interest in David and began teaching him the alphabet at home even before he enrolled in school. By January 1956, when the new school year began, David was just about five-and-half years old, and could not meet the standard requirement for enrolment in elementary school in those days: the prospective pupils would have to put their right hands over their heads and touch their left ears. This was only possible for a child of at least 7 or 8 years of age. However, because of the learning that David had already accomplished at home through the help of his kind neighbor, Mr. Wuave Malu, he was admitted into primary one in 1956.

Attending a mission school was a major shaping factor for the young David's life. School began each day with the singing of Christian songs and a devotional reading of the Bible, followed by biblical instructions. These, together with the exemplary lives of the teachers, left an ineffaceable mark on David's life. It was here that the gospel was explained to him and he embraced it whole-heartedly. What hampered the spiritual growth of the young pupils was the lack of conscious effort in discipling them. Nonetheless, David remains grateful for the seed of faith that was sown in his life both in the elementary school and the Sunday school classes he attended. David naturally loves music and the school period devoted to singing, when the basics of music and new songs were taught, both from *Golden Bells* and *Sacred Songs and Solos*, were always his golden moments in school.

Another major influence in David's life was his father, Iordaah Agabi. Mr. Agabi taught his children the virtues of hard work, personal integrity, and discipline. It was unthinkable that on a non-school day, Mr. Agabi would go to the farm and leave his sons behind. He brought them up to be self-reliant, and to earn their own living rather than depend on others. Like the preacher says in Ecclesiastes 9:11, it was customary to hear him instruct his children, *"Whatever you want to do, do it with all your heart."* David similarly acknowledges the godly influence of his mother, Mama Kwaghtsule Iordaah, though only a nominal Christian at the time.

David had early exposure to interaction with people of other ethnicity, which was uncommon in his day. His family homeland shares a common boundary with what is today known as Cross River State. His family had long standing friendship with the Agabi family in Cross River, and it was out of this friend that his great grandfather had named his grandfather Agabi.

CAREER DEVELOPMENT

After his primary school education in Zaki-Biam, David proceeded to what is today known as Government College, Katsina-Ala, for his secondary education in 1963. He graduated from there at the beginning of the Nigerian Civil War, in 1967. David admits of having made some bad choices with regards to the subjects he had registered for in the final WASC examinations. He registered for a combination of science subject but without chemistry, similarly he also registered some art subjects but without English Literature. This made it practically impossible for him to have a good subject combination to proceed on to HSC studies, even though he had passed his WASC with distinction. This made him to journey, on December 31, 1967, to Jos the state capital of the defunct Benue-Plateau state in search of a job.

The journey to Jos in those days was usually undertaken on the haulage trucks, the kind David's family had boarded to migrate to Zaki-Baki. So it was a long and tiring trip, part of it being in the night. They arrived in Jos in the frigid morning of January 1, 1968, which was very characteristic of the city during the Harmattan season back then, without knowing where he would go for accommodation. God brought his way a kind-hearted student of Gindiri Secondary School, who graciously offered temporary accommodation at his uncle's two-room tenement unit for David for a period of two weeks. Thereafter, he would be on his own. The saving grace for him and many other young job-seekers, who were flocking into the city, was empty houses abandoned by the Ibos, who had fled at the beginning of the crisis that led to the civil war. There were many of those houses in the city, so the municipal authorities were looking for people to stay in them so as to prevent them from being hide-outs for hoodlums and miscreants. That was how they were able to find shelter from the biting Harmattan winds, while they paid minimal rents to the local authorities.

It was, however, impossible for him to survive for long on the meagre money he had brought with him from the village before he found work later in June that year. Amazingly, just when he had ran out of money, God made it possible for him to reunite with an alumnus of the secondary school he had attended. This fellow was David's senior, whom David had fagged when he was in his first year in secondary school. He provided David with room and board in his house, and in exchange David served him as a houseboy; and his duties included cooking, doing laundry and ironing his clothes, and running errands for him.

David recalls that in those early post-independence days, there was a thriving private sector. The banks were growing, and there were major chain stores like Challerams, Chanrai, Kingsway, Leventis, and motor dealerships like General Motors. At that time, David admits, he had no knowledge of what banking was, but as he went round the city looking for work, he submitted his application letters to the chain stores as well as to the banks. The Standard Bank of British West Africa (as today's First Bank was then called) happened to be the first place to have invited him for a pre-interview written examination, on which he scored very highly. He was subsequently invited for interview and offered the job of a clerk. While he was going round the city, submitting applications, when he came to the Standard Bank building, he was simply enthralled by it, and he remembers telling himself how glorious it would be to work in a place like that. That was a kind of premonition of what was coming for him. He started work with the bank on June 17, 1968.

David had learned well the lessons concerning dedication, integrity, and industry from his father. Now that he was an employee of a bank, he pressed these virtues into service, and his superiors were not slack in taking notice. Within a short time of three months he was promoted to the position of a cashier, whereas it usually took people years to make that transition. This was the beginning of his meteoric rise within the banking sector.

As he was rising in rank on the job, he still nursed the ambition of furthering his education. He had already enrolled with London Institute of Bankers and was preparing for the professional examination. At about that time, Ahmadu Bello University (ABU), Zaria, had just advertised its newly introduced Diploma programmes in Banking, Accounting, and Insurance. David immediately applied and secured admission into the Banking programme. His next concern was how he would finance his education. For this, he applied for the state government scholarship, but God was working out something better for him. When he took his reference forms for the Benue Plateau State scholarship to his manager to recommend him, the latter decided on his own to request the Bank headquarters in Lagos to offer David sponsorship throughout his studies since it was in a field relevant to the Bank. This is a testimony to how much his manager valued his work. His manager was able to obtain full sponsorship for him, and he would still enjoy all his benefits as a worker while he was in school. The icing on the cake was that upon graduation, he would not be bound to return to the bank. This was more than what he had bargained for, although it is not too surprising because his manager was a white man. In that setting, the vices of either tribalism or nepotism that often colour the decision making process in contemporary Nigeria were non-existent. Thus, merit was rewarded rather mere ethnic balancing. He therefore, left his work station for school in the next school year and by 1973 he completed his diploma in Banking.

Earning a diploma instantly changed his job cadre in the bank, from the clerk line to the officer cadre, and thereafter his promotions came in quick succession. He served in diverse places including Jos, Kano, Kaura Namoda, Maiduguri, Gusau, Kaduna, and Lagos. He rose from his last position of cashier to manager's assistant, to branch manager, then area manager, to principal area manager, to assistant general manager, to deputy general manager, and then General Manager. Dr. David Iordaah eventually rose to the position of an Executive Director of First Bank from 1996 until 2000, when he voluntarily retired, after more than three decades of meritorious service with the bank. Suffice it to say that during those years of service in the bank, David continued with his educational pursuit through distant learning programmes leading up to an MBA, and eventually a PhD. He also attend courses in Britain, South Africa, and Switzerland (at the renowned Lausanne School of Business).

DAVID IORDAAH'S FAMILY

David met his wife, Rose Anya, in Jos. At that time David was already working with the bank, while his wife was a student, first at the Queen of the Rosary Secondary School, Gboko, for her secondary education, and later at St. Louis College, Jos, for her HSC. He met her while she and her sister were holidaying with their mother, who was working as a nurse in Jos. This chance meeting grew into a loving relationship that was nurtured for five good years, until it blossomed and culminated into their marriage in 1973. Their marriage was very fruitful, being blessed with four children, two boys and two girls; and they now have ten grandchildren.

David and Rose were true lovebirds. It was hard to see one without the other. They were a perfect team. Though Rose was a school teacher, because of her husband's transfers, she gave up her career so that the family would always be together—not separated by their different careers. Instead, they poured themselves into the service of the Lord (i.e., outside of David's professional work as a banker). They were heavily involved with the local ECWA congregations where they worshiped. They were also deeply committed to the ministries of Child Evangelism Fellowship and the Gideons International. This partnership continued for nearly forty years until Mama Rose (as she came to be fondly called) was called to glory on May 1, 2012.

SERVICE TO GOD THROUGH SERVICE TO HUMANITY IN THE WORK PLACE

The perspective a person has on life determines how that person's life is lived. For David, when he began working in the bank, one of the things the Lord did was to impress on his mind that all human beings bear God's image. Thus, he was to know that anytime he was serving somebody, he was to remember that the person before him was an image-bearer of God. Therefore, it was incumbent on him to treat everyone that he served, while on duty, as befitting the image-bearer of God. This divine instruction was undergirded by the demand of Jesus on his disciples when he said to seek first the kingdom of God and his righteousness and all other things will be added (Matthew 6:33).

The constant overriding passion of David throughout his long working life was to bring God honour and glory by every aspect of his life. To keep himself on this track, he learned early to pray fervently about his work, understanding that it was his station of service to God. Thus, he began each day at work with prayer, committing the day's tasks and challenges in the Lord's hands and believing him for victories as well. For this purpose, he always came to work earlier than the usual opening hours so that he would not be taking his work hours for prayers. It did not take long for customers of the bank branches where David worked to realize the kind of person he was. This frequently saved him from unnecessary pressures and temptations, since many of those who come to banks with shifty deals would normally avoid him. Amongst many examples, he recalls a time when in 1977 he was serving in Gusau as a branch manager, and he had facilitated a loan offer to a customer. After the loan had materialized, the customer return one day, and offered Dr. Iordaah a cheque of ₦6000.00 (that amount, back then, could purchase two brand new Toyota Corolla cars and there would still be some hefty change left over). At this Dr. Iordaah turned in surprise and asked the man,

"What is this for, sir?"

The man's cool reply was, "It is my 'thank you' package for your assistance."

Dr. Iordaah's succinct response was, "I am here to serve, not to collect money from people. The bank pays me my wages, and if I have a need greater than the pay the bank gives me, my God, who has placed me here, is more than able to provide for all my needs according to his riches in glory."

This scenario, in years to come, would repeat itself in all of the mega branches of First Bank in such cities as Kano, Kaduna, and Lagos, where Dr. Iordaah served. Time without number, customers had brought back bags of money to give him for services rendered, and each time without fail he turned down their offers—pointing out that he was only doing his duty for which he was being remunerated by his employer and shall be rewarded for it by his Maker and Saviour. His attitude tellingly embodies the teachings of our Lord and Saviour Jesus, who said,

> So you also, when you have done all that you were commanded, say, "We are unworthy servants; we have only done what was our duty" (Luke 17:10 ESV).

The faith of those who step out and take a stand for God would always be tested. One such incidence, Dr. Iordaah recalls, occurred when he was the Deputy General Manager (Banking Operations) in Lagos, and he was being tipped to move north and head the First Bank's operations in Kano zone, as a General Manager. There was a serious concern among the top echelon of the bank, that if he went to Kano, his religious fervor would stymie the fortunes of the bank, since Kano stood religiously at polar ends with Dr. Iordaah's faith commitment. The concern arose because news had filtered to the management that Dr. Iordaah was holding prayer meetings in his office before the commencement of the working day. At this, the alarmed management directed the Managing Director (MD) of the bank to confer with him of the matter, in view of his impending transfer to Kano.

On the appointed day, the MD summon Dr. Iordaah to his office, and informed him that he was being considered for promotion to the rank of a General Manager to be posted to Kano, but that the management was entertaining reservations on account of his religious activities; that they had heard that he even prays in the office. Dr. Iordaah's answer was as blunt as can be, *"Guilty as charged."* He went on to tell his boss that it is we, the Christians, who are afraid of owning up to our faith that contemplate such concerns; but the Kano people they were worried about understand the value of faith—they don't pray only in offices but everywhere. He pointed out to his boss that if he observed, he would have noticed that the Muslims, for whom he was expressing concern, even erect prayer places within bank premises. Only Christians don't appear to treasure their relationship with their God. Furthermore, Dr. Iordaah advanced other reasons why he prays in the bank:

> *The bank needs prayers more than other places because all sorts of characters come to the bank. Armed robbers come to the bank; they don't go to my house because there is no money there. If you pay heed, you would observe that since I've been in charge of banking operations in Lagos, there has been no armed robbery in any of the branches that I supervise [which was unusual for Lagos in those days, and as soon as Dr. Iordaah left that position the story changed also, with several of their branches being robbed repeatedly]. Besides, I pray for you—that you would succeed. I pray that God will give us business. I pray that God will keep us healthy, and make us stronger. I also pray that God will protect our customers. I don't only pray in the office, sometimes I also pray with customers who come to the bank but carry heavy burdens that only God can lift off their shoulders. At the end, they become even happier for coming to our bank. So if you were to stop me from praying you would be denying yourself, the bank, and many others the blessings for which God brought me here. However, if you are still*

skeptical, you could post me to Kaduna, which supervises my home state of Benue.

Not surprisingly, Dr. Iordaah was instead transferred to Kaduna, where he had a very successful second tenure as a General Manager, and moved on higher to be an Executive Director of the bank for four years before retiring voluntarily. Dr. Iordaah was able to stand up for what he believed in because earlier on, in his younger days in the bank, God had helped him understand that the compartmentalization of life by Christians into the sacred and secular was alien to biblical faith. Dr. Iordaah believes that in the divine economy, there is nothing like full-time ministry, as all God's servants, wherever they are found (whether in the bank, in judiciary, in market square, in the mechanic workshop) are all meant to be fully in service (ministry) to God every single moment of their lives. For him, that indeed is true worship.

God's word has always been central in the life of Dr. Iordaah; it both saved him from troubles and also served to build up his faith. Working in the bank, the temptation to make quick money was ever present. What helped him maintain his sanity was the rhetorical question Jesus asked, *"... What will it profit a man if he gains the whole world and forfeits his soul? Or what shall a man give in return for his soul?"* (Matthew 16:26 ESV). This question constantly reminded him that all of the riches of the world dismally fall short of the worth of a single human soul, so why would he mortgage his eternal destiny for fleeting pleasures of sin. Secondly, there was a point in his career at which it was revealed to him that the Lord had raised him up for signs and wonders (Isaiah 8:18). Besides, it was deeply impressed on his heart that God will never share his glory with any other person (Isaiah 42:8).

Thus, throughout his career, he had to rely on God for his preferment (Psalm 75:6). On this note, he recalls vividly when he was due for elevation to the Board of

Directors of the bank. Several people had suggested that he should go to see various people as a way of securing his elevation. However, with the deep conviction of absolute dependence on God, he would not. He and his dear wife, Mama Rose, just spent some time seeking the heavenly Father's face about it. They came out with the conviction of God's assurance. God's message to them was clear,

> *"Rely on me. For if I am with you, even if there are seven billion people against you, they will have no success. But if I am against you, even if seven billion people stand for you, you will make no progress."*

At the end of the day, his elevation came to the amazement and wonder of many who had made the rounds, lobbying those who mattered in the process. What he came to learn from all this is that when God stands for you, even those who would have ordinarily opposed you would recommend you at the critical moments, and then afterwards they would be regretting their action. This agrees perfectly with Scripture, as it says, *"When a man's ways please the LORD, he makes even his enemies to be at peace with him"* (Proverbs 16:7 ESV). Experiences like this, helped strengthen his faith in God.

On the whole, Dr. Iordaah looks back over his career with deep gratitude for opportunities it offered him to serve God. Working with the bank made it possible for him, through transfers, to live in different parts of Nigeria. There were opportunities for him to serve the Lord in all those places, serving as an elder in local ECWA churches in all the cities in which he worked. In all of those cities, he regularly had invitations to preach in local churches and fellowship groups—these would not have being possible without his work with the bank. He recalls many people he had led to the saving knowledge of Christ, a number of them within the banking precincts. He is thankful that his banking salary enabled him to attend programs of the

CEF and Gideons International (both within and outside the country). He is also thankful for the opportunity he and his wife had to support the gospel financially. He recalls one pastor, who had told him once that he was still in ministry because of the encouragement and support of the Iordaah family. This is just one example out of many such testimonies. He testifies to the fact that when you stick out your neck for God, God takes up your cause. He had seen many of his colleagues dismissed from work because of the mad pursuit of money. He had seen the Lord help him sort out, within mere minutes, labyrinths of complicated work situations that would otherwise take long agonizing hours. Our God is a loyal covenant keeping God. One only needs to be faithful to see his goodness in the land of the living.

POST-RETIREMENT LIFE

When still serving with First Bank, Dr. Iordaah recalls, every so often when customers came to offer material gifts in appreciation to him for services rendered, and as he refused to collect such, he would tell them that the time they could really show that they were his friends and they appreciated him would be the time of his retirement. He used to say this knowing fully well that, in our context, such show of appreciation to a retired person would seldom take place. This is because even though people call such gifts appreciation, they offer them so as to smooth their path when next they have to deal with the person. A retired person ceases to be of any business facility to the clientele of his or her place of employment, and as such there is usually no business sense in offering any gift to such a person. In other word, Dr. Iordaah knew very well that those gifts were investments for the future (bribes paid in advance), not appreciations of the past.

Dr. Iordaah's adamant refusal to collect the so-called "appreciation gifts" from customers was held in derision and disdain by some of his colleagues. He remembers one time when he was serving in Lagos that a colleague came to him and told him,

> *David, this your Christian whatever has made you so stupid that you reject gifts that could help you and your family plan for the rainy day, especially retirement. Listen well, and let me tell you some hard facts, if you continue in this way, you will eat shit when you retire.*

Dr. Iordaah's response was to point this colleague to his abiding faith in the veracity of the word of God, in which the sweet psalmist of Israel testifies, *"I have been young, and now am old, yet I have not seen the righteous forsaken or his children begging for bread"* (Psa 37:25 ESV). Thus, in view of this promise from God, he wasn't going to begin worrying about what was yet to come, knowing fully well that because Christ lives he can face tomorrow with confidence and certainty (He will cross that bridge when he gets there. In the final analysis, he told his colleague,

> *The God that I serve has not promised 'shit' to his children, but loving care and adequate provision for their needs. I have no doubt in my mind that the way God will work with me, even in retirement, will be a sign and wonder to many and a challenge to his children to learn to trust him and live in faithful obedience.*

Now in retirement, Dr. Iordaah is waxing stronger in his faith and service to God, as he continues to bear testimony to God's faithfulness. He says that God has over blessed him in retirement: He says he is neither eating "shit" nor begging. In his words he says, *"When I look at God's blessings in our lives, I sometimes wonder, 'why does God spend so much time working on the lives of others when there are many others needing his attention also.'"* It is a known fact that God lavishes his blessings on those who, he knows, would not hoard such blessings for themselves only, but would share with others, as Jesus said, *"Freely you received, freely give"*(Matthew 10:8 NASB). Dr. Iordaah gives as much as he has been blessed.

His giving heart has pushed Dr. Iordaah to continue working as hard in retirement as he did when he was in regular employment. This, he acknowledges, has made him equally busier than he was when he worked with First Bank. Upon his return to Benue State, after retirement, Dr. Iordaah was taken aback by the level and pervasiveness of poverty in the state. There is untold need everywhere one turns: widows without anyone to provide for them; orphans with no one to pay their school fees; the aged who can no longer work and have no source of livelihood; the sick who have no means to pay for medical attention; churches need help; para-church organizations need help; and ministers of the gospel need help. The list is endless. Dr. Iordaah's compassionate heart compelled him to action. He knew that he could not meet all needs, but some of them had to be met. Even then, he still realized that his pension wasn't going to suffice for him and all the needs that he desired to address. All the same, to do something, he must; it remained to decide what it was that he and his wife were going to do. As he and his late wife prayed about this, they felt God leading them to meet a need as a business investment: they started a private water-bottling company, **Waterfirst Rehoboth Ltd**, which produces the **Waterfirst** bottled water brand using the process of reverse osmosis. This business has not just kept him busy, but has also proved to be a veritable source for meeting as many of the needs he was burdened about as possible, while at the same meeting the need of clean table water for many of the cities in North-Central Nigeria.

CONCLUSION

One of the things that have baffled Dr. Iordaah is

the abysmal decline of ethical standards in Nigeria nowadays. What troubles him most of all is that there is little difference between Christians and non-Christians when it comes to this problem of ethical decay. One regret he has relates to once being swindled of his money by some fraudster, who had come to him under the guise of being a Christian. What was hurtful about the whole thing was not just the loss of money, but the fact that people could use the name of the Lord for criminal acts. Being a man of the word, Dr. Iordaah is quick to point to the Bible, where God had challenged King Solomon that if he walked before God in the integrity of his heart, as his father David did, God's blessings will overflow to him and his progeny, which would result in the perpetuity of his dynasty (1 Kings 9:4–5). So for him, living in accordance with God's word is a surer way of securing blessings than the pursuit of sordid gain. Dr. Iordaah is convinced that Nigeria is where it is today because many of those who profess to be Christians no longer embrace truth, honesty, and integrity in their daily lives and in the conduct of their businesses. He believes that if there is going to be any change in Nigeria, it must start with professing Christian behaving their beliefs.

CHAPTER EIGHT

THE PACESETTER

ENGR. DR. EZEKIEL NWOSU IZUOGU

FROM THE START

Engr. Dr Ezekiel Nwosu Izuogu hails from a polygamous family: His father had four wives, his mother being the first with eight children and he was the firstborn. While his parents had no Christian commitment, they actively encouraged their children to attend church. Notwithstanding the nominalism of the Christianity in the days of his youth, Ezekiel loved God from a very young age. It was his common practice from an early age to go into the bush to be alone, fasting and praying. One could almost say that the love of God was innate in his young heart. Even though his juvenile heart was restlessly seeking after God, there was no one, who knew the gospel enough to help him find his rest in Christ alone by grace alone through faith alone. This yearning for God made him hate evil and set himself apart from all other children. Yet, it was not until the end of the Nigerian civil war before he was first introduced to Christ as his redeemer and friend.

Born on November 4, 1949 in Akokwa, Imo State, Ezekiel attended the Native Authority school, both the nursery and primary school segments, in his village. He completed his primary school education in 1963. However, because his was from a very large family, with limited resources, he could not proceed straight to secondary school. He was sent to stay with his uncle in Onitsha. He helped his uncle with his retail business in Onitsha for one year. Through this, he was able to save the money with which to start school, and the following year he went to Iheme Memorial Grammar School, Arondizuogu, in Imo state. Ezekiel, by all standards, did well in school. He frequently took the first position in his class, right from primary school to now that he was in secondary. His stellar academic performance often stood him in good stead with his class teachers and school authorities. Thus, from an early age, he regularly had responsibility thrust upon him. He had served variously as class prefect, house prefect, school prefect, and time keeper: He had these positions severally both in elementary and secondary schools. He also loved sports but he did much better at tennis than soccer.

Though a very brilliant chap, Ezekiel's path to schooling was not smooth. As noted above, after his primary school, he stayed at home for a year before proceeding to secondary school. By the time he was in form three, his education was rudely interrupted by the Nigerian civil war in 1967, as all schools in the defunct Republic of Biafra were shut down for all the thirty months that the war lasted. Notwithstanding, as he reminisced over all this, all he can recall is the deep gratitude they all had at the end of the war for still being alive, in view the huge numbers of people that lost their lives during that war.

Not only did the war disrupt his education, just like it did to all other Ibo youngsters, it also brought untold hardship. There was immense poverty, hunger, and suffering. To survive, Ezekiel became a dancer and used to organize entertainment for the Biafran soldiers. As with most war situations, these youngsters were not only being used as child soldiers and labourers, but the soldiers also sought to corrupt their morals. It was not uncommon for the soldiers to seek to introduce the children to such barrack vices as alcoholism and drug abuse (e.g., smoking marijuana and the like). However, with his antecedents, Ezekiel had resisted such a lifestyle, and, thankfully, no one attempted to compel him to indulge in it.

Finding new life in Christ was a great milestone in Ezekiel's life. This momentous event took place in January 1970, immediately after the end of the civil war. Although folks in his village generally thought him to be very good and well behaved, Ezekiel was not unaware of his little hidden sins: lying, deceiving his parents to get money and such other misdemeanors. God had used the ministry of the Scripture Union (SU), to bring this servant of his to himself. Through an evangelistic outreach of the SU, he was made to realize that having a personal relationship with God was the way to eternal life: that it didn't matter whether or not one went to church and was a communicant member therein. What matters is whether one has the assurance of one's destiny at the end of one's life. Ezekiel had no such assurance regarding where he would be in the hereafter: whether in heaven or in hell. At that point, he saw through the emptiness of his vain religion, knelt in surrender to the Saviour, and asked him to come into his life. Since then, life has not been the same; it changed for the better, as he ruminates with wonder,

> ...looking back, my life has never been the same. I wonder what would have become of me, if I didn't give my life to Christ—if I didn't have a personal relationship with him—because it turned out to be what has sustained me over all the turmoil I've been through, over all the ups and downs, over all the problems one has gone through. I just wonder—it's simply amazing! I think I would have perished a long time ago—I would have perished a long time ago if I didn't

know Christ.

The following year, Ezekiel went to the University of Nigeria, Nsukka, and graduated with the Bachelor of Science degree in Electrical Engineering in 1977. During his undergraduate days, he was a member of the campus SU fellowship. God used this fellowship to establish him in the faith. He became a prayer warrior and spent an enormous amount of time in God's presence in those early years of his Christian pilgrimage.

CALLING AND MINISTRY

The battle for the direction for his life ensued shortly after graduating from the university. In those good old days, job opportunities awaited university graduates at the gate upon graduation. With his own qualification as an electrical engineer, even the oil companies were coming for him. Yet he had decided to place his life at God's altar. He eventually accepted to serve as an itinerant evangelist with the SU (as a traveling secretary, as it was then called). In this capacity, he had no salary. As one who hails from eastern Nigeria, this act of sacrifice was looked upon as the height of irresponsibility and idiocy. He was disowned by everyone: his family, friends, and even fellow Christian friends. Indeed, one of his uncles loaded his gun one day and went out in search of Ezekiel, with the singular aim of silencing him with one shot of the gun for disgracing the family. It was a hard time for him. He almost gave up. Yet he found strength in God to keep trudging on in faith and absolute surrender to God's will.

Besides all these outward persecutions, there was the inward struggle of giving up one's passion. Ezekiel was very passionate about engineering research. He had keen interest in researching into the field of alternative energy sources, at the time when no one in the entire world was really thinking of such a subject. His desire was to pursue this line of research further after his undergraduate studies. To give all this up for the ministry was like giving up his Isaac. In retrospect he says,

> *I was very much in love with engineering, very much in love with it to the point of obsession. Now, God was asking me to leave all of that and just carry the Bible and preach. It was just too much for me. My thought was that he was calling me to permanent full time ministry, to eventually become a pastor. In other words, it was as if God wanted me to turn my back on engineering forever. This was a bit too much for me, but through much prayer, I found the divine help I needed to surrender to God's will, just like Abraham surrendered Isaac. Abraham was able to sacrifice his only son for God. I didn't know that God was going to confront me with a similar challenge. So, when I was confronted, I discovered it wasn't easy—surrendering one's Isaac is never easy. But thank God, miraculously he helped me to surrender, and surrendered I did.*

Through this experience, Ezekiel learned to tear down his idols and allow God to be truly preeminent in his life. The amazing thing is that surrendering his professional passion did the unexpected; it freed him from the self-pity that had resulted from being rejected by family and friends. From this point on, nothing else mattered more than his relationship with God: The Lord really became enthroned in his life as his Sovereign.

Ezekiel was soon to find out that God is no debtor to anyone. As Scripture says, God is not unjust as to forget the labour of love of his children (Hebrews 6:10). He certainly remembered Engr. Izuogu and visited him. Six month into his full time ministry with the SU, while serving in Benin City, God revealed to him the intricate workings of the Self-Sustaining Emagnetodynamic Machine (SSEM) as an alternative energy source—the very area into which he had wanted to research. However, it would take another thirty-three years of labour to bring the revelations to fruition: this invention has now been patented in about one hundred and forty countries. Emagnetodynamics is a way of extracting energy from permanent magnets. It is a safe way of generating atomic energy that avoids the kind of nuclear disasters that occurred at Fukushima and Chernobyl. Scientists had thought this impossible, but Engr. Izuogu had the breakthrough into this groundbreaking invention. This is what obedience to God brings. Indeed, Engr. Izuogu likens his experience to those of Daniel in the courts of the Babylonian monarchs.

Meanwhile, Engr. Izuogu points to his life to demonstrate the grace and patience of God, who sometimes acts like an indulgent father. He recalls how when he was answering the call, he was making demands of, like God had to give him a new house in which no one had stayed before, God had to give him a new car, and the like. Surprisingly, just like a kind and compassionate father would be patient with his child, who is throwing tantrums without shouting at the kid, God patiently indulged him and gave him all that he asked for me. It was in his 7 bedroom bungalow in Benin that he received the revelation into the science of emagnetodynamics. Experience has taught him over the years that it is immaturity that leads people to pray such kinds of prayer, but God does understand their need to grow up and as such is patient with them.

Leaving the so-called full time ministry was not the end of his ministry. Engr. Izuogu, upon moving from Benin to Owerri, became the evangelism director of his diocese (which has now been divided into 10 different dioceses). He continued labouring for the Master just the same as if he were really full time; the only difference was that he was doing these now without pay. He was preaching in churches and at conferences throughout the diocese, organizing open-air evangelistic campaigns, and planting churches. When he veered into politics, coupled with his research, his time became more limited but he continued to serve whenever called upon by his church (the Anglican Communion). He has preached at several synods, and recently was even invited by the Primate of the church to preach at the conference of all the Anglican bishops in Nigeria. Now that his research in emagnetodynamics has reached a good level, he is more disposed to availing himself all the more for service to the Lord.

CHANGING CAREER PATHS

By and large Engr. Izuogu spent three years in full time ministry with the SU. Whereas his initial impression when he first got the call was that of a lifelong commitment, after just three years, he felt God telling him, *"it was enough; he just wanted to test my obedience."* God had already, through this experience, established his sovereignty over Engr. Izuogu's life; he could now free his servant so as to use him in other sectors of the society. God helped him to see that these other things he would be giving himself into were of no less significant service to him than the so-called full time ministry.

Engr. Izuogu experienced career changes in rapid succession. After three years of service with the SU, he took up a lecturing job with the Federal Polytechnic, Owerri. He lectured in the department of Communication and Electronic Engineering for another three years. Thereafter, he left to establish his own business, Major Lab (Nig.) Limited, which was the first scientific equipment manufacturing company in Nigeria. Prior to the existence of his company, science laboratory tools and equipments for schools were being imported from abroad. His company, at the peak of its production, was manufacturing 500 different types of scientific and laboratory tools and equipments. While the company began as a viable investment, it was later ran aground by the huge debts owed it by various state governments in the country. These governments would order the equipment for their schools (in the form of contracts), but once the equipment were supplied, various government functionaries, who were responsible for paying the company for the supplies, would start to demand bribes before they would effect the payments. Because Engr. Izuogu was unwilling to play along, the monies owed him were also not paid. Till date, the hundreds of millions (which at current value would be scores of billions) of Naira owed his company have yet to be paid. Corruption, he says, has taken its toll on honest business in Nigeria, and is a major factor that is hindering the country's development.

He eventually decided to divert some of his resources at the company into other lines of research. The first was his research into the production of the first African car. With this vision, he set up **Izuogu Motors Limited**. This effort paid off with the production of the first entirely African car, which he christened Z-600. It had the initial maximum speed of 140KM/hour and had the fuel consumption rate of 10 km/litre. This car was presented to the Nigerian public in 1997, with the then Chief of General Staff (the equivalence of the Vice President), Gen. Oladipo Diya gracing the occasion. As the case is with other inventors in the country, there are no funds available for their researches, and even after they have sweated through it, no one is willing to invest in the mass production of the product. This has been the fate of Z-600.

Aside from the challenge of funding, the ingrained desire of our people to hinder the advance of the progressive elements of our population is mind boggling. Engr. Izuogu had made a presentation of his research and production of Z-600 in South Africa in 2005. At which point the South African government showed keen interest in investing in the production of this car. Subsequent to this, in 2006, out of nowhere, supposed armed robbers attacked Engr. Izuogu's laboratory in Owerri and made away with all the moulds that he developed for casting all the major components of the car. This incidence stalled any further development of the Z–600 project.

Undeterred by all these adversities, the indefatigable Engr. Izuogu, turned his focus to his first love in engineering; he renewed his research into emagnetodynamics as an alternative energy source. God once more smiled on the effort his servant with success, leading to this new scientific breakthrough. It remains to be seen, from where and when the resources for the mass production of this machine will come. One pay-off of this research, however, is that the Commonwealth University, administered from London and Belize, evaluated his research findings in the subject of Emagnetodynamics, **the branch of Physics that studies the conversion of the energy of static magnetic fields into work**, and decided to admit him to the Doctor of Science degree. The Tiv people say that the talking drum sounds much clearer to those further away than to those close to it. Whereas Nigerians may not have cherished the work of Engr. Dr. Izuogu, the rest of the world has not failed to take note.

FAMILY LIFE

Dr. Izuogu got married to his wife, Ngozi, on October 6, 1977. That was when he was still serving with the SU as a travelling secretary. They made their home in Benin City after their wedding. Ngozi was a school teacher. The Lord has blessed their marriage with four boys and one girl. His was a very busy life from the beginning: Serving as a travelling secretary meant that he was constantly on the road, visiting schools and SU groups. This meant that the burden of raising the family to a great degree fell to his beloved wife, who most of the time stayed home with the children as he traveled. Even after leaving the SU, he continued to receive invitations for speaking engagements, and he still had his research going on. He and his wife were determined to raise a godly family, and were making conscientious efforts to give their children a Christian upbringing. His frequent travels made him not to have as much time with his family as he would have loved to. His decision in 1988 to join partisan politics made him to have even less time with his family, as his travels increased. Notwithstanding, he tried to spend quality time with the children at every opportunity he had. Thus, his children remained close to him, as any father would desire.

JOURNEY INTO POLITICS

When Dr. Izuogu made his surrender to God in 1977, it was a surrender to always seek to be at the centre of God's will for him. With time, he came to grapple with the fact that there was the need to bring the redemptive grace of God to bear upon the Nigeria's national polity. At the height of the religious tension in the country brought about by the Babangida military administration's action of surreptitiously smuggling the country into the full membership of the Organization of Islamic Country (O.I.C.), Dr. Izuogu accepted to be the National President of Youth Wing of the Christian Association of Nigeria (CAN). This assignment brought him into a close working relationship with Engr. Samuel S. L. Salifu, who was then the Youth CAN President, Northern Zone.

In 1986, they had organized a national Youth CAN conference in Ilorin. One of the features of the conference was a fierce debate on Christian involvement in politics. Present at the debate were such prominent Christian leaders as Gen T. Y. Danjuma, Amb. Jolly Tanko Yusuf (of blessed memory), Chief Bola Ige (of blessed memory), and some others. Some of the panellists were of the view that politics is a dirty game, which true believers should shun like a plague so as to not soil their testimony and not miss heaven. Others held that it is an incumbent duty on Christians to serve as light and salt in every segment of the society, including politics. So intense was the debate that it lasted eight good hours.

At the end of the day, there was a consensus that Christians could go into politics with certain caveats. First, Christians venturing into politics must do so after much prayer and with a clear understanding that it is a calling to serve God and country in that arena, and as such must advance with a resolve to bring their light into the darkness that prevails in the political theatre. Second, they must determine to maintain the Christian hallmarks of honesty, integrity, and faithfulness. Third, they must also resolve never to indulge in corrupt practices and primitive accumulation of ill-gotten wealth at the expense of the people they are supposed to serve. Fourth, those who would like the support of the youth must make definite commitments to them on these issues so that they would not be like others who go into politics for self-enrichment. Dr. Izoguu's personal decision to enter the political arena, after this debate, was not immediate. He took two good years to pray with his family about the issue before deciding to join politics in 1988.

Having the assurance that the Lord was leading him into politics did not make things easier for Dr. Izoguu. If anything, it made life harder for him. For example, joining politics took an even heavier toll on his business. Already his business was suffering from his refusal to connive with government officials in their corrupt practices. Now that he joined politics, many of his customers (since the business had largely government patronage), saw him as a competitor. Their conception was that if his business prospered, he would even become a greater rival. Thus, they made all effort to ruin his business. Dr. Izoguu, remains eternally grateful to Chief Victor Attah, who as governor, ensured that his state government promptly paid Major Lab (Nig.) Ltd. for the laboratory equipment it had purchased from the company.

A major test of his faith came the very first time he ran for gubernatorial elections in his home state of Imo. One of the prominent leaders of his state approached him and told him pointblank that everyone in the state knew he was the best candidate, but that he was not going to see the state house unless he swore an oath of allegiance to the occultic group to which this prominent politician belonged. The man told him that this was their way of protecting their interests. It is kind of like Satan telling Jesus in the Judean wilderness, *"All of the kingdoms of the world will be yours, if you only bow the knee to me."* Here he was, with every chance of being the next governor of his state and making a difference for his people, the very thing he had always wanted to do. Yet, here is a first hurdle: What was he going to do? It was not too much of a choice for him. His allegiance to his Saviour and Lord, Jesus Christ, trounces any other passion: This was settled in 1977. He turned down the offer, and your guess is as good as the reality—he never became the governor. The interesting thing is that at that very time, there were twelve candidates for the same position, and all of the other eleven candidates took the oath. Of course, only one person could be a governor at a time. The devil had used that bait to purchase the souls of the ten others for nothing. This is the reality of our contemporary political terrain: It is increasingly becoming the exclusive preserve of occultic perverts. It is little wonder that our country is sliding dangerously into rottenness and decay toward a perilous precipice.

In his characteristic inexorable manner, Dr. Izuogu was not deterred from standing for elections. Between 1989 and 1999 he thrice ran for the governorship of his state, and thrice he won, yet thrice he was denied the mandate given to him by his people. After one of the elections, the proclaimed winner, who had an ounce of conscience, came to Dr. Izuogu with some "settlement." He plainly told Dr. Izuogu that he knew that it was the latter who won the elections, but it has been given to him (the proclaimed winner); that he was here to compensate Dr. Izuogu for his losses. He, thus, offered Dr. Izuogu the sum of ₦50 million Naira and three commissionership slots into which he could appoint any of his surrogates. Standing on principles, Dr. Izuogu preferred to retain his integrity instead of making merchandise out of the people's mandate. He turned down the offer to the chagrin of even some of his supporters, some of whom became disillusioned because Dr. Izuogu's hardcore Christian principles have denied them access to the corridors of power. In spite of all his travails and losses, Dr. Izuogu has no regrets. He says,

> *Nigerian politics, if you apply Christian principles, you will never get anywhere. So, it is not surprising that in spite of the tremendous goodwill and support that I have enjoyed over the years, and the fact that I won the governorship elections on three occasions, it was repeatedly snatched from me. This makes people conclude that, in Nigeria, you don't use principles, forget about principles; just do what others are doing and gets somewhere—that is the belief among politicians now. Anyway, I personally don't know how to diverge my principle from my practice in the things I do. So, that has been my albatross, but I thank God, because I cannot eat my cake and have it: I cannot be enjoying such a wonderful relationship with God, and at the same time be enjoying the other side. You have to choose your priorities, and no doubt, I have made my choice.*

Looking back over his political career, Dr. Izuogo is thankful that while some of his followers are resentful that his strict principles have denied them the progress they could have had if his own political career had been more successful, many others have expressed gratitude for the influence of his leadership and lifestyle in their lives. Many have written personal heartwarming letters to say how thankful they are for the insights and perspectives on life they gained based on how they watched him make significant decisions at critical junctures over the years. A number of his political protégés have risen to various public offices all the way from local government council chairmen, commissioners, senators, ministers, to governors, many of whom remain grateful for the role he played in their lives.

CONCLUDING THOUGHTS

Looking at where we are in Nigeria today, and in view of the Ilorin Accord, Dr. Izuogu is pained that many Christians have bailed out. One could feel the agony in his voice when he moaned,

> *I must tell you that I am very, very disappointed at the performances of the Christians who have gotten into important positions, especially political positions. There have been a lot of compromises. Integration of faith and vocation has not done well at all in Nigeria. You will find that what people **say** before they got into positions is quite different from what they **do** after they get there. The looting and plunder that is characteristic of Nigerian political leaders is also true of Christians (I mean those professing the born again Christian faith) who have got there. If I tell you that I am impressed, I will be lying to you—I will be a hypocrite—I'm not impressed. Their lives*

are not different from the lives of any other politicians from north to south. Rather, I even know of a few Muslim politicians who live more decent lives than so-called born again Christian politicians; that is true. You will find some Muslims who become ministers and they don't amass wealth; you will find Muslims who become Central bank Governors and they are no richer than they were prior to their ascendency to that position. On the other hand, you will find Christians, supposedly born again Christians, who become managing directors of banks, and billions of stolen money is traceable to them. I am embarrassed to know that no less than 60% of bank CEOs indicated by the recent cleanup activities of Dr. Sanusi Lamido Sanusi (the Central Bank Governor) were prominent leaders in key Pentecostal churches in this country.[6] *I feel very embarrassed and I don't like to deceive myself.*

To counter this current despicable trend, Dr. Izuogu proposes a return to the lost biblical virtues of honesty and truth. Christians, he insists, must remain loyal disciples of Jesus, no matter their positions, whether presidents (of Nigeria or of the world) or ministers or governors or whatever. Integrity (in morality and stewardship) must remain the hallmarks of Christians, whether in low or high positions. When you meet Engr. Dr. Izuogu, you meet a man thoroughly disappointed with the Nigerian project thus far, and yet you also encounter a man who is hopeful of a better Nigeria. It remains to be seen if succeeding generations of Nigerians (especially, Nigerian Christians) will work conscientiously towards the new Nigeria of our dreams.

CHAPTER NINE

THE LEADER'S SCEPTRE SHALL NOT DEPART

DR. CHRISTOPHER KOLADE

EARLY YEARS AND CAREER LIFE

From his early years of growing up in the countryside of present day Ekiti state, Dr. Christopher Olusola Kolade was taught to begin his day with a time of seeking God's direction through Bible reading and prayer. His parents were not only devout Christians, but his father, Archdeacon Kolade, was an ordained minister of the Anglican Church. Both the instruction and, especially, the godly examples of his parents sealed in his young mind principles that would guide him for the rest of his life.

After his elementary education, Christopher had his secondary education at Government College, Ibadan, from where he went to Fourah Bay College, Freetown, Sierra Leone. Though he was raised in a Christian home, it was during his days at Fourah Bay College that he was led to make the faith of his parents his own. In his providence, God began drawing the young Christopher into fellowship with himself through a grateful attitude. In retrospection,

Christopher was led to review the events of his life, as a result of which he was awestricken with the realization of the guiding hand of God, which had orchestrated these events up to that point in time. Having already being well taught by his parents, he knew exactly what he needed to do: He turned over the rudder of his life to the Lord, and began cultivating a personal walk with God. This experience would prove pivotal for the rest of his life, because it was at this time that it also dawned on him that God had a special purpose for him in life. Without any clarity or certainty, he was willing to commit himself unreservedly to whatever mission the Lord will have for him. This strong sense of destiny has guided him in his long working life, and it brings him back again and again to the place of dependence on the Lord.

Following God has never been an easy road. Sometimes it is as if the closer one draws to God the sorer is his faith tested. This was Christopher's experience while still at Fourah Bay College. On Sunday evenings, there were two places that he was likely to be found, namely, either in the chapel for Evensong or, thereafter, his room. One fateful Sunday evening, Christopher along with others students went to the chapel for the usual Evensong. During the service, an unexpected turbulent tropical storm descended on the city. The deafening crashing sounds of the stormy rain forced them out of the chapel. As the frightened students scampered out of the chapel, Christopher, who was the organist, was the last to leave his seat. Before they had exited the chapel, there was a sudden flash of lightning, then a piercing clap of thundering that rumbled into a rambunctious boom that scared the youngsters out of their skins. In a rush they poured into the darkened wetness of the soaking torrential downpour as they scurried to their dormitories. On getting to his dormitory, Christopher discovered that the lightning had struck his hall and its roof had caved in on his room area in particular and all his belongings were afloat as in a lake. The next day, when he got to the chapel, he found out that the roof of the chapel was also struck by the lightning and had imploded and fallen right on the organ where he had been sitting a few moments before their hurried exit, prior to that outburst of thunder. Shivers run down his spin, and his lips let out an involuntary whistle that betrayed the mixed emotions of shock and relief. He had had a close shove with death, but for divine intervention. Death had waylaid him in either of the places he was accustomed to be at that time of the day on a Sunday. Heaven came to the rescue. Looking back over the miracle of that day, Christopher ever lives with the awareness that it was none of his doings, but the mercy of God that worked mightily to deliver him. This would engrave indelibly on his mind the biblical truth: *"My times are in your hands"* (Ps 31:15).

In view of the impact of his teachers on his life, Christopher had always wanted to be a teacher himself. Upon graduation from Fourah Bay College, he secured a job in the old Western region of Nigeria as an education officer. To be a true professional, he undertook further studies in education. He took his job with every sense of pride and dreamed of rising through the ranks to the position of a school principal someday. With every sense of accomplishment and satisfaction, Christopher had thought teaching was his life's career, but that was never to be, as God had other plans for him. Indeed, as he would testify later, the application he wrote for the post of an education officer was the first and last he has ever had to write for a job. Every other job he has held ever since has always been by invitation, beginning with the invitation he received from the then Western region to join its broadcasting corporation. Once again Scripture finds fulfillment in his life as it states, *"The heart of man plans his way, but the LORD establishes his steps"* (Pro 16:9; ESV).

What has always served Dr. Kolade well has been his dedication to hard work and an avid commitment to the pursuit of excellence in whatever he does. The seriousness he attaches to duty comes from his understanding that whatever work he does is, first and foremost, a service being rendered to God and for his glory (cf. Col 3:23–24), and as such must be done as work befitting service to the King of kings. This is what stands him out from the crowd. His orientation toward excellence has persistently opened new and higher opportunities for service for him, as his superiors and other people never fail to take notice of his dedication to duty. A testimonial to this is his meteoric rise to the rank of Director General (DG) of the National Broadcasting Corporation (NBC) within twelve years, subsequent to the merger of the regional broadcasting corporations into a national corporation, even though he had no formal training in journalism. At the time he was made the DG of NBC, Dr. Kolade was barely thirty-nine years of age. Many people had thought he was rather too young for that position, in the day and age when people were much older before they got to those kinds of positions. Yet, he looks back to the five-and-half years spent on that position with delight. Even as a very modest man, he could say that there are a few things he did in those days that have remained reference points in broadcasting in the country to this day. All this, he is quick to attribute to God's sustaining grace.

From public service at NBC, Dr. Kolade moved to the uncharted waters in the business world in Cadbury Nigeria. Within four years of serving as a director in Cadbury he was promoted to the position of deputy managing director, a position he held for only eighteen months and then became the managing director (MD) of the company. After serving for about five years as the managing director, Dr. Kolade became the executive chairman/CEO of Cadbury Nigeria for the rest of his years of service in the company. After twenty-four meritorious years of service Dr. Kolade voluntarily retired as the Chairman/CEO of Cadbury Nigeria in 2002, believing it was time to quit and rest, as he thought he was also getting along in age. Once more God had other plans for him—it was not yet time to rest. In the early years of the Obasanjo administration, he was called upon to serve as Nigeria's high commissioner to the United Kingdom.

As a man who never loses the sense of divine call and providence in his career life, in reminiscing over his life, Dr. Kolade sees nothing extraordinary about his life save the grace of God—the grace which God in his covenantal loyal love extends to all his chosen vessels, as is evident from biblical characters. He does not fail to see his place and role both in the public and market squares as service to God, through service to humanity and his fatherland. He, thus, deeply appreciates the manner in which God has ordered his life, bringing him to places he never thought of and giving him the ability to perform beyond what was expected of him.

FAMILY LIFE

Dr. Kolade was born in 1933, and it took another nine years before his only sister would come. Thus, the family in which he was raise was a small family by all standards, consisting of his parents Archdean & Mrs. Kolade and their two children. Perhaps, it is this background that also influenced Dr. Kolade and his wife, Beatrice, to have only two daughters. He is also blessed with three grandchildren (a girl and two boys) from his two daughters.

Dr. Kolade's years in NBC coincided with the period when his daughters were young and growing up. His schedule was busy and involved traveling often. Yet his family held a special place in his scheme of things. He feels blessed to have had children that cherished his presence. He continued building his family on the foundation that his own parents had laid. He, like his father, maintains a family altar: consistently observing times of devotionally reading of God's word, and seeking his face for the challenges that lay ahead in the dawning day. This constantly inspires them to go forth into the day and live out for the glory of God, with honour and integrity. Dr. Kolade is appreciative of the support that his family has given him all through his working career, without which, he affirms, he would not have been able to do the things he accomplished. For instance, he is quick to point to the anchoring role his wife played in watching over the family during his busy and traveling years when their daughters were still very young. He also readily points to the active role his wife played during his stint with the Foreign Service in London. He believes that she may have made as much impact on British society during those days as he himself.

Though a very busy career man, Dr. Kolade never neglected active participation in the community life of the church. Having never formally studied music, he consistently served as church organist from his college days (at Fourah Bay) and throughout the years of his career up to 1996, when he gave room to younger people. Since then, he has given more time to ministering through teaching and preaching God's word, even though he has never had the opportunity of obtaining formal theological training. God's grace still avails for him even in this ministry also, but he also continues to give himself to a disciplined study of God's word on a personal basis.

CHALLENGES IN WORK LIFE

Dr. Christopher Kolade has had a visibly public life both in broadcasting and in the corporate world. Yet he remains one of the few public figures in Nigeria whose image remain untainted. He is aware that some folks argue that the days in which people like himself served were saner and devoid of the hydra-headed monster of corruption that now bestrides the Nigeria public and corporate landscape as a colossus. While he concedes that corruption may have as yet not gained the notoriety that it now enjoys, he nonetheless holds that nothing is new under sun: the basic problem of degenerate and depraved human hearts have been with us from time immemorial. He attributes his own success to the foundational role God and his word play in his life. He says that early in his life, God had taught him to understand that the issues of life are structured in a hierarchical order. His task, therefore, was to learn to place everything in its rightful place. Thus, he learned not to worship creatures (possessions) as the Creator (God)—the malaise of our contemporary society. Besides, he is always guided by a sense of stewardship, knowing that at the end of life, a time of reckoning will come, and as such he has to remind himself to so order his life and work that Christ will not be ashamed of him when he stands before him to render account of his stewardship, but would gladly receive him into his bosom. It is only those who live in oblivion to these eternal truths of Scripture that will allow themselves to be swept off their feet by the tide of greed and hedonism that leads to all kinds of corrupt practices.

For Dr. Kolade, the benefits of walking in obedience to God are manifest even in this life. One area in which this is demonstrated is the uncanny wisdom that God gives to those servants of his who desire to please him and be the best that they could ever be for him in this world. As an illustration of this, he cites an incident that occurred in his early days in Cadbury in the awful years of import licenses during the Babangida military era of the late 1980s. An official who was in charge of issuing import licenses demanded bribe before one could be issued to Cadbury for the components they needed for their factories. As a deputy managing director, it was his lot to deal with the matter. As he prayed about the issue, he felt led to tell the officer that his request will have to be presented to the board of directors for approval before the money will be released to be given to him (which would be the normal process for the kind of money that the officer was demanding). And when the approval is made, he continued, a member of the board of directors will bring the money in an envelope to this bribe-demanding officer. Of course, this officer was well aware of the calibre of people on Cadbury's board. The mere fact that this demand would become public knowledge and some of the people who may know of it may have influence on the fate of the officer in his own career, made him recoil from the demand and issue the import license for which Cadbury had applied.

Maintaining consistent principled living is the key to overcoming battles that may come one's way. Dr. Kolade recalls another incident in his days in Cadbury. In those days, government was a lot more protective of local entrepreneurs. For instance, a company could import packaging for its product, but there had to be some local content value added, namely, the printing on the packing had to be done in Nigeria. So there was a time Cadbury had imported some packages for some of its products from the UK for its products, and they had made it clear to the supplier that the printing had to be done in Nigeria. However, the supplier thought to pull a fast one on them, and went ahead and did the printing in the UK. When the packages arrived in Nigeria (of course, with the name of Cadbury Nigeria on it), they were found to have been culpable for breaking the law. Cadbury's managing director was arrested and detained. As the DMD, it was Dr. Kolade's lot to go and bail out his boss. In the process, he decided to seek audience with the then Attorney General of the Federation (AGF). The AGF directed the appropriate officers to investigate the matter properly before rushing to conclusions. Dr. Kolade recalls the AGF in his own words saying, *"I know this Cadbury people. They would not do something like that."* This incidence was to leave an indelible imprint on Dr. Kolade's mind, to know that he did not have to give bribe for his boss's bail, but that their reputation of integrity in Cadbury had gone ahead of them to make way for them.

One thing that Dr. Kolade brings out of all these is that the Christian should not have two lives or two ethics but one. He should have one ethic for both his private and public lives. Those principles that undergird how he operates in the church or at home, should also guide him in the public square. While he is not oblivious to human frailty and fallibility, Dr. Kolade points out that the key thing is the orientation and goal that drives one's life: it should not be self and vainglory seeking but the search for the common good and ultimately the pursuit of God's glory in all that one does. People who work with this goal will find God's guiding hand to be a constant in their life's equations, as God has promised never to leave nor forsake his people (Josh 1:5) but to provide guidance for them (Ps 32:8; Isa 30:21). God has promised wisdom for the simple minded and for those who admit their lack of it (Ps 19:7; James 1:5).

The foregoing has been Dr. Kolade's own personal experience. Right from 1960 when he was the Comptroller of the Western region's Broadcasting Corporation at the young age of twenty-seven, he has been thrust into one leadership role or another. After his ambassadorial posting at the beginning of the millennium, he was invited to be the Pro-Chancellor and council chairman of Pan-African University, Lagos. For nearly three-quarters of his life, Dr. Kolade has been a public figure, yet he can stand with his head high in the context in which many, who have had less than a quarter of the length of his public service, dare not show their faces in public, where integrity is being discussed. It is in view of this long track record of his that the

Goodluck Jonathan administration, at the moment when it was facing credibility deficit with the Nigerian populace over the fuel subsidy removal at the beginning of 2012, came knocking at Dr. Kolade's door, inviting him to be the chairman of the recently created Subsidy Reinvestment and Empowerment Program (SURE). As a true patriot and one who has been prepared for such times as this, and one who would not shirk where duty calls, he accepted once again to offer his services to his fatherland.

Moving from one leadership position to another has meant that Dr. Kolade always has people over whom he superintends; people whose career paths he has had the duty of shaping. To him, this is no light responsibility, but one that comes with the moral burden of consciously modeling before these younger generations the path of honor, integrity, and professional excellence that they ought to take. Indeed, early in his working life, it had become evident to him that the best way to lead and guide others was by the strength of personal exemplary living. For him, leaders have no moral justification to expect their followers to attain to the level (whether morally or professionally) that they have not attained themselves. That is a high calling to which people are unable to attain in their strength, hence the need for him to interminably draw up the inspiration and super abundance of providential grace through a studied devotional life of prayer and daily meditation on the word of God. In this way, his Christian faith has been a deep source of strength in his professional life.

One other way that his faith has had profound impact on his career is the high premium it places on human life and human dignity. While human effort can produce capital and other factors of production for the creation of wealth, the most potent factor of production, labour, is the creation of God. The investiture of humanity with the divine imprimatur (the *imago Dei*, God's image, Gen 1:26-27) inalienably endows humanity with inherent worth and dignity. For this reason, it has been Dr. Kolade's practice never to despise or to treat anyone with contempt (especially those who work with him), nor to underestimate the inherent potential for good in anyone. His constant aim is to understand the people that work for him and see how best he could motivate them to actualize their latent potential. His belief is that he lacks the capability to predict the height to which God intends to take anyone. Rather, his role is that of providing the enabling environment for people to thrive and optimize their potential. Ultimately, he has learned over the years to trust God with his best effort, in the spirit well captured in the thought of the blessed Apostle Paul who wrote, *"I planted, Apollos watered, but God gave the growth"* (1 Co. 3:6; ESV).

Dr. Kolade testifies of his dependence on divine grace even in the running of an industrial giant like Cadbury Nigeria. Running such a conglomerate is no child's play: every decision one takes has monumental financial implications (positively or negatively), and decision making is the major, if not the primary, task of a chief executive of an organization. This calls for sagacity at every moment. A case in point, as Dr. Kolade recalls, was a time when his corporation was faced with the need for building a new factory for one of their products. A major option, at the point in time, was to take a World Bank loan of $6.5 Million. The approval for the loan came after an eighteen month negotiation process in which both the then chairman/CEO of Cadbury Nigeria and his vice were also involved. Dr. Kolade, as the then MD of Cadbury Nigeria, was invited by the MD of the then Nigerian Industrial Development Bank (NIDB, the local agent of the World Bank) to come and sign the contract for the loan. He recalls that the event took place in the year that the Babangida military government had begun the devaluation of the Naira, and the exchange rate at the time was ₦1.4 to $1.00. While he was in the office of the MD of NIDB, suddenly he thought of the daily downward spiraling of the Naira and the implication this would have on the repayment of the loan that had a three year moratorium. As this devaluation of the Naira was a new phenomenon, this thought had not previously crossed the mind of any of them from Cadbury that were involved in the negotiations, not even the Chairman/CEO who was a financial guru in his own right. So the following conversation ensued between Dr. Kolade and the MD of NIDB:

> "Would you assure me that this money that I am borrowing now, when I start paying back after three years, the rate of the Naira to the Dollar at which I'm borrowing is the rate I will be repaying the loan?" Dr. Kolade queried.
>
> "No way," retorted the NIDB MD, "when the time comes for you to start paying, the Naira-Dollar rate that is current at the material time will be the rate at which you will be repaying the loan."
>
> "Hey, are you telling me that this loan I'm taking at the rate of ₦1.4 to $1.00, you might ask me to pay back at the rate of ₦2 to $1?" asked Dr. Kolade.
>
> "Yes," replied the NIDB MD.
>
> "Or ₦5 to $1?" demanded Dr. Kolade.
>
> "Yes," came the unwavering reply for the NIDB MD.
>
> Dr. Kolade, in the fashion reminiscent of the dialogue between God and Abraham in Genesis 18, thought to himself, *"Let me quote the most outrageous figure,"* then he inquired further, "What if the exchange rate climbs up to ₦20 to $1?"—an amount that

was unimaginable in the mid to 1980s.

The NIDB MD affirmatively replied, "Absolutely. If that is the going rate on that day, that will be the rate at which you'll be repaying the loan."

At this point, Dr. Kolade was left in not doubt that taking this loan would bog down his company in a quagmire of a long debt repayment that would prove unprofitable. He consequently declined the loan offer on the ground that taking it was tantamount to mortgaging the future of his company. He returned empty handed and reported the decision he took at the behest of his gumptions, a decision that was deeply appreciated by the company leadership. By their projections, in view of the tumbling value of the Naira in the years that followed, it would have taken them not less than eight years to repay the loan with many more millions of dollars than they had borrowed in the first instance. They had to wait patiently for another nine months to source the funds they needed through the foreign exchange market, but it was a wiser choice.

Looking back at the decision, Dr. Kolade attributes it to the hand of Providence over his life. It never ceases to amaze him that all through the eighteen months of the negotiation, none of them had thought about that. All the same he is ever thankful that the thought came to him at the nick of time. He believes that God is pleased to help his children succeed, when he sees that they are relying on him, and on him alone, not any other thing or power, for their success. Dr. Kolade recalls the words of the psalmist, *"I lift up my eyes to the hills. From where does my help come? My help comes from the LORD, who made heaven and earth"* (Ps. 121:1–2; ESV), and confidently adds, *"If you know that your help comes from the Lord, and you don't go looking for help elsewhere, he will always deliver you."*

In spite of such a successful life, Dr. Kolade makes

no claims to being superhuman. He unabashedly admits that he has his own fair share of human fallibility and frailty. Like every other person, he has his own regrets as well. In decision making, for instance, with hindsight, he can clearly ascribe some decisions he made to poor judgment. Such errors of judgment, he says, are reflections of the limitations that his understanding at the moment had imposed on him. Given similar situations today, given the knowledge, experience, and wisdom gained over the years, he would definitely act or decide differently.

On the whole, Dr. Kolade looks over his long working life with a deep sense of gratitude to God for his generous endowments on his life. As he counts his blessings, he points to the fact that he has been called to do things for which, from the human standpoint, he has had no formal training. These include his many years as a church organist and choirmaster without musical training, his time at NBC with no prior training in journalism, his labours in the corporate world without any formal training in business or economics, and his diplomatic assignment without any diplomatic antecedents. Yet, in all these places he has always received genuine commendations for good services rendered, for which he is thankful to God for his gifts of grace. He reviews his life story in the light of God's workings with David. When David was called to kingship, he was a mere shepherd boy, and there is such a vast chasm between watching over sheep in the back woods of the Judean hill country and ruling in the Jerusalem palace. Yet, that was God's choice and he endowed David such that he became Israel's greatest king. Dr. Kolade believes that God is still in the business of elevating his servants to heights they themselves never dream of attaining, if their hearts are right with him, as his word says, *"For the eyes of the LORD run to and fro throughout the whole earth, to give strong support to those whose heart is blameless toward him"* (2 Chronicles. 16:9; ESV). He also sees this truth in

Paul's statement that he could do all things through Christ his strength (Philippians 4:13). The indwelling Christ accomplishes his purposes in those who surrender to him so that they can reflect his grace and glory in the society. This is Dr. Kolade's life philosophy.

COUNSEL OF THE AGED TO THE YOUNG

In counseling others with regards to outlook on life, Dr. Kolade waxes philosophical as he points outs that no one has the power to decide as to whether he should be born at all, or who his parents should be as well as in which country he should be born. Similarly, normally, no one decides when, and how, and in what manner her life would end. All these decisions are made by God. Thus, if we have no control over the beginning and ending segments of our lives, how could we ever arrogantly think of wresting authority over the mid-section of our lives from the sovereign control of a truly loving and caring God? Instead, he believes, we would be better for it, if we learn to hand over the reins of our lives willingly to the Lord of life, in whose hands our destinies are most secure.

One point that Dr. Kolade would not want people, especially the young, to lose sight of is that there is purpose to life—we are not here by accident. God who brought us into this world has a definite purpose and task for each of us. It behooves us, then, to seek his face to understand his purpose for us and to commit our lives unreservedly to it, and to solicit God's help in remaining true and faithful to the vision until we fulfill our calling. He has no doubt in his mind that such prayers will never go unanswered. But to fulfill one's destiny, one must realize that God's purpose cannot be served in a life that is full of greed, avarice, deceit, and every kind of vice. Thus, those who desire to live out the true meaning of their lives must turn away from every form of filth and perversity—not walking in the counsel of the wicked, or standing in way of sinners, or sitting in the seat of scoffers, but delighting and meditating on the word of the Lord daily (Ps 1:1–3). This is the path to a blessed, fruitful, and fulfilled life. It is not a call to sinless perfection, but it is a summon to work at becoming more like Christ in every facet of our lives (our career lives inclusive) on a daily basis, Dr. Kolade insists. The Christian, he cautions, must be weary of temptation toward primitive accumulation of wealth, since at the end of life one will take nothing out of this life (cf. Eccl 5:15–16; 1 Tim 6:7). It is the pursuit of vainglory through unbridled acquisition of possessions by all means that drives people to indulge in sharp and shameful practices for the sake of filthy gain. Dr. Kolade would like the readers to reflect and think of some of the wealthiest people they know. At the point of death, how much of their wealth did they take with them? Even if their family members go ahead to buy a million pound casket and do a lot of things to give the person the so-called befitting burial, will that person even know or will that change his or her eternal destiny? The parable of the rich fool (Luke 12:16–20), Dr. Kolade reminds us, paints a vivid picture of the vanity of a hedonistic life, lived in oblivion to matters of eternal consequences.

To sum it all, Dr. Kolade holds that those who venture into business need to remember that God says that it is he who gives them the power to make wealth (Deut 8:18). What he has seen in his life experience is that wealth does not drop from heaven like manna. What God has promised is *the power to make wealth*. The divine purpose for the bestowal of this power to generate wealth is to bring God glory. So people need to be wary of short cut formulae to wealth. The labours of those who use that power properly and toil patiently, waiting upon the blessing of God, will never be in vain. When their honest reward for earnest labors comes they will truly appreciate and be thankful for the harvest of divine blessings that visits their effort; and how they use their wealth will also lead others to praise and glorify God on their account.

He also cautions those who attain to positions of authority, whose decisions have far reaching implications for the lives of others: He warns them not to treat their positions with flippancy, knowing that a time of reckoning will surely come, either in this life, or in the life to come. Thus, he sets forth a key petition in the Lord's Prayer as a cardinal directing principle for life, *"Your will be done on earth, as it is in heaven."* When this becomes people's vital guiding principle in life, they would not deliberately go out of their way to do things they know are contrary to the will of God. Those who hold to this principle will discharge their stewardship of public trust faithfully, rather than defrauding the public for personal enrichment or other self-serving purposes. True success and the true meaning of life, for him, is living out God's purpose for one's life and doing that on God's terms. Even when people appear to be successful because of their ostentatious lives, but have failed to comply with God's standards, it is all hollow, and there is no abiding value to it. It is vain, therefore, to toil and labour for that which has no abiding value, he says.

CHAPTER TEN

THE PRUDENT MANAGER

JONATHAN ONIGBINDE

THE BEGINNINGS

Jonathan Olusola Onigbinde's father, Moses Onigbinde, and his mother, Dorcas Oyebisi Onigbinde, were very committed Christians; and their lifestyles as an outflow of their faith commitment would impact Jonathan for the rest of his life. Unfortunately for the young Jonathan, his mother died when he was only eleven years old; he was born in Bukuru, Plateau State, in 1948. Though she died when he was quite young, Jonathan's mother's impact on his life within that short span of time was monumental. For example, it was customary for her to pick him up after the church service, put him on her lap, and review the day's sermon. Her constant aim was to break the sermon down to the level of a child's understanding, since there were no children's Sunday school services back then. By this means, Mrs. Onigbinde imprinted her faith indelibly on her son's young mind (cf. Deut 6:5–9).

Life was not easy for Moses and Dorcas Onigbinde in their earlier days. Dorcas came from a Muslim family, and her parents had a hard time accepting her conversion to Christianity. When she wanted to marry Moses, it took God some time to persuade her parents to allow her to do so. When Moses moved to Jos in 1928, he was a mere lad accompanying his uncle, who was a businessman, a trader to the core. Believing he did not come to the Plateau to see the beautiful rock formations, he made business unequalled in his priorities, while religion ranked very low on his scale of things. Moses, on the other hand, had come to faith very early in his life and showed unparalleled interest in following the Lord. He walked every Sunday from Jos to Bukuru to attend church services, while his uncle opened his store for business even on Sundays. Moses' uncle could not stomach his stupidity for long, and on one particular Sunday, as Moses got ready to go to church, his uncle accosted him and told him, "You have to choose between church and helping me out with my business as an apprentice, in order to build your future." That was not a hard choice for the young Moses—to church he must go. He let his uncle know this in no uncertain terms, and his uncle equally wasted no time in throwing Moses out in the street.

It was not as easy as it may now sound for a mere youth from faraway Ogbomosho—in those days people rarely traveled more than ten kilometres from their birthplaces—with no other relatives around to be suddenly homeless. Moses left for church that morning knowing neither from where his next meal was going to come, nor where he was going to spend the next night. Nonetheless, he was satisfied with being able to lay claim to his fundamental human right to the free exercise of his conscience and the right to associate freely, for he knew that meeting for fellowship with other Christians was vital for his spiritual growth. With nothing to begin with other than a strong faith and a strong determination to succeed, Moses set out to chart a path for himself in business. Faith and hard work combined with divine blessing saw Moses rise to become a successful businessman in Jos.

The life and faith of his father would inspire Jonathan to tread the same path later on in life. To

Jonathan, his father is the noblest man he had ever known: a man of vision, courage, character, and spiritual strength. By the time Pa Onigbinde died in 2010, at the ripe age of 106, many people came from far and wide to testify to his impact on their lives. Jonathan remains ever grateful to his parents for their legacy in his life.

While wealth and property may be inherited from parents, saving faith is never inherited. Individuals have to make their own faith commitment and have their own personal journeys of faith with God. Jonathan is no exception. Though having very godly parents, he recalls his growing-up years during which he would wake up at night pondering over questions of his eternal destiny because he did not want go to hell. He remembers that during those days, a certain Christian morning crier used to walk through his neighborhood every early morning, at about 5 o'clock, ringing a bell as he proclaimed in Yoruba, Hausa, and English, "Repent! Jesus is coming back soon. Repent and believe in him or you will go to hell!" This certainly used to scare the hell out of the young Jonathan. This is the atmosphere in which he was growing up. Yet that personal commitment to Christ was not to come until he went to secondary school at Titcombe College, an SIM school in Egbe, in present day Kogi State. Jonathan was led to Christ during an Easter weekend programme by one Tony Wilmot, of blessed memory. Tony was a Lagos-based businessman, who frequented Titcombe College to minister to the young students. An enduring friendship would ensue between Tony and Jonathan, a relationship that in its own right had consequential influence on Jonathan's life.

No one comes to faith without any challenges. For Jonathan, his challenge was a debilitating struggle with doubt. Any time he fell into sin, Satan would come to him with words like, "Well, you see what you've done? You claim you're a Christian; you can't truly be one. You've just told a lie. God's children don't lie, so you can't possibly be one, and you can't be sure you're going to heaven." This torment persisted until 1964, when he attended a weeklong leadership course organized by the Fellowship of Christian Students (FCS) at Baptist High School, Jos. As Jonathan listened to the fiery sermons of the guest speaker, Rev. Piepgrass, who was then with Baraka Press in Kaduna, he thought to himself, "This is my opportunity to sort out my doubts with this preacher." He, therefore, sought an audience with Rev. Piepgrass . Once Jonathan had Rev.Piepgrass attention, he opened up and began: "Rev. Piepgrass, I've got to tell you this: I have these doubts in my mind—am I really a Christian? I can't say anymore." He then went on to recount to Rev. Piepgrass all of his struggles. After a brief but penetrating interview with Jonathan, Rev. Piepgrass finally told him, "Your faith experience is real!" The reverend gentlemen then pointed him to the Scriptures as the source of the assurance of his salvation. A key passage among others that he employed was John 6:37, which reads, "All that the Father gives me will come to me, and whoever comes to me I will never cast out" (ESV). In view of the scriptural truth, Rev. Piepgrass told the young Jonathan, "Jesus will never cast you out; he will never leave you; he will never let you go. Since you believe in him, you are his, and he will never let you go." The Spirit of God used the profundity of this simple truth to settle Jonathan's disquieted mind. It was an occasion that would remain ineradicable in his memory; he would know that his salvation was assured not because of what he did or failed to do but by the finished work of Christ on Calvary. 2 Corinthians 1:4 says that God comforts us in our trials so that we may be able to comfort others in diverse trials. Jonathan has used this truth over the years to encourage other young believers troubled by doubts.

EDUCATION AND CAREER

Jonathan has had the unique privilege of attending

Christian schools all through his life. As noted above, he attended Titcombe College, Egbe, for his secondary education. After graduation, he went to Boys Secondary School, Gindiri, for his Higher School Certificate (HSC), as it was the norm them. Subsequently, he went to Wheaton College, in the United States, where he studied economics. He then studied for his Master of Business Administration (MBA) at Tulane University in New Orleans (then a conservative evangelical university). Studying in Christian environments furnished a solid foundation upon which to build his life to withstand the storms of life, which were sure to come.

In his younger years, Jonathan did not pay much heed to consciously engaging in service for the Lord. He was rather preoccupied with the pursuit of career and money. After graduating from Tulane in 1975, he was recruited to work for the accounting giant Arthur Young & Co. (which later merged with another accounting firm to become Ernst & Young). After one year of working with the company in Dallas, he was transferred to the London office. Jonathan worked in London for another year, but the lure of home was too strong, so at the end of the year, he resigned his promising career in the multinational accounting firm and returned home in 1976 to work in the family business.

The hand of providence had been at work to bring Jonathan into the business world, giving him both a father who was a businessman himself, and also a spiritual father, Mr. Wilmot, who was likewise in business. Yet his venture into the business world was not a straight path. In secondary and high schools, he had studied the sciences with an eye to studying medicine. In those days, there was roughly one year's lull between higher school (HSC) and university, and people generally found jobs to do during that time. Pa Onigbinde and his family were now living in Bukuru. He was banking with the Standard Bank of British West Africa (today known as First Bank). Pa Onigbinde had good rapport with the branch manager (a white man, as all managers at the time were), and while Jonathan was waiting for university admission after his HSC, the bank manager requested that his father send one of his sons to work for the bank. Since Jonathan had just returned from school, he was the one sent to work for the bank. He recalls that after working at the bank for barely a month he found himself soliloquizing, "I like business, I like economics, and I like banking; I'm not going back to science or medicine." That singular kind gesture from the bank manger completely changed the direction of his life: it ignited his interest in business, ultimately leading him to a lifelong commitment to business.

THE ARROWS OF GOD

The arrows of God are healing balms, one may say. He takes the bitter and ugly things that life hurls at us and makes the most beautiful things out of them. This is Jonathan's story.

Though he grew up in a Christian home, came to faith early in life, and attended only Christian schools, he never thought much about truly making all of life a commitment to God. His primary commitment was to business and money until he hit a brick wall. The mismanagement of our national economy by the National Party of Nigeria (NPN), coupled with the concocted landslide victories at the polls, ended the second republic in a fiasco. The military then rode to power at the end of 1983 on the crest of its popularity as the newly found messiahs. Yet, by 1986 the regime's corruption stymied and eventually killed many industries in the country. The national reserves had been completed depleted, and Nigeria begun to slide into abysmal debt to the foreign creditors collectively called the Paris Club. Foreign currency was scarce and had to be rationed. So those who needed to import raw materials and/or machinery for their businesses had to go cup in hand begging the military junta for import licenses, which were issued only to the well-connected and those with money to dole out to the corrupt officials who issued the licenses. A thriving industry arose out of this for touts and middlemen, who could navigate the corrupt terrain and ferret out import licenses. Many of these middlemen were mere crooks and common criminals, who were ripping people off of their hard-earned money. To these charlatans Jonathan fell prey.

By 1986, Jonathan had been back to Nigeria for ten years. He was saddled with managing the family business, which had grown and was involved in food processing (ice cream, fruit juice, and the like) and also producing the plastic containers for these products. Suddenly, it was becoming impossible to import the materials they needed to stay in business. Then one day someone introduced him to a fellow in Lagos, who supposedly would help him obtain the Foreign Exchange he needed. The fellow was even touted as a pastor. So, after due negotiations, Jonathan took a bank loan of N2 million and gave it to this fellow for the pursuit of the Forex. Once the fellow had collected the N2 million, he vanished into thin air. After a while Jonathan became frantic. Things had turned sour: the family business was on a downward spiral and the bank was after him. He had to report the matter to the police. Life came to a standstill. He recalls,

> The experiences I had in those days were terrible. I couldn't do my work. I couldn't stay in my office here in Jos. I had to be going to Lagos. I had to be going to the police every now and then, until the police picked the guy up, and then the court case started.

The arrest of the conman of a pastor did not end Mr. Onigbinde's woes. The court case that ensued was itself a seven-year journey into futility. Even more distressing, the documents the police recovered from the bank account of this supposed man of God showed that he spent the money on hedonistic living with prostitutes. The apparent lack of justice from the hallowed (or should it be hollow?) halls of our justice system drove him to his wits' end. The interest on the bank loan was piling up. Something had to be done. With nowhere else to turn, he had to sell stock piles of raw material, and dispose of factory machinery and other assets to pay off the loan. In his Slough of Despond, he said to his wife one night, *"Charity, do you think I'll ever be happy again in my life?"*

As Don Meon says, *"God can make a way, where there seems to be no way."* The way that God began to make for Mr. Onigbinde was to shift his attention from wealth to God himself. The first vessel God would use in this work of moulding his servant, Mr. Onigbinde, was his wife. In response to his desperate question, Charity pointed him to Psalm 40. Mr. Onigbinde began to trust God to take him out of the miry pit in which he found himself and to place him upon the rock. With time, he would come to know that that rock is Jesus Christ the Messiah. He was now looking onto the Lord to put a new song in his mouth. He came to see how all of his offerings meant nothing to God as compared to his own love, obedience, and loyalty to his heavenly Father, and he was drawing ever so slowly closer to the Lord.

Even though Jonathan has several siblings, two from his late mother (one of them older than him) and six from his stepmother, no incident of sibling rivalry ensued, even at this moment of adversity. The godly example of their father helped them all weather the storm together. The loving support and encouragement of his family provided the succour he needed. His father set the stage with these words of encouragement:

"You're worrying too much, Jonathan. Don't worry about this thing; just know that it's a

lesson that you have to learn and that you have just started business anew. So, learn the lesson and move on. God will see you through it all."

He also encouraged him with these words of Scripture: "Mercy triumphs over judgment" (James 2:13 ESV). That was the attitude of the whole family. Mercy was shown to him rather than critical judgment. Every member of the family worked hard to find the resources with which to pay off the bank loan. Jonathan says this proudly of his family,

> *"I don't think anybody has a family like mine because there is love; there is kindred spirit; there is cooperation and team spirit. That is how we act in all our businesses."*

God did not judge him either, but extended mercy to him. Through the mercy of God, as they worked assiduously, they were able to pull the family business out of the doldrums, and it has continued to grow and diversify, with investments in such diverse enterprises as distributive trade (through the Onigbinde supermarkets), food processing, and farming.

FAMILY AND MINISTRY

Mr. Jonathan Onigbinde was married to Charity in 1978, and God has blessed their family with four children, two boys and two girls, all of whom are adults now. They are all career men and women in their right, both within and outside the country. Their first daughter is married, and through her Jonathan and Charity are grandparents. While they were raising their children, Jonathan and Charity laboured to pass on the legacy of the faith of their parents to their children. Some of the means they used to introduce their children to their faith included a daily family altar (morning devotion), evening family prayer time, and a weekly (every **Thursday**) family Bible study. They also regularly took their children with them to church for Sunday and mid-week services. It is a blessing to them that their children have gladly received their instruction and continued to walk with the Lord. In this, the observation of the wise teacher becomes poignant, *"Train up a child in the way he should go; even when he is old he will not depart from it"* (Proverbs 22:6 ESV).

Jonathan has continued in the stead of his father and has remained in the United Gospel Faith Tabernacle Church. Of this church, he says:

> "This is the church my father attended. It is a small church, but that is the church that my father helped in building—that is the church that helped in building my father. So, it is a church to which my whole family goes."

He and his family are actively involved in and support the ministries of the church. For instance, besides serving as an elder, he also doubles as the acting pastor of one of the recent church plants of their local congregation. It is his lot to nurture this church until it reaches the point where it can sustain a pastor.

Mr. Onigbinde has somehow found the way of balancing between business and ministry. His commitment to kingdom services goes beyond the bounds of his local church. He supports and serves on the boards of such diverse local and international ministries as Children Evangelism Ministry, Joint Project for Christian Learning Materials, Campus Crusade for Christ, Word of Life, Harvest Leaders Network (which supports pastors and churches in preventing the burn out syndrome), International Leadership Foundation, and Petra College of South Africa (a premier South African institution that offers training on evangelizing children).

LIFE LESSONS AND THE TRUE SOURCE OF SUCCESS

In business, as in all of life, one cannot always

speak of great success. Along the path of great successes are strewn many failures. No one is immune to this. Mr. Onigbinde says that any honest businessman would acknowledge the failures he has experienced, and he is quick to add that he is no exception: he has had his fair share of failures. He could list a number of ventures he started but had to shut down, not the least being branches of the Onigbinde Supermarket. Indeed, he says that he has closed more branches than those that are operational. Yet, he points out that those who have faith, vision, and determination will smile at the end of the day:

> "The truth is, it's not the number of failures one has experienced, because you may have failures, but if you trust in God, he will guide you and you will eventually succeed, if you don't give up."

In addition to an abiding faith in God, Mr. Onigbinde points to integrity and credibility as the hallmarks of those who strive to earn honest gain from honest and earnest labour. He says that his late father taught him and all his siblings to always strive to earn credibility and trust with their customers and creditors. He insisted that they must always honour their word to customers; they were never to issue a cheque that would bounce, and before they borrowed money, they must first of all have clear alternative plans on how to redeem the debt. These and many other sound principles were inculcated into them early in life.

Sound principles must be balanced with a clear vision and a lucid mission. A vision gives one the sense of destination, while the mission provides the path to that destination. In explaining these principles, Jonathan says that for you to succeed,

> "you've got to have a vision and a mission. Even if you don't have it written down, you need to have one. ... A vision is a picture of where you want to go and it must be very clear in your

mind. For a Christian it must have divine authentication."

A vision and a mission are different in that *"a vision is the place where you want to go; a mission is a lot like the vehicle that takes you."* By this, he lays out fundamental philosophical principles in management that are necessary for fashioning out attainable objectives, the three basic questions one must constantly keep in mind are:

- ❖ Where do I want to be in x-time?
- ❖ How am I going to get there?
- ❖ Who can help me get there?

These are questions to which those who want to succeed must find feasible answers.

An instance of the outworking of the foregoing is seen in the late Pa Onigbinde's life. One may say that his clear vision was to live a life that is honouring to God so that at the end of life on earth he would never be ashamed when he would stand before his Maker. His mission was to take business as a "calling" and to conduct his business as a servant to his customers and employees alike, not exploiting anyone. This way of carrying on informed how and where they invested. For example, Pa Onigbinde considered Nigerian banks to be too exploitative and usurious in their practices. Thus, for him, though the returns on investment in the banking sector were huge, he did not choose to invest his money there. Thus, he shunned many of proprietors of the new-generation banks that were birthed in the 1980s, who had courted his partnership. Furthermore, the Onigbinde family chain of businesses avoids investing in brewery and tobacco industries and others like them that have untoward moral and health implications on families.

Mr. Onigbinde holds that the management style that one adopts will determine how far one will go in his endeavour. He learned early that in view of the scope of things he had to oversee vis-à-vis his frequent travels, he could not attempt to micro-manage things himself in a hands-on fashion. He learned to identify promising young folks within the corporation and train and empower them to attain their full potential. Then he gives them the chance to prove their worth. Many people are likely to take those challenges seriously and do their best. It is to his credit that many people he has trained in this way have moved on to become either accomplished professionals in other corporations and banks or successful businessmen in their own right.

Delegating responsibility is good, but if not executed well can become a nightmare. Mr. Onigbinde says that his first step towards identifying people in his business that he would work with closely is spending a lot of time in prayer and seeking God's face about the issue. From there, he looks through his staff to discern those who seem to be concerned with integrity. He holds that one who has integrity is 50% on the way to being successful. Next to integrity is "industry." It is not enough to be honest; one must also be hard working and competent. This is especially so in our context, where people want money but do not want to do the work that produces the money. Thus, for delegation to be successful, responsibility has to be given to those who are both honest, dedicated to duty, and adroit at their tasks.

In addition to all this is the element of divine grace. As Scriptures says, *"So then it depends not on human will or exertion, but on God, who has mercy"* (Romans 9:16 ESV). One has to do one's best, but at the same time one needs to appreciate God's favour in his or her life. Jonathan illustrates this point vividly with regards to his own health. He recalls a time he had gone to a doctor for routine checkup. After examining him, the doctor turned to him and asked, *"What kind of sports do you do?"*

"I don't really have time for sports, I'm sorry to say," was his reply.

"*No, no, no, but you do sports,*" insisted the doctor.

"*No,*" Jonathan maintained. "*I don't do sports,*" he continued calmly.

"*Tell me the truth, because your heart beats like that of a sportsman,*" complimented the doctor with an innocent and cheerful smile.

Jonathan simply asked the doctor, "*Do you know about something called the grace of God?*"

Of course, the doctor, being a Christian himself, knew exactly what the grace of God is. It was this grace that kept Mr. Onigbinde's father alive for 106 years. God, in characteristic loving nature, extends a measure of common grace to all humanity, but the special province of redemptive grace is reserved for those who are in covenant relationship with him. Herein lies the necessity of saving faith for those who desire to dwell in the realms of special grace.

Finally, Jonathan advises that success is closely related to the pursuit of happiness. One must employ oneself in the things that one enjoys doing. It is not enough to do things purely for the sake of money, but it is even much better to do things that one truly delights in. It is equally not enough to pursue a career merely to please one's parents or to impress one's peers. This is where experimenting with different things can prove beneficial in helping people discover their heart's true passions. Mr. Onigbinde recalls how he had thought of pursuing a career in medicine or the sciences just because he was good at them. The experience of working in a bank changed his life. For a Christian, seeking God's will for one's life is also important, because at the end of the day, what matters most is how one can best be Christ's ambassador in his world, and only God can lead one to that place.

CHAPTER ELEVEN

ON THE JUDGMENT SEAT

HON. JUSTICE JAMES OGEBE

THE STARTING POINT

James Ogenyi Ogebe was raised by his grandmother because his own mother died very early, when he was only nine years. A native of Igumale, Ado Local Government Area of Benue State, James was born in the dry season of 1940 to the family of Ogebe Ogbu. His father was an interpreter with the colonial administrative officers and judges. His father, a polygamist, had many children. Though pagan from his roots, through interaction with the administrative machinery of the northern region, Mr. Ogebe Ogbu was converted to Islam. However, he reverted to paganism towards the end of his life.

One would have thought that coming from this kind of background would be a negative influence on James, but this was not to be because his grandmother sent him to a Christian school—the Methodist primary school in their village. Through this school, which was the first primary school in Idomaland, he was introduced to Christianity. However, it was when James went to Government College, Keffi, that he accepted Jesus into his life as his personal Saviour and Lord. While in Keffi, James had joined The Challenge Reading Unit, and in one of the meetings, their leader explained the gospel to them, pointing out that all human beings had sinned against God and as such were liable to eternal damnation in hell. Yet, God in his infinite mercy had sent his Son, Jesus Christ, to bear their sins vicariously and the consequences thereof, thereby making available God's gift of eternal life to all who in faith accept the death of Jesus Christ on their behalf. To this clear gospel message, James responded that night of February 13, 1957. As he got back to his dormitory, James knelt down beside his bed and prayed asking God for forgiveness, inviting Jesus into his life, and surrendering his life to the Lord. That was the beginning of his Christian walk.

CAREER PATH

James's first experience of ever working was in teaching. While he was in Form Three in Government College, Keffi, a tropical storm blew off the roofs of their school buildings. Thus, the school was closed down for repairs to be done. They were home for a fairly long period of time. It was during that time that he took up a temporary teaching assignment and helped establish a Methodist primary school in Ikpemnbe, a village near his hometown.

His second stint with teaching took place during the interregnum between when he completed his HSC and when he went to the university, which was about nine months in all. During that time, he was offered a teaching job at the Boys' Secondary School, Gindiri. It was a great experience that he still treasures. It provided him with the opportunity to interact with missionaries and other Christian people, who became very close friends, some of these friendships have lasted throughout his lifetime to this very day. It was an opportunity for him to impact younger people, a number of whom have made tremendous strides in their chosen professions; a good example of these being Professor Nenfot Gomwalk.

As a child, James had no idea what it meant to be a lawyer nor had he met one previously. By nature, however, he was very inquisitive, at the time when children were supposed to be seen but not heard. This was a constant source of irritation and displeasure to the adults around him. Many of such people would often, in exasperation, say something like, *"Leave me alone, are you a lawyer?"* It was through these cynical rebuffs that he first heard the word "lawyer" and the unintended consequence was that this cynicism planted the idea of becoming a lawyer in his young mind, and he resolved, *"That's what I will become when I grow up."*

James's destiny in the legal profession was divinely ordained. In early post-independence Nigeria, knowledge of the Latin language was a prerequisite for admission to the study of law. It was very providential that his class in Keffi was the first to be taught Latin, and he took to it with alacrity. He took Latin up to HSC level and was very good at it. James was an all-round student; he did well in both the science and art subjects in his WASC. This meant that he could have fitted into any other area. However, with the desire to study law, he had to choose the arts when he entered the HSC class. He eventually studied law at Ahmadu Bello University (ABU), Zaria, and after attending the Nigerian Law School, he was called to the Nigerian Bar on the June 28, 1968. Thereafter, he entered the service of the then Benue Plateau State government as a pupil State Counsel rising gradually until he went on to the bench as a Senior Magistrate and later Chief Registrar. After the creation of Benue State, he was appointed a high court judge of the state judiciary in July 1976, a position he held until he was moved to the Court of Appeal 1991, and subsequently advanced to the Apex Court in the land, the Supreme Court of Nigeria in 2008, from where he honourably retired after many years of fruitful and meritorious service to his fatherland in 2010.

At the time he joined the judiciary as a magistrate, there was a dire need of judges in the newly created Benue state. Because of the dearth of qualified people, who could have been appointed straight away as judges, pioneers like him, who had just spent eight years at the bar, were appointed judges to fill the gap, even though the constitutionally required length of experience is ten years. Thus, they were appointed as acting judges for a period of two years, and thereafter were confirmed as substantive judges.

The tone of Hon. Justice Ogebe's long career was set the day before he was to be sworn in as a judge of the Benue State High Court in 1976: It was a word from God, which reads,

> And I charged your judges at that time, "Hear the cases between your brothers, and judge righteously between a man and his brother or the alien who is with him. **You shall not be partial in judgment**. You shall hear the small and the great alike. **You shall not be intimidated by anyone**, for the judgment is God's. And the case that is too hard for you, you shall bring to me, and I will hear it" (Deuteronomy 1:16–17 ESV).

He considered this passage the oath of God, which he took before the oath of the nation that was administered the next day by the state governor. This has been the guiding light of his career. He understood that in his career on the bench, he was essentially representing God, the great and righteous judge, here on earth.

The enormity of the task of a judge gripped the heart of Hon. Justice Ogebe very early in his career on the bench. He realized what powers the judge has: his job gives him the power of life and death over fellow citizens. A judge can do so many things to fellow citizens: he can sentence a person to death, confiscate his properties, give him hope, or bring ruin and disaster to him. Such enormous powers, he came to grasp, were not to be exercised with flippancy. Consequently, while he served on the bench, he always sought to do that which he believed was in accord with the divine order for the dispensation of justice. He always made it a point of duty to seek God's face in all cases, and especially so when critical cases were before. On occasions, he would even solicit prayer support from trusted brethren (of course, without divulging the details of the cases to them).

As an example of how divine guidance helped him in the correct interpretation and application of the law and, hence, in the administration of justice, Hon. Justice Ogebe mentioned a case that came before him as an appeal in his early days in the Benue State Judiciary. He took the appeal with a senior colleague of his. It was a land dispute case that arose from a lower court in the Gboko division of the state judiciary. In this case, the appellant was represented by a counsel, while the respondent, a poor man, had no legal representation. As they heard the case, he and his colleague were sharply disagreed as to the verdict. While he was deciding in favour of the respondent—the poor man, his senior colleague, was inclined to uphold the appeal—in favour of the richer appellant. After a long period of arguing back and forth, his colleague finally yielded to the superior arguments of Justice Ogebe as he said, "It's alright. I will agree with you; you go ahead and write the judgment." In favour of the poor man, who evidently was in the right, the appeal was disallowed.

Unbeknownst to the justice, this was almost like the biblical case of the powerful Ahab going full throttle to grab the land of the poor Naboth. Just like the Naboth in the Bible, this poor man was not about to diffidently lose his ancestral patrimony to any person because of the person's wealth or social status. It was only after the case had been decided upon that Justice Ogebe learned from the court registrar that the poor man had vowed that if the case was decided in favour of the rich man he would hang himself. The Lord had guided his servant to do what was right without compromise or deference to wealth or social status, not even the status of seniority, which is so much venerated in the legal profession.

Following the path of integrity and justice is never an easy road. Indeed, as Scripture says that all who desire to live a godly life will be persecuted (2 Timothy 3:12), so was the experience of Justice Ogebe. He recalls that during the Buhari/Idiagbon administration's purge of the public sector, many judges in the country were sent out of service in 1985, at which point he became the most senior judicial officer, and indeed, he had twice previously acted as the Chief Judge of Benue State in the absence of the Chief Judge. Naturally, the leadership of the state judiciary should have devolved on him and he should have been appointed the Chief Judge of the state, since no one had questioned either his competence or his integrity, at least, not to his knowledge. But that was not to be. Instead, two of his juniors were promoted over him: one was made the Chief Judge of Benue State and the other elevated to the Court of Appeal. Afterwards, he learned that someone had written an eighty-page petition against him, the crux of which was that he was a religious fanatic who was not really doing his job. Sadly enough, no one showed him the petition, neither was he given any fair hearing—a fundamental doctrine in jurisprudence usually stated in Latin as *audi alteram partem*, i.e., "hear the other party." So, he was denied his rightly deserved elevation on account of these snide accusations, without being afforded the opportunity to defend himself. It was a difficult trying period for him.

As is the case with someone facing tough times, people came to Justice Ogebe with all sorts of counsels, ranging from asking him to petition the federal government about the matter to advising that he should seek transfer from the state to the federal judiciary. However, Justice Ogebe decided to seek the Lord's face about the matter. He took some days off and went on a personal retreat. The Lord's message to him was from Psalm 37:5–13, which states,

> *Commit your way to the LORD; trust in him, and he will act. He will bring forth your righteousness as the light, and your justice as the noonday. Be still before the LORD and wait patiently for him; fret not yourself over the one who prospers in his way, over the man who carries out evil devices! Refrain from anger, and forsake wrath! Fret not yourself; it tends only to evil. For the evildoers shall be cut off, but those who wait for the LORD shall inherit the land. In just a little while, the wicked will be no more; though you look carefully at his place, he will not be there. But the meek shall inherit the land and delight themselves in abundant peace. The wicked plots against the righteous and gnashes his teeth at him, but the Lord laughs at the wicked, for he sees that his day is coming. (ESV)*

He felt the Lord telling him to be still and rest in Him and he will see the end of the wicked. All this took place in May 1985 and by August of the same year, the government that had perpetuated this injustice against him was swept away in a coup. This more than anything else, taught him to allow God to fight his battles for him.

When he moved to the Court of Appeal, the tempo of work changed completely. While he enjoyed his work, it was nonetheless daunting. More often than not he was moved to trouble spots. Justice Ogebe recalls,

> *When I got to the court of appeal, I enjoyed my work but the main challenge I had there was*

the difficult cases I had to handle. Whenever a division was in trouble, they would send me there to go and put things right; and as soon as I did that, they would send me on another trouble-shooting mission. They were always sending me to difficult stations like Port Harcourt, Lagos, and Enugu. We had especially difficult cases in Enugu.

The Enugu division of the Court of Appeal is a haven of election tribunal cases. It is, thus, a sort of death zone or Bermuda Triangle for judges, especially those with corrupt inclinations, some of whom have been sucked out of the judiciary for accepting bribes from election petition litigants. Because of this, even justices of the Appeal Court who were there were applying to be transferred out of the division. It was in the midst of all these that he was uprooted from Lagos and sent to go and take care of the troublesome Enugu division. The President of the Court of Appeal chose him specially for this assignment, and Justice Ogebe, accepted it as a vote of confidence. His conclusion was, "As a child of God, I knew it was God who was sending me to all those places to be light in the midst of prevalent darkness." And, indeed, he did not fail his Master; he let his light shone brightly for all to see.

Hon. Justice Ogebe remembers that when the then President of the Court of Appeal Hon. Justice Umaru Abdullahi was appointed, he went to congratulate him and assured him of his full support both as a friend and as a classmate; and the Appeal Court President took full advantage of that support. That was why he never hesitated to send Justice Ogebe to those tough situations or cases, knowing that he would not let him down. One of those landmark cases was that of the wrongful removal of Gov. Ladoja as the governor of Oyo State under questionable circumstances. Justice Ogebe, at the time, was in Enugu, but he was sent to Ibadan to preside over the panel which handled the case. At the end of the day, Gov. Ladoja was vindicated and restored to his position. This enraged the then Nigerian President, who thought he could use the Supreme Court to upstage the Appeal Court's ruling, but that never worked. Justice Ogebe feels, it was the bold steps of the judiciary like his that helped (and continue to help) sustain our fragile democracy. Decisions like his helped to restrain the use of federal executive might in wresting the people's mandates from duly elected officials. This was what put a stop to the spate of kangaroo style impeachment processes that were being foisted willy-nilly on state legislatures in the first decade of this millennium.

The climax of Justice Ogebe's career experience, however, was sitting over the 2007 presidential election petition. Indeed, at a point, he came to view this case as being central to his life's calling, and much of the survival of the country or, at least, its democracy depended on it. He also realized the divine purpose, even in his stagnation at the Court of Appeal for sixteen years, for if he had been advanced to the Supreme Court when he was due, he would not have had the chance to preside over this case. He once more sees God using him, through this case, to bring the stability in our polity that was very much needed at the time. His was an active and full career; he never had a dull moment, and he is thankful for the opportunity he has had to serve his fatherland in this capacity.

The abiding source of strength in the discharge of Hon. Justice Ogebe's duties was his firm Christian commitment, of which he has no apologies. He saw his work on the bench as a divine calling in much the same way as others receive the callings to be religious priests or ministers. From this perspective, he always commenced his day at work by praying together with his staff. These prayer sessions were open to all staff but they were not compulsory. They served the dual purpose of calling on divine help for the challenges of the day as well as sending a clear signal as to where he stood. People clearly knew then that he was not up to playing any shady games. His Christian principles guided him both in private and public lives.

One thing Justice Ogebe is quick to tell you is that being a Christian is not synonymous with being sloppy or espousing mediocrity. Giving his own testimony he says,

> *I made sure that I lived a Christian life within the court and also outside of it. With regards to my work, this meant that I was diligent; I was punctual to court. I made sure that whenever I adjourned matters for judgments, the judgments were delivered on the set date so that I would not be sending wrong signals that would allow anyone to make any innuendos that this judge is waiting for money before he would give his judgment. I researched on cases before me thoroughly before reaching conclusions. In other words, I made sure that my work was done properly and as promptly as possible. Then when I became a presiding justice of various divisions, I also sought to influence my colleagues to be diligent in their work.*

When working in concert with others, he knew that he could not impose his views on them. What he learned to do was to have his ground in law and work hard in persuading his colleagues to come to the same perspectives as his on the interpretation of both the law and the facts of the case before them. Very often he was successful in doing this.

Choosing to live by his conscience continued to be Hon. Justice Ogebe's albatross even in the federal judiciary. He served on the Court of Appeal for sixteen years before his well-deserved elevation to the Supreme

Court bench. By the time he got to the Supreme Court, he discovered that some of those who were now his seniors at the Supreme Court had not yet been lawyers when he was already a high court judge. During those sixteen years on the Appeal Court, any time his name came up for promotion to the Supreme Court, he was often left behind on account of his faith. He was thought of as being unbendable because he was a religious fanatic. In spite of all that, Justice Ogebe was not bitter. He waxed philosophical as he reminisces over it all,

> It didn't bother me. I will not compromise my faith because of any position. My belief is that you can make your mark no matter where you are. The important thing is to understand the purpose of one's life and to live it out. This I did for the 34 years of my service in the judiciary.

FAMILY LIFE

Hon. Justice James Ogebe is married to Mary formally known as Mary Madaki, the first female doctor in northern Nigeria. He met her in Gindiri during her years in secondary school. They met when he taught there briefly before going to the university. She was the president of the Fellowship of Christian Student (FCS) in her school, just as he had been the president of the FCS in Government College, Keffi, the previous year. With this common spirituality between them, it was just a matter of time for something unique to develop from this interaction; and develop it did, as on July 5, 1969, they were happily united in holy matrimony in the Methodist Church. The union has been blessed with four children: two boys and two girls. The first girl however has gone to be with the Lord due to a motor accident in 1995. The two boys have followed in their father's footsteps and are in the legal profession while the last girl is a medical doctor like her mother. The girl and her eldest brother are based in the United States, while the second son lives in Lagos.

Having followed Christ early in life, Justice Ogebe's faith has been a guiding principle for every member of his family. This is even more so because his wife Mary is also a Christian. All the children were brought up within the church and received Christ early. They are all practising the faith and are all serious with their commitment to the Lord. Interestingly, even their grandchildren are beginning to follow in the steps of their parents. When the Ogebes go visiting their children, their grandchildren enjoy having devotions with them and they are visibly excited about their Christian faith.

The life of a judge is a peculiar one; one that does not permit socializing, on a general note. Besides, it is also a very busy life that often involves taking on assignments that come up without (or with very short) notice. Thus, the family's support is critical in helping the judge to stay focused on his very sensitive tasks. Justice Ogebe has had the full support of his family throughout his long career. His wife had a brilliant career as a medical doctor and rose to be the Executive Secretary of the Benue State Health Management Board. Notwithstanding, when he was appointed to Court of Appeal and had to move to Benin City, his wife did not hesitate to quit her job in order to accompany him and provide all of the support he needed. In other words, she sacrificed her career so his could be advanced. Her step was in consonance with their firm belief that a husband and wife should always live together in order to fulfill God's established order for the family as well as to avoid the complications to family life that results from living apart. Dr. (Mrs.) Mary Ogebe has had to move around the country with her husband to all the various areas of his posting, and has been very supportive as a wife, friend, prayer partner and cheerleader to him.

The nature of the job of judges is such that they are limited in their associations and the kinds of friendships they can cultivate. Therefore, the closest people to them are members of their families. When he had a difficult case, Justice Ogebe would urge his wife to pray along with him, which she always did gladly. A good example was when he was presiding over the Gov. Ladoja appeal case in Ibadan. The Lord impressed the significance of that case upon his wife, and she chose to be close to her husband. She, therefore, left their home base in Enugu to join him in Ibadan for the time he was there, and she was ceaselessly on her knees as the case lasted.

Finances are very critical in the life of any family, and much more so for the family of a judge, because this is the area in which people are easily tempted. Even in this regard, Dr. (Mrs.) Ogebe proved to be a true supporter to her husband. Early in their marriage, at the point when the wages of judges were meagre, they learned to pull their resources together. Besides, putting her salary into the family purse, Dr. (Mrs.) Ogebe also brought all of her earnings from her gardening business to her husband as well. Justice Ogebe remains forever grateful to his wife, knowing that it was her unflinching support to him that made it possible for them to train their children at time when his income alone would have been grossly inadequate. Justice Ogebe is similarly appreciative of their children, who at very young ages grasped the sensitive nature of his work and followed his instructions to them never to accept any gifts from people in his absence.

IMPACTING OTHERS

Hon. Justice Ogebe's life has had a huge impact on many others. On the bench, those he had mentored and has had more direct influences on their careers include, Justices Utsaha, Ogbole, Puussu, Igbetar, Ejembi Eko, Tom Yakubu, Aboyi Ikongbeh (of blessed memory), and many others. Justices Eko and Yakubu are currently serving at the Court of Appeal, and the fact that they are following the trail blazed by Justice Ogebe is not lost on keen observers. A case in point is where the presiding justice of the Port Harcourt Division of the Court of Appeal, told Justice Eko that the latter is operating in the mould of his mentor (in reference to Hon. Justice Ogebe).

Justice Ogebe's efforts to raise the next generation of godly people were not limited to the judiciary only. He was actively involved in Christian ministry as well. In his younger years, he was deeply involved with the Fellowship of Christian Students (FCS). Beginning right from secondary school where he was once an FCS president at Government College, Keffi, he continued after school to serve as an associate member of the fellowship. He became the National Vice chairman of FCS for several years. In the same light, the Ogebe's home served as the venue for the weekly Bible study fellowships of the Makurdi Chapter of the Associates of FCS for most of the years they lived in Makurdi. They were likewise deeply involved in FCS school outreaches and visitations in Benue State while they lived there. Not only that, Hon. Justice Ogebe also served for many years as an elder in the ECWA Church in Makurdi. Although he was raised Methodist and was married there, he felt uncomfortable with the bickering and eventual split that led to long drawn litigations. Since he did not believe spiritual matters should be resolved in a court of law, he eventually left the Methodist Church and joined ECWA. Justice Ogebe has also been involved in rural church planting, being a founding member of the defunct Benue State Evangelistic Association (BESEA), the organization that in the true sense of the word pioneered rural church planting in modern Benue State. He and his family continue to support many of these churches and tent-making indigenous missionaries working with them.

Charity, they say, begins at home. This is true of Justice Ogebe as well. Though he came from a pagan background, with nobody in his family to show him the way to salvation, he became God's vessel for bringing many in his extended family to the saving knowledge of Christ, including his grandmother, who raised him up. It was through him also that most of the other members of his family came to the light of the Gospel of Christ. To him, the opportunity to bear witness to the redemption that is in Jesus our Saviour is one of the greatest advantages of the extended family system. He looks back with great satisfaction at the many relatives, who lived with his family over the years, and through this came to embrace the Christian faith. Many of these folks are now established men and women with their own families, but continue to walk with the Lord.

A THANKFUL HEART

Hon. Justice Ogebe is grateful to God, who took him from a lowly background and did not only give him a noble career but also took him to the pinnacle of the profession in the land. This was not something he had dreamed about neither could he have achieved it in his own strength—it was purely an act of divine grace. Although he cannot pinpoint any outlandish issues that he particularly is remorseful about, since he knew the Lord in his youth, there certainly are moments in his life that he regrets, especially ways in which he had handled some issues with youthful zeal. As a human being, he does acknowledge moments in which he failed God, and he is ever awed at the loving heart of our God, who is slow to anger, abounding in steadfast love, and ever eager to receive back his erring children as they return to him in repentance.

Justice Ogebe has no greater joy than to see young people come to the saving knowledge of Jesus Christ as their Saviour and live daily in submission to his Lordship—bringing every sphere of their lives to his sovereign control. His assurance to those who would consider taking such significant step in their lives is that to those who commit themselves to the Lord, the Lord will also unreservedly commit himself, and he will lead them through the valleys and hills, through moments of sadness and moments of triumphs: He will never leave them nor forsake them. There is nothing to lose in following the Lord, he insists, rather there is everything to gain, as Scripture says, *"seek ye first the kingdom of God and his righteousness, and all these things shall be added unto you"* (Matt 6:33 KJV).

The oft peddled notion of bifurcated lives (sacred and secular) is alien to the legal luminary. From his experience, he has learned that being in the centre of God's will for one's life is the most important thing; otherwise someone may even be in the so-called full time ministry and be living the worst lie one could ever imagine. His successful career in the legal profession (just like many other believers) is sufficient proof that God desires to have his children in all sectors of the society: If Lot was a righteous man in Sodom, one can remain faithful to God (by his grace) in any place or profession.

The learned justice is quick to point to several avenues the Lord provides for the support of his children who desire to remain loyal as his servants in the public arena. For example, he says, there is a Christian fellowship group in virtually every professional guild in Nigeria today. In the legal profession, there is the Christian Lawyers' Fellowship of Nigeria (CLASFON). There are local churches and many other groups. All of these are avenues that provide support groups for those who want to stand with God. He recalls that whenever he had very crucial cases in his court, like the presidential tribunal of 2007, he would solicit the prayer support of his church members (ECWA Maitama). Through these, he never failed to find God's abiding protection, wisdom, encouragement, strength, and courage to do what is right. He rightly points out that what makes many Christians in public positions err is when they begin to feel too important to associate with their fellow brethren and thereby deny themselves the fellowship and support they need to help them remain steadfast (cf. Hebrews 10:25).

He remembers that when he first started reading law, even up to when he became a lawyer, the one question young people asked him often was how can you be a Christian and be a lawyer because according to them lawyers are liars. His career has disproved this notion; he has proved by his exemplary life that you could actually be a Christian and make it in the legal profession without soiling either your own name or the name of the Lord. There are many Christian lawyers as well as Christian judges all over the place. All of these have gone to show that it is possible to go into any career and stand your ground as a child of God. He feels that we need Christians everywhere, even in politics, as we cannot afford to leave sensitive matters only to the unbelievers, otherwise they will make laws and/or policies that will impact us negatively.

Equally important in this matter is the willingness to make one's position known. Hon. Justice Ogebe says without fear of contradiction that throughout his lifelong career on the bench, he never for once felt any pressure from Government or any group to sway his decision one way or another in any matter before him, notwithstanding the many high profile cases he handled. This he attributes, without equivocation, to the fact that people already knew his stand. Once a matter was before his court people simply resigned to the wheels of justice. It was not uncommon to hear comments about him on this tenor,

> *"Ah! That judge you can't go near him; you can't bribe him; you can't tempt him with women, money or material things. He is unbendable; he is unapproachable."*

With this, they simply left him alone. But you must first

make people know where you stand. You cannot be professing one thing and be seen doing another—people are quick to detect the inconsistency and they will exploit it.

CHAPTER TWELVE

GIVING IDEAS WINGS TO FLY

ENGR. WILLIAM RUMBERGER

This autobiography is a partial summary of my career history with specific reflections on how my "professed faith" related to "practiced faith" in the workplace during a 50 year career at Boeing Helicopters in Philadelphia. Included as well are details about my service to the Lord in the Church and in the home.

What means did God use to enable me to live out my faith and experience his blessing during my career at Boeing? Looking back, the evidence of God's hand is unmistakable. I will mention about various individuals and events that affected or dictated certain outcomes, challenging me to be the Lord's man in the marketplace. Also included are reflections on how attitudes and protocol changed at Boeing in response to the Cultural Revolution that took place during my 50 years of employment.

ORIGINS

I was the first born of parents who came to faith in Christ out of godless homes. In the womb I apparently heard much hymn singing. As a consequence, I sang hymns before ever talking; and now, 75 years later [in 2011], I often wake up with a Christian song going through my mind. Through my mother's teaching I came to faith while very young. Mother taught me the importance of making a public confession of faith. With her urging, I remember going forward from a church balcony to take a stand for Christ around six years old.

While growing up I saw my father with his Scripture memory cards that he memorized during his work day. Evening meals were filled with stories of Dad's exciting experiences sharing his faith with men at his workplace. I remember sharing my faith at street meetings where my Dad would preach while I handed out Christian tracts. Both my mother and my father were active and effective Christian witnesses in our neighborhood.

I was impacted in my teenage years at church through a faithful and powerful Bible teacher, Dr. William Allan Dean. He also taught at the Philadelphia College of the Bible, now Cairn University. My church activities included leadership roles at Christian Rescue Missions in Philadelphia. Mission conferences at church influenced me greatly and were times of enrichment which I remember to this day.

CAREER DIRECTION

Mother encouraged me toward engineering. She saw instincts and abilities similar to those of her father, who was an outstanding tool and die maker at Westinghouse Electric. My father graduated as an electrical engineer from Drexel Institute of Technology; my career was aimed in that direction. Upon graduating from high school, I enrolled at Drexel Institute of Technology, now Drexel University. I married while at college to a believer whose parents led the young people's ministry at church. During my college years I joined Inter-Varsity Christian Fellowship, which strengthened my Christian faith within the academic environment.

My career started in 1959 at Boeing Vertol which had just started hiring after a downturn. I was placed in the Transmission Design Group and I was excited about it. My employment at Boeing offered many opportunities over the years to stand for my convictions in the face of opposition.

STANDING FOR GOD'S PRINCIPLES IN THE WORKPLACE

Thankfully, my childhood training at home had implanted a willingness to stand alone and not follow the crowd. This attitude protected me in my new career experience since I lacked Christian fellowship in the work environment. Psalm One was ingrained in my thinking; I did not want to become "like the chaff which the wind drives away." God taught me lessons during those early years at Boeing as I observed firsthand the "dog eats dog" world of office politics. These observations assaulted the sensitivities of my Christian training, but in retrospect I can see many lessons I learned through people and circumstances the Lord brought into my life. I determined not to follow the ways of the ungodly.

An essential part of being God's man in the workplace is establishing credibility by one's honesty and work ethic. Being known as a believer, causes one's attitudes, actions and words to be observed by curious and critical eyes. Worldly observers want to see if one "walks the talk." The walk needs to be humble, including asking for forgiveness when we fall. The child of God cannot be like the Pharisees with only a set of do's and don'ts, but must also demonstrate love for God and neighbor.

EARLY DESERT EXPERIENCE

The first couple years at Boeing were very challenging. I elected to move to the Engineering Test Laboratories. This group treated me with disdain. By God's grace, I did not return evil for evil during those desert days. The test lab technical knowhow I acquired during my work experience in the Engineering Test Laboratories proved invaluable to my future career.

During this desert period, the Lord sent Clyde, a Christian brother, for mutual encouragement. We started a lunch time Bible study that encouraged the faith of a seeking friend, John Paul. I invited John Paul's family to our home for meals and they reciprocated. He came to the Sunday morning men's Bible class at church, but when his wife objected we were sensitive to her fears and discontinued the class together. Some years later, John Paul's wife received the Saviour a week before she died. She was in great fear of her approaching death, but we witnessed a dramatic and unforgettable coming to faith. Her face was radiant as God's marvelous peace filled her soul.

SIMPLE GRACES AND THE BLESSING THEY BRING

A friendly lunchtime visit to my boss's supervisor brought eventual rescue from the "desert" place. He was evaluating the cause of a tragic helicopter crash which killed five people. Because of my previous experience in the Transmission Design Group I was able to correct some wrong information he had regarding the cause of the failure. Recognizing my experience and background, he immediately reassigned me to the Transmission Test Labs.

Looking back over the years at Boeing, I can mark significant and positive career changes that were facilitated through simple kindness and friendliness that I extended to others. I experienced the truth of scripture: *"Do not despise the day of small things."* I can attest to the blessing that comes from extending simple graces.

INNATE TALENTS ARE GIFTS FROM GOD

Gifting is something that one has been given. I

inherited my grandfather's engineering genes along with a gift of creativity. On occasion when trying to solve a particularly difficult problem, I would wake up in the morning with the answer running through my mind. These God-given gifts were developed in my teenage years through my hobby of model railroad building and in later years through automobile repair work that developed my mechanical skills.

The initial occasion to express my gifting came through a new job assignment. The opportunity occurred due to an unusual event during an acceptance test of a CH-46 Sea Knight helicopter. This event prevented the delivery of the helicopter to the customer. I found a simple yet ingenious breakthrough solution to this particular problem and resolved a particularly frustrating problem that the design group had been unable to fix. This breakthrough solution earned me a reputation that would build during the remaining 40 years at Boeing. It was just the beginning of workplace blessings and opportunities far beyond my imagination. In subsequent years, I saw God's hand orchestrate exceptional breakthroughs, resulting in the awarding of fifteen US patents.

BUILDING BRIDGES THROUGH RELATIONSHIPS

I believe an essential part of being God's person in the workplace is to make the home an extension of one's work. Many times I invited new people, hurting coworkers or temporary international visitors from overseas to our home. These international visitors were thrilled to be invited to an American home. My wife and family enjoyed participating in this, making it a mutual blessing. Looking back, I realize how special those times were. They offered opportunities where hospitality could be extended and the gospel shared, but not imposed, on our guests. I believe our children benefited from the demonstration of hospitality and sharing Christ, along with the exposure to different people and cultures.

Living out the gospel of grace develops friendships that often lead to special opportunities. This was the case with Joe. Joe's expertise was recognized within Boeing, and when he moved up in the organization, he requested that I assist him in his new assignment. My friendship with Joe lasted over forty years and included attending Christian men's retreats and a home Bible study group. Years later, I visited Joe weekly at his home where he lay dying of cancer. To be God's man in the workplace is to seek out and care for those that are hurting, and it often leads to opportunities to share the Gospel message.

CREATIVE OPPORTUNITIES, HONOUR, AND BLESSING

The next chapter in my career was the most creative as it provided opportunities for exciting inventions and U.S. Patent awards. It also included dramatic encounters of challenge and intrigue. I had the privilege of partnering with an elderly engineer, Chuck. Together we developed an advanced failure detection device for helicopter gear boxes. This shared effort would result in the award of two US patents. Unfortunately, he had no interest in spiritual matters. I was learning that unless God has prepared the heart, our efforts are in vain.

Boeing licensed our failure detection device for marketing and sale to other helicopter companies. The Boeing Company's incentive program for invention licensing gave a monetary reward from the licensing agreement. I promised the Lord that if he would bless me with a license agreement I would give him all the incentive money. God blessed us with a license agreement and we honoured him with the income.

We found great joy in being able to partner with our missionary brothers and sisters. Recognizing that all our financial income was a blessing from the Lord, we decided to increase our giving beyond the tithe. As a result we have been able to participate more fully in Kingdom work over the years and around the world. These investments have been one of the most rewarding spiritual experiences of our lives. We testify to the truth of God's Word where He says, *"For them who honour Me, I will honour"* (1 Samuel 2:30).

As an example of the joy God has given to us, the Lord brought into our lives a native Burmese missionary who is like the apostle Paul in commitment and sacrifice. He has traveled thousands of miles throughout his country winning hundreds of souls to the Lord, including over 100 monks, providing for widows and orphans, establishing schools, helping typhoon victims recover, feeding the poor and hungry and much more. In one of the most persecuted nations in the world, he has established a training and sending missionary organization that has reached many more of his people. We were also privileged to help his son, Nishit (Not real name), get his Ph.D. at Reformed Theological Seminary in the U.S. Nishit has started a Bible School and his students are now going out to evangelize and establish churches.

MY MOST UNIQUE INVENTION

As a follow-up to the failure detection device for gear boxes, I developed a unique concept called the Sparker, which I subsequently sent to the Boeing Patent Office. This idea had great potential and whoever would market the Sparker concept would have the opportunity for great financial benefit. The Sparker device offered significant advantages over the existing failure warning systems for helicopter gear boxes by greatly minimizing false warnings. However, I was not to be part of the Sparker success story. Collusion with an outside company and conflict of interest by my supervisor resulted in the stealing and fraudulent patenting of this device by this outside company.

The marketing of the Sparker by this company was extremely profitable for them. I can take consolation, however, that the use of this device has benefited and improved the flight safety for the users of helicopters and other aircraft worldwide. This painful experience brought me face to face with the greed and dishonesty that exists within the market place. My response to this theft and injustice would test my Christian faith. I had a choice to make: I could become bitter and pursue this through the courts attempting to obtain just recompense for this theft that would have consumed all my time and energy for years or I could let it go and put it in the Lord's hands. With God's help and advice from a Christian patent attorney at Boeing, I chose to let go and give it up to the Lord.

SHEPHERDED THROUGH A FAMILY CRISIS

The need for creative and experienced engineering talent took me away from the group that practiced such blatant collusion and dishonesty. In my new assignment with the Surface Transportation Department I was blessed to have an ethical supervisor. Al was a gracious and talented boss and my relationship with him was such a blessing. Many years later, I had the privilege to share Christ with Al on his death bed.

I was still working for Al when my daughter became very ill needing to be in a special hospital which was 800 miles away just north of Chicago, Illinois. There were neither the funds nor the means to make this trip possible. At this crisis time the Lord, used Al to arrange a trip for me to install a special fan in a transit car in Chicago as part of my work assignment. To my amazement the Transit Authority in Chicago was close to the very location of the hospital where my daughter was to be hospitalized. I was able to make the trip taking my wife and daughter with me. I never cease to be amazed when I recall this event and how the fan project created the exact circumstances that required this trip, to that very place and at that very time. How gracious of the Lord to arrange these events for the blessing of my daughter, my wife and me.

BEYOND MY CHOOSING

The unseen Hand continued to guide my career changes that were beyond my choosing. On one occasion I was forced by orders from the Vice President of Engineering to return to the organization from which I had "escaped." Little did I know that my return to that department would present new opportunities and put me in the place I needed to be to make a significant contribution to the V-22 Osprey program at Boeing.

It was at this juncture in my career that a "messenger from the Lord" by the name of Gene came to challenge me in my vision and spiritual care for those in my new group at Boeing. As I introduced Gene to my Christian co-workers, he was amazed by the number of believers in our workplace. He would often come and stand in front of my drafting board with arms upraised and say, "Praise God! This place is like being in church!" Gene recognized my stance as a believer at Boeing so he suggested that we spend time during our lunch breaks praying for the men in the group. He also encouraged me to pray more earnestly to the Lord for a breakthrough in the difficult design challenge that I had been assigned to help resolve.

I think that Gene provides the best example of one whose faith is lived out boldly in the workplace. Through a divorce experience, Gene had been broken. Humbled and forgiven, Gene was totally "sold out" to his Lord and Saviour. There was a quiet boldness in his attitude, for his allegiance was no longer to himself; he had been set free from self. As abruptly as Gene came into my life at Boeing, so he was taken out through a tragic auto accident.

Consider how my testimony contrasts to that of Gene's. There was passivity in my stand for the Lord in the workplace compared to Gene's. The godless atmosphere of my workplace often tended to intimidate me. Although I would never deny the Lord, there was a muted boldness in my witness. My coworkers knew where I stood in my faith, but I wasn't the firebrand that Gene was. Perhaps personality played a part in this; for although I possessed initiative ingenuity in my assigned tasks as a designer, I lacked assertiveness in my interactions with others.

My experience has shown me that a believer who grows up in a Christian home tends to be more passive in his witness for the Lord as compared to the believer who has had a dramatic conversion experience. These believers often act as a catalyst for the more reserved believers and encourage the timid believers to be bolder in their stand for the Lord.

A DESIGN ACHIEVEMENT OF SINGULAR SIGNIFICANCE

Remember Gene's prayer for a **breakthrough** in my design challenge? Shortly after Gene's passing, I, with the assistance of a young stress engineer, came up with an idea that would become the basis for the patented **Flex Ring** concept which is used on the V-22 Osprey. The Flex Ring component *connects the wing to the fuselage.* The mechanism also *permits the stowing or folding of the wing* when the aircraft is used on board ships. The steps leading to the process by which this design became incorporated into the Osprey were certainly providential. For this change to take place at this particular time in the Osprey program required a myriad of events to take place:

1. The retirement of the Chief Engineer
2. A crash of an Osprey during flight test

3. My reassignment to the Research and Development Group (R & D)
4. A temporary stoppage of the entire program by the Customer
5. A customer demand to reduce the existing cost and weight of the current Osprey design
6. A $1,000,000 grant from Boeing Corporate for Research and Design (R & D) at Boeing Helicopters
7. A decision from the new Vice President and Chief Engineer to assign the $1,000,000 R&D grant money for the development of the Flex Ring.

These extraordinary events all took place. However, for the Flex Ring program to move forward the following processes also needed to be resolved:

1. In the aircraft business the process required to go from a design concept to actual incorporation into the aircraft is an extraordinarily complex process. It usually requires years of testing and multiple step-by-step design refinements. How could all of this be accomplished in the limited time we had?
2. Boeing and Bell helicopter companies shared joint responsibilities for the design of the Osprey. Because of their competing interests, agreement between them was difficult to achieve. How could consensus be reached on the novel Flex Ring concept in time?
3. The "customer" represented several military groups and each of these had their unique interests. Could common ground

be found that was acceptable to all parties?

4. The Flex Ring was a novel concept. To replace *the existing qualified hardware* on the Osprey would break precedent. Could precedent be set aside?

It is for the above reasons that a senior consultant at Boeing Headquarters said that he had never seen a novel design concept become incorporated into a production aircraft in such a short time. These events that constitute the Flex Ring story and its incorporation into the Osprey will always stand out to me as an example of how a series of exceptional events and my gifting were used to accomplish something significant to benefit my fellow workers and to honour the Lord. Reflecting on the many years at Boeing simply testifies that God's hand orchestrated the breakthroughs and 15 patents that were awarded to me.

REFLECTIONS ON "STANDING TALL" IN THE MARKETPLACE

I recently heard a pastor from Bangladesh explain the necessity for a convert from Islam to boldly express his allegiance to Christ. This public declaration was necessary for the sake of the individual as well as for the integrity of the Gospel witness. He testified that the individual who declares his faith **openly** will surely have to endure a **limited** time of extreme hardship, ostracism and possible death. However, the **secret** convert, will experience a **lifetime** of hardship and isolation since the philosophy of life within Islam is in such stark contrast to the grace of the gospel of Christ that the believer has embraced. The secret believer has cut himself off from the fellowship of the openly declared believers which compounds his pain. As I reflect on this pastor's testimony who lived and continues to live out this experience, I believe what he said relates directly to the challenge before us of "standing tall" for the Lord in the workplace.

For a Christian to stand boldly for Christ in the market place he must have been truly born from above. He must have opened his heart's door to the Saviour—a true conversion.

1. He must count the cost of identifying with Christ, much the same as Moses did in casting his lot with the people of God rather than continue to enjoy the pleasures of sin in the Egyptian palace.
2. He must be taught how to respond to persecution in a godly fashion.
3. He must continually hide God's word in his heart as a resource for truth and comfort.
4. He must seek out other believers for encouragement and he must encourage others.
5. He must be transparent, credible, humble and compassionate in all his relationships.
6. He must speak the truth in love.

THE BELIEVER IN THE WORKPLACE IN A POSTMODERN WORLD

It was 50 years ago when I was hired by Boeing, and significant cultural changes have taken place in the U.S. since then. They reflect the social revolution taking place in the society. These changes have had a major impact on the authority structure within the workplace. The attitudes that accompany these changes affect a believer's response to faith questions from fellow employees and his stand.

Fifty years ago, Boeing had strong authoritarian figures and a strong chain of command. Thirty-five years later when a supplier asked me "Who's in charge here?"

My answer was "No one!" This expressed the frustration under which we had to work. Cultural changes in the society were occurring through the rapid demise of ethical standards that influenced the way we did business. As a consequence, Boeing felt the need to initiate an ethics education program which all employees are required to take.

The "Team Concept" was introduced in the 1990's. We received training in this new approach with the intended purpose of appreciating each person's contribution in resolving a particular problem. However, in implementing this management model, agenda–driven people required us to give equal validity to all input from all staff, notwithstanding their knowledge and competence in the matters at hand. I remember a training session that required us to give **no** consideration as to whether the contributing individual was **qualified** to give an opinion on the subject or not. **All contributions were to be considered of equal value.** If the problem was technical in nature and I was not trained to think technically, it didn't matter. **All opinions were considered of equal worth!**

I had previously been taught that for tasks in the desert, a team chooses a camel for its transportation instead of a horse. However, this new teaching implied that camels and horses were equivalent if "the team" came to that conclusion. **Accommodation** became the new rule. The decision making process under the new "team concept" became a beclouded and complex process. With "group ownership," the "team" was now in charge. This meant that "no one was in charge."

With the questioning of the existence of ultimate truth came a diminished amount of common sense. Into this vacuum and the loss of critical thinking came the imposition of "political correctness." Many had embraced the belief that all truth is relative. This revolution in societal thinking affected, not only the way we did business, but it also greatly affected the words and the approach that the believer would need to use when giving an answer to the hope that was in his heart. We had arrived in a post-modern and post-Christian culture, and it became apparent in workplace ethics.

THE LAST TEN YEARS

My reputation as the inventor of the Flex Ring provided me the opportunity to be hired as a consultant after my official retirement from Boeing in 1995. This reputation gave me a respect in the design office and on the assembly line, enabling me to be more effective in sharing my faith and the giving of honour to the Lord. My initial assignment was to help solve a problem on the Boeing 777 aircraft, but my final assignment took me back to the Osprey and the Flex Ring that I had invented and developed prior to my retirement.

As a consequence of my accomplishments and respect awarded me, I was asked to be a mentor to a young engineer in the Structures Department. This assignment was part of a mentoring program that the Boeing Company has recently inaugurated to transfer the experience and judgment principles of senior engineers to the next generation of junior engineers. I was assigned a young Hindu man, Ankit, to be my protégé. This gave me the opportunity to analyze the methodology I use in seeking solutions to mechanical design problems and failures. I was able to articulate the mechanism and philosophy used in identifying problems and solutions. I emphasized to him the importance of establishing respect and rapport within the design community. I also shared with him that I was a Christian and the principles of humility, truthfulness and integrity were to me essential in successfully implementing identified solutions and corrective actions.

During this period I was privileged to be part of an active Christian fellowship group. Charles, a committed believer, asked me to be part of a discipleship group which was very rewarding. Another believing friend, Harley, was a foreman on the Osprey assembly line. Men like Harley with his committed lifestyle, were a positive influence down in the shop and through his witness many were blessed. His Christian attitude had a positive effect on the quality and the quantity of the tasks performed.

As an aside, during this time, on my Friday lunch hour, I was blessed with the opportunity to teach at a small Christian school nearby. I led the children in participating in a dramatized Bible story which we all enjoyed. I am continuing to do this in my retirement years.

In the final months of my consulting employment, a young engineering graduate, Scott, was assigned to the cubical next to mine. I had the opportunity to explain to him some of the features of the Flex Ring design. While visiting the aircraft assembly line with him I acknowledged God's blessing by recounting the events that made the design possible. The young man said, *"I can see you're a man of faith."* Following this encounter, I invited Scott to my home for a meal and to meet my wife. He was untaught in the faith, but God had recently put a deep hunger in his heart to know him and to study his word. It's been a year and a half now and Scott continues to come each week to our home for a meal, Bible study, prayer and fellowship. What a wonderful token of God's blessing this experience has been and continues to be as a final chapter to my 50 years of investment at Boeing Helicopters.

FAITH, FAMILY, AND CAREER

As parents we are instructed to *"train up a child in the way he should go."* This admonition is for the good of the child, the honor of God and the joy of the parent. We are also told in Deuteronomy 6:6-7 that the parents are to *"impress them (the commandments) on your children. Talk about them when you sit at home and when you walk along the road, when you lie down and when you get up"* (NIV).

We read Bible stories and Christian books to our children, had Bible reading, prayer and sang a hymn before supper, Christian records for the children to play and prayed with the children at bedtime. Scripture memorization was done outside the home at church and at the Christian school. However, we did not follow the Deuteronomy 6:7 instructions explicitly.

In 1965 when our oldest son was in grade 6, he wrote an article for the class newspaper in which he said that God gave the beaver the ability to build a dam. His teacher removed the reference to God from his paper. He came home upset and told us that the word "God" had been removed. When I asked the teacher about this she told me that it was against school policy for the name of "God" to be used in the classroom. I realized then how hostile and opposed to our Christian values and beliefs that some teachers were in the public school system. As a result, we enrolled our children in the private Christian school nearby. Although it stretched our budget, it was an investment that we were willing to make. We recognized, however, that the most effective means of faith transfer was accomplished in the home from parent to child. We attended a Bible believing church faithfully with our children. However, only one of our children had a Christian friend to play with who lived close by.

Although raising godly children was our desire, to our great sorrow, we apparently did not impart our faith to our children as we should have. We realize that faith is a matter of personal commitment and that each child must make this commitment for himself. Two of our 4 children are following the Lord and are committed to raising a Christian family. What joy this brings to our hearts. Our children who aren't following the Lord are continually driving us to our knees in prayer and faith before the Savior.

Thankfully, I don't believe my career as an engineer at Boeing had a negative impact on my family. I think the opposite is true since the children saw caring and reaching out to those in my workplace. My job provided an adequate income and it did not require my spending long hours away from home or taking extended trips. However, upon looking back, the time I spent with my family needed to reflect a closer walk with the Lord which would have helped to support my wife and would have impacted my children's lives more profoundly.

FAITH AND PRACTICE OUTSIDE THE WORKPLACE

"But Lord, we did all these things in your name." The Lord answered, *"I don't know who you are."* Christian activities without relationship with Christ Himself can be a waste. In recalling my involvement in Christian service outside my workplace at Boeing, I realize how God often prospers his truth even though the messenger is lacking.

My early years were spent enjoying singing in the Aldan Union Church choir. The great hymns of the Church expressed my heart of worship to the Lord as much as the teaching of children and other means of serving. I also enjoyed directing the Junior Department for 4th through 6th grade children over a ten year period.

Through the years that followed there were opportunities to serve on a Christian school board and church boards. My skills and training as an engineer were utilized when I served as chairman of the Building Committee for the new middle school and gym for a well-established Christian school that our children attended. My faith was strengthened at this time as the Lord provided a strong Christian brother on the board who came to my rescue defending truth in the face of a major deception being perpetrated by the "Christian" contractor, who was responsible for the construction project. I experienced seeing the

Lord answer my urgent prayers in a wonderful way.

In serving on two of the church boards, severe problems arose due to sin in the members of the leadership which brought disgrace on our Saviour's name and resulted in splits in the churches. Many of us were broken and cried out to the Lord for his help, forgiveness and mercy. What stands out as my most poignant memory of my serving on these boards is the pain, discord and destruction that resulted from the pride and the desire for prestige that existed among some of the Christian leaders with whom I served. Pride is an enemy that keeps us from entering the Kingdom; and that same enemy, pride, destroys our relationships within the Kingdom. Thankfully when reflecting upon those difficult times, it is God's grace in the face of human pride that has become even more precious to me than anything else.

My current board assignment is with Plesion International, whose mission involves providing pure water for children through mission outreach in developing countries. This requires the design and arrangement of drinking water system components such as pumps and filters. These design responsibilities have taken me to Vietnam, Romania and Nigeria as part of the Plesion ministry.

Our home has served as an outreach as well as a home care group. For ten years we hosted a large group for Bible Study and prayer in our home for Church of the Saviour. We have often hosted international students from local colleges during Thanksgiving and Christmas Holidays and we still do some of this type of ministry. Our home became a home for a Chinese woman for a ten year period during which she learned English and earned her master's degree in counseling psychology.

We have been so blessed and our lives enriched with the many opportunities the Lord has given to us to reach out to those who are hurting and lost as well as to our Christian brothers and sisters in need. The Lord has given us meaning and purpose in life through being in partnership with him as he enables us in promoting his kingdom by loving him and loving others as ourselves.

CHAPTER THIRTEEN

CONTENDING FOR THE FAITH

ENGINEER SAMUEL S. L. SALIFU

Samuel Sani Lando Salifu was born toward the end of the Second World War, between 1944 and 1946, in Lando village in Basa Local Government Area of Kogi State, Nigeria. At his birth, his grandfather gave him the name of Sani Hitler because Adolf Hitler was well known throughout the world during those war years. When he grew up, went to school, and got to know what the person after whom he was named really stood for, he dropped Hitler from his name and only retained Sani Lando Salifu and, then, took up the Bible name of Samuel at his baptism. Because his parents were not literate, his birthday was not recorded, so his assumed date of birth is August 18, 1946. In 1958, when he was about twelve years of age, an evangelist came to evangelize their area: his name was Noah Ogbangia. Even though Sani (as he was then called) came from a Muslim background, he loved the songs the evangelist was teaching the children at that time, so he would stealthily go and listen to them. Eventually, he openly came out and declared his faith in the Lord Jesus Christ, and on October 24, 1958, he was baptized into his new faith, at which point he took on the name Samuel. At that time he was in primary five. He completed his primary education in 1960, and through divine providence, he ended up in a mission secondary school—Ochaja Secondary School. He had missed the rare privilege of going to the government secondary schools in either Keffi or Okene, which were the schools to which intelligent students in his home area used to go. However, his going to Ochaja Secondary School afforded him the opportunity of being strengthened in his faith there.

In those days the determination of who proceeded to high school (the intermediate state between secondary and university) was not infrequently done at the secondary school level, based on the students' performance in the mock WASC examinations. When Samuel completed his secondary education at Ochaja, only one person's mock WASC result was better than his, yet twelve students were selected to proceed to either Keffi or Okene for high school and he was bypassed. So he left Ochaja and returned to his village of Lando. While he was there, someone providentially told him that the entrance examination into the Kaduna Polytechnic was about to take place. On hearing this news, he left home immediately and headed to Kaduna. When he arrived at the Polytechnic, he was told that the candidates were already writing the entrance examination and that only thirty minutes remained before the entire examination would be over. However, he was allowed to take the examination anyway, and thereafter he returned to Lando.

On January 8, 1966, Samuel returned to Kaduna to check on his admission into the Polytechnic. That was around the time of the first coup d'état, when many prominent Nigerians were assassinated. Coming from the village, Samuel had heard nothing of this. When he dropped off at the motor park, he saw people running helter skelter, and he overheard others talking about the coup and the killings, but he had no idea what it was all about. The Radio Kaduna station was not far from the market, and he saw soldiers standing sentry. He approached them and inquired with the naïveté of a villager, *"What are you people doing here like this?"* Typical of uniformed men in Nigeria, one of the soldiers charged at him like a mad dog, hitting him hard with the butt of his gun. *"Ah! These people can kill! I must run for my life,"* he screamed in fear, more to himself than to anyone else. Like a scared cat in the midst of ferocious wolves, he scampered off for his life. By and by, as things calmed down, Samuel was able to get to the Polytechnic. To his delight, he found out that twenty students from his school had taken the examination; three of them had passed; two were to be admitted; two out of the three needed to go through an interview process; and one passed well enough that he needed no interview. The one who needed no interview was Samuel Salifu.

Samuel's father was influential in determining the course of his life. When the WASC results were out in 1966, Samuel had division two, having missed division one narrowly. His thinking was that with this kind of result, he should be taking a path that would lead him to university studies and not a polytechnic. So he went to meet the permanent secretary of the Ministry of Education at the regional headquarters in Kaduna, and requested that he be sent to the Federal School of Science, Lagos.

"You sound so brilliant, why didn't you go for your HSC in the first instance?" inquired the permanent secretary.

"You people did the selection from here and you dropped my name so ..." Samuel began bluntly.

"Not so," the permanent secretary cut in. "The selection was based on your mock WASC results. What was your aggregate?"

"Aggregate 18," Samuel responded.

"And your principal didn't send your name?" The permanent secretary asked with bemusement. "Did you run into any trouble with your principal? In the mock result of your school that I have with me here, you had aggregate 48."

"Yes," replied Samuel. "I had some issues with her."

"What was the problem"? the permanent secretary queried.

"Our principal is an Irish lady, and she happens to also be a Christian. However, I saw that some of her actions were incongruent with the Christian life. She used to order talismans from India. Mark you, she is the principal of a Christian school. I knew she was wrong. I came to know about it because her messenger, who used to go to the post office to bring our mail, used to show her correspondence with the Indian talisman folks to me. So, I used to go to her to challenge her that what she was doing was wrong. That was why she developed hatred for me and now tried to undermine my future."

The permanent secretary was touched by Samuel's integrity, his courage, and the injustice he had suffered, and told him that even though it was already June (the school year in those days began in January, not September), if he wanted to go to the Federal School of Science, he would send him there. However, when Samuel returned to Lando to confer with his father, his father counselled him to stick to Kaduna Polytechnic:

> Go back to where you already are. .... If it is a degree that you want, God knows how and when to give you a degree. In the meantime, return to where God sent you; don't go to Lagos.

Samuel took his father's advice with gratitude and returned to Kaduna Polytechnic. It can be seen that very early in his life, Samuel began to stand for what is right, and naturally he also began to suffer the woes of daring to speak out for the truth.

In time, Samuel came to see God's purpose in providentially ordering his steps to the polytechnic. At the polytechnic, he was receiving a monthly scholarship allowance of £14, while those who were at the Federal

School of Science received only £2/month. With this allowance, he was able to train his younger siblings while he was still in school himself. His father was a polygamist, having three wives: Samuel's mother, to whom Samuel was an only child, and two others. One of the other two wives was childless, while the other had eight children. It was Samuel's lot to train all the other children, and he started doing this when he himself was a student, which was not an uncommon phenomenon in his day. At present, only his childless stepmother is still alive; his father, mother, and the mother of eight have all passed on.

MARRIAGE AND FAMILY

Samuel married his wife, Alice, in 1970. He was doing his internship in Zaria, where Alice and her family lived. Alice herself was attending a commercial college in Zaria at the time. Meeting Alice was love at first sight, yet at the time Samuel was not financially buoyant enough to embark upon the marriage venture. However, Alice's parents had noticed the potential in him, and as such did not want Alice to dither. Once her parents noticed the affection between him and Alice, they nudged them on. They encouraged Alice that she could pursue her education even after she was married. Her parents were so kind that they waived all of the dowry requirements for him, so they went right on ahead and got married.

Samuel had a lot to learn from his wife. He soon realized that even though he had been a Christian for a long time, his wife was more grounded in the faith than he was. Amongst many other things, for example, he learned much about praying from her. He also came to know that his marrying Alice was not just happenstance but an answer to prayer. Alice had prayed and put out a fleece to God—that the first gift she would receive from the person God wanted her to marry should be a Bible—and that was exactly what happened. His first gift to Alice was a

New Testament. After more than forty years of marriage, Engr. S. S. L. Salifu remains ever grateful to the Lord for giving him such a wonderful wife. He cannot believe that his life would have been as good as it has been if he had not married his wife. In his own words, he said, "We have been married for over 40 years now, I'm not sure anybody else would have loved me the way she does. I know God prepared her specifically for me, and after these years I have no single regret at all for marrying her. She has wonderfully brought up our seven children, as well as those of my brother and my sister. She has been the stabilizing force in my family and, indeed, in my whole clan. She is the spiritual and physical stabilizer—the binding force in my universe—among other things that she has been to me." The Lord blessed the Salifus with seven children: six boys and one girl. All but one of these children are university graduates, and some are married. His greatest joy is that all are believers.

CAREER PATH

After obtaining his higher national diploma (HND) in mechanical engineering, Engr. Salifu took a teaching job with the Ahmadu Bello University in the agricultural mechanization department, where he taught from 1971 to 1973 and was also the department head. In 1973, however, he received a Macedonian call from his alma mater, Kaduna Polytechnic, to return to the mechanical engineering department as a lecturer. He obliged them and taught there for three-and-a-half years. He then proceeded to the University of Detroit, in the United States, for further studies and undertook a master's degree in manufacturing. He completed his studies in 1980 and promptly returned to Nigeria, continuing to teach at the polytechnic until he retired in 1991.

Engr. Salifu has also dabbled—or rather, he was thrust—into partisan politics. It all began during the early days of Gen Babangida's experiment with a return to democracy. Because their involvement in the fight for the rights of northern Christians, Christian youth began to nudge young professors like Dr. Harrison Bungon and Engr. Salifu into the political arena. It began with Engr. Salifu's close friend and ally, Engr. Dr. Harrison Bungon. Both Engr. Salifu and Dr. Bungon[7] were in the office one day when Christian youth from all over the country besieged them, demanding that Dr. Bungon contest for the governorship of Kaduna State. Dr. Bungon laughed. He protested. He pointed out that he had no money to run a campaign. The youth were insistent. They locked him up in a toilet and took the key away. They were not going to let him out until he wrote his letter of resignation from his work with the polytechnic. Protest as he did, the youth still had their way; he resigned, and, indeed, did contest the election. He did not win, but he made an impact as the first Christian in the state ever to rise to such an occasion. So strong was his impact that when the military reshuffled the government at the state level, they at first contemplated making Dr. Bungon the deputy governor of Kaduna, which they failed to do eventually, nonetheless he was made the commissioner for works.

What happened to Dr. Bungon was just a foretaste of what was coming for Engr. Salifu. He was in his house that memorable day when Christian youth from sixteen out of the then nineteen states of the federation descended on his house. It was déjà vu: the youth came to demand that he contest for the presidency of the country.

Engr. Salifu, like his friend Dr. Bungon, laughed. Pointing to the flip-flops he was wearing, he asked them, "Are these the shoes of a president?"

Their reply was, "We don't know, but when you get there you will buy the right shoes."

When he stopped laughing and began to reflect, he began asking himself, "What if the Lord was speaking through these young people?" So rather than dismiss them with the wave of the hand, he told them, "OK, let's pray about it, but you all know we don't have money."

"No, we don't have money but we will do it by faith," was their reply. To cut a long story short, that was how Engr. Salifu ended up running for the presidency of this country at the beginning of the 1990s.

Submission to divine purposes often makes people look foolish, but the important thing is the ends are served. In these days of multi-billion Naira campaigns for even gubernatorial elections, it might sound crazy to imagine someone running a presidential campaign with an old car. But that was what Engr. Salifu did. He traversed the length and breadth of Nigeria with his old car. Along the way, some brethren donated their vehicles, while others made themselves available to travel with him. On occasion, he had convoys of up to nine vehicles. He belonged to the defunct Social Democratic Party (SDP), and at the national convention of the party in Jos, Chief M. K. O. Abiola emerged as the party candidate for the aborted 1993 elections, still touted today as the freest election in Nigeria. With hindsight, Engr. Salifu believes that his standing for that election achieved its goal of creating the awareness that Christians too could lead this country in a civilian era, and it paved the way for the emergence of Christian presidents in the post-military era.

Engr. Salifu continued with politics for a while in the current political dispensation. He worked with Gen Obasanjo for a while during his first term in office as an elected President. It all began with a chance meeting of the men in Malaysia. When the General became President in 1999 and wanted to make Engr. Salifu a minister, it was Engr. Salifu's own Christian brothers who rose up against him, going to the President and beguiling him with lies against their brother. Unfortunately, the President acted on those lies without checking them out, and that was how Engr. Salifu lost out. When he stood for governorship in his home state of Kogi, it was again some of the supposedly Christian folks that rose up against him, claiming that if he became governor, his strict Christian principles would deny them access to what they would otherwise be enjoying. It was at that point that he kissed partisan politics goodbye: he had had enough of its back-stabbings.

THE COST OF DISCIPLESHIP

The price of standing for the truth, which Engr. Salifu began to pay in his encounter with his Irish secondary school principal, continued to trail him throughout his life. When he was at Kaduna Polytechnic, he held one rank for twelve years in the days when promotions came routinely every two years. His offense was his commitment to Christ. Even those who were supposedly Christians, because they wanted to secure their own positions, often became tools in the hands of those who did not want to see him progress. *"They felt I was too Christian; let's put it that way. I was too much of an embarrassment to a lot of them because of my Christian faith,"* Engr. Salifu remembers. Even during the directorship (in his department) of a southern "Christian," one Dr. Essay (not the real name), things were not any better for Engr. Salifu. He recalls going to meet Dr. Essay one time to ask him about his promotion. Dr. Essay's response was that Engr. Salifu was too busy distributing Christian tracts. Engr. Salifu presented the facts of the case before Dr. Essay: First, he gave his evidence that he was one of the best lecturers in the school. His students always did excellently, even in external examinations like City & Guilds and Full Technology Certificate examinations. Second, he asked Dr. Essay about the other people who go to pray four times before the work day is over and yet their promotions continue to run regularly. These were facts that Dr. Essay could not controvert, but there was an unwritten script concerning Engr. Salifu that was always followed.

The above encounter with Dr. Essay would eventually bring Engr. Salifu to a face-to-face encounter with the rector of the polytechnic, one Alhaji Kutur Mallam Kutur (not the real name). Alhaji Kutur was so irked when he heard Engr. Salifu's statement that he blurted, *"Let him go to the Christians to give him promotion! Let him go to CAN [Christian Association of Nigeria] to give him the job promotion he desires."* Well, because Engr. Salifu was not promoted, for many years many of his juniors could not be promoted either, because there would be no justification for bypassing him and promoting his junior, as he could not be faulted in terms of his work performance. Perhaps one could say all this was going on in the days when there was still some level of sanity in the country. Today, those juniors could have been promoted right over his head without any qualms.

Engr. Salifu was accustomed to facing glaring injustices in the workplace. There once was a vacancy for a principal lecturer in his department for which he was the most senior and also eminently qualified. However, because the rector wanted to give the post to someone of the same faith as himself, he decided that two people should be promoted to the position. To give an appearance of fairness, the rector constituted an interview panel made up of folks from the town; these people knew little about the make-up of the polytechnic politics, and it appears they were not well briefed about the rector's intentions. Three lecturers (Engr. Salifu, Dr. Bungon, and one Alhaji Junaid, the last name is fictitious) were invited for the interview. At the end of the day, the panel recommended the first two for promotion, and they typed their letters accordingly. However, when the rector heard of it that night, he directed that Engr. Salifu's name, in one of the promotion letters be erased and Alhaji Junaid's name typed over it; and that was what was done, even though Alhaji

Junaid could hardly even express himself intelligibly in the English language. The next day, it was a co-religionist of the rector, who was present when all these things had happened who divulged the information to Engr. Salifu. His informant was riled at such brazen injustice. Several people had urged Engr. Salifu to lodge a complaint with the Public Complaint Commission, but he refused to do so. He rather chose to let God be his vindication.

Those who hated Engr. Salifu also attacked his wife, who was also a staff of the polytechnic for some time. At one point, after she had been moved to the secret registry of the school, her over all boss began to subject her to gender-based harassments. But she did not yield, and naturally she would inform her husband of what was going on in the office. The boss, alarmed that things were not going his way, called Alice and asked her to swear by the Bible that she would not reveal office "secrets" to her husband. She refused to swear, on the ground that the Bible forbids her from swearing. The head of her department, a Christian, very eager to protect his boss so as to secure his own job, told her in frustration, *"You are carrying your Christianity on your forehead, why are you behaving like this?"* Soon they sacked Alice from her job and told Engr. Salifu that she had been derelict in her duties. Engr. Salifu, having already known exactly why she was sacked, told them in response, *"That is her faith. You either keep her with her faith or you relieve her, as you have done. But I know that she will never exchange Christ for anything."*

Engr. Salifu's belief in divine vindication continued to sustain them, and they did not bother to seek legal redress. God proved himself faithful, and just one month after his wife lost her job, she got another job at which she was paid twice what she had earned at the polytechnic. The Salifus could even now say, *"It was even good that they sacked her."* It is true, as the saying goes, that every disappointment is a blessing in disguise. Indeed, my good friend Earle Senn once said, *"Any disappointment is an appointment with God."* Shortly after this incident, Engr. Salifu also was promoted. Perhaps these people were smitten in their consciences for the ills they had visited on the Salifus. Truth be told, Engr. Salifu retired with the rank of a senior lecturer, in spite of his many years of dedicated and meritorious service. But he was not bothered by all these things, knowing fully well that he had counted the cost of following Jesus. Besides, despite his stunted progress on the job, they never lacked financially: God always provided for all of their needs.

Deciding to stand with God requires a conscious choice of daily cross-bearing and dying with Christ—the denial and crucifixion of self. This is the choice the Salifus made early in their lives. This is what informed Engr. Salifu's return to Nigeria in 1980, in the first place, after the completion of his master's degree in the United States. He turned down admission into the PhD programme of the school, even though the admission came with full sponsorship from the General Electric Company. He also turned down a job offer from General Electric for him to be their country representative in Nigeria after he had refused to continue with doctoral studies. He judged that taking the job would be a breach of trust (and contract), because he had signed a two-year bond with the Kaduna Polytechnic, his employer and sponsor of his graduate studies, which required him to return after his studies to serve the polytechnic for two years. As a follower of Christ, integrity mattered to him above personal profit.

Not only that, Engr. Salifu also could very much say with the Apostle Paul,

> *"I do not account my life of any value nor as precious to myself, if only I may finish my course and the ministry that I received from the Lord Jesus, to testify to the gospel of the grace of God"* (Acts 20:24 ESV).

His personal life philosophy comes from the hymn *Stand Up, Stand Up for Jesus*: early in his life the lines *"Where duty calls or danger, be never wanting there"* caught his attention and became his driving philosophy. This buoyed him, upon his return from the United States, to stand firm for Christ and his kingdom, especially in his work with the Christian Association of Nigeria (CAN), in the face of the emergent militancy of Islam in Nigeria at the beginning of the 1980s, which only kept increasing in intensity as the years rolled by.

It is not a coincidence that the rise of Islamic militancy in Nigeria followed on the heels of the Iranian revolution of 1979. It is rather unfortunate that those who run the Nigerian state are either daft, accomplices, too engrossed with the more important matter of looting the national treasury to be bothered with such insignificant issues as violent injustice, or simply are fiddlers playing while Rome burns. Whatever the reason, they have paid little heed to Iranian (and other foreign) meddlesomeness in the religious turmoils that have engulfed our dear country for over three decades now. Engr. Salifu returned to Nigeria in January of 1980 and resumed teaching at the Kaduna Polytechnic immediately. By March 1980, Muslim students from the Ahmadu Bello University (ABU) began to serve as stooges in the hands of those intent on fomenting trouble for Christians in Kaduna State. One fateful morning in March 1980, as Engr. Salifu set out to go to work, he found the hitherto sleepy city of Kaduna thrown in a tumult. Hordes of Muslim students from ABU had flooded the city and were inscribing "ISLAM ONLY" on any surface (roads, billboards, buildings—including churches) within their purview. On the roads, they were compelling commuters to chant ISLAM ONLY, and they would inscribe the same words on their cars, irrespective of the commuters' religious affiliation. Engr. Salifu was bewildered by such craziness, which the country had never experienced heretofore. He thought to himself, *"Have they forgotten that there are Christians in this country"?* Little did he know that this was only the tip of the iceberg—the real thing was yet to come.

The seed of religious tension and discord had already been sown. When he eventually got to school that day, he found the Muslim students of the polytechnic chanting the same slogan as well. He made bold to challenge the Muslim students in class: *"How can you people say ISLAM ONLY? I'm a Christian and I'm a Nigerian and I'm your lecturer."* When he saw the intensity of passion exhibited by his Muslim students, it then dawned on him that this was only the beginning of the unfolding of the big challenges ahead for the Christian community in the north, and Christians needed to brace up for it. This was part of the motivation for his involvement with CAN.

SERVICE THROUGH CAN

The drive toward ecumenical cooperation amongst Christians began in northern Nigeria because of the unique challenges that northern Christians have had to contend with over the years. Key figures in this regard include such Christian pillars as the Archbishops Peter Jatau and Gabriel Ganaka, Amb. Jolly Tanko Yusuf, and Evang. Paul Gindiri, all of whom have been called to glory. However, the coalescence of these efforts, at the national level, took place in Lagos in 1976. At the time, the Murtala/Obasanjo regime was about to take over Christian mission school all over the country. They, therefore, called the Christian mission proprietors of these schools to Lagos (then the federal capital of Nigeria) to brief them on this issue. At the end of the briefing, the gathered Christian leaders then decided that it was in their best interest to continue meeting regularly and working together for the common good of the Church of Christ in Nigeria. These, as Engr. Salifu recalls, are the origins of CAN.

From these humble beginnings, within a few years CAN grew to become a force to be reckoned with nationally. The galvanizing force was the ever-increasing intensity of violent religious aggression against Christians in the north. Not long after his return from the United States, Engr. Salifu was neck deep in CAN from the time of the religious riots of 1984 (the Maitatsine riots), but especially from the Kaduna riots of 1985 and the Kafanchan riots of 1987, during both of which there were unprovoked mass attacks on Christians, their businesses, and their places of worship. These thrust him into the thick of things (The Task Force Secretary of CAN): creating awareness of the plight of these hapless Christians in the state within the larger Nigerian church, collecting and collating information on Christian casualties and their losses for presentation before the commissions of inquiry that were set up. These efforts resulted in book-length publications that catalogued all these atrocities (*Kaduna Religious Riots*, 1987; *Do you know*, 1987); *Leadership in Nigeria*, 1989). His struggles for his brethren brought Engr. Salifu to national limelight. He eventually became Youth President of CAN, Northern Zone.

The road to becoming the General Secretary of CAN was not a smooth one for Engr. Salifu, neither was the job itself any easier. When the tenure of his predecessor was coming to an end, and since it was the turn of the TEKAN/ECWA block of CAN (to which Engr. Salifu belongs) to produce the next General Secretary, some Christian leaders began calling on him to take up the mantle. However, resistance began also to build up against him all the way to Aso Rock (is the Nigeria's equivalence of the American White House or the British No. 10 Downing Street). When he saw the fierceness of those who were opposing his candidacy—some of whom he had expected would support him—he was tempted to throw in the towel: He felt the whole thing portended too much danger. But as he shared his concerns with his wife, she urged him on:

> *Of what danger are you afraid? If the Lord charges you to go, then go forthwith. After all, many of the Lord's servants before your time gave themselves unreservedly to his service. Some he allowed to be killed, some he delivered, and others he simply allowed to suffer and be mistreated. So whether you die on your duty post or not, you will surely die one day and go to meet the Lord. How much better it would be to stand before him with the assurance that you did his bidding!*

Engr. Salifu delightfully recounts, *"When she said that, her faith and courage gave me strength and made me love her more."*

Even with such encouragement coming from the faith, courage, and support of his wife, Engr. Salifu did not take this matter lightly. Before applying for the job of CAN's General Secretary, he decided that he and his wife would spend two hours every day in prayer for forty days. At the end of the forty-day period, he did not yet have the assurance he desired, and so they spent another twenty days in prayer before the Lord, at the end of which the assurance came. The urgings of friends (both civilians and military generals) further encouraged him. He thus submitted his application, with the likes of Archbishop Peter Jatau and Prof. Ishaya Audu writing letters of recommendation for him. At the end of the process, he was shortlisted for the job, along with Prof. Yusufu Turaki and one other fellow.

As his things always go, the selection process was not an easy one. At the interview, Engr. Salifu scored 76%, Prof. Turaki scored 80%, and the other candidate 56%. The second stage was to select one person out of the three of them to present to the National Executive Council (NEC) of CAN for confirmation. There were five people on the interview panel, one person from each of the blocks of CAN. When the panel balloted, Engr. Salifu received the majority of the votes, Dr. Turaki came second, and the third candidate had no vote. News of this outcome brought enormous angst to Aso Rock. Machinery was set in place to scuttle Engr. Salifu's confirmation by the CAN NEC. The results were to be announced the next day, but the CAN leadership decided not to wait until the next day. Instead, a decision was reached to hold the NEC that very night. At the NEC gathering, one of the officers that came from Aso Rock abused the assembled bishops and Christian leaders, calling them corrupt. He alleged that Engr. Salifu, whom he labelled as a failed politician whose businesses had also all collapsed, had bribed them. This infuriated the Christian leaders, who there and then decided that they could not be teleguided by Aso Rock into choosing their leader, and therefore voted unanimously to confirm Engr. Salifu as their new General Secretary. That was the miracle the Lord performed to bring him into that office. Unbeknownst to those who were accusing him of having bribed the bishops was the fact that Engr. Salifu had borrowed the ₦3000 to fuel his car to attend the interview.

As a firm believer in the Bible as divine Scripture, he believes it when it says, *"Righteousness exalts a nation"* (Prov 14:34 ESV). By application, righteousness exalts families and individuals as well. The only thing is that there is a high price to pay in trying to live an upright life, but at the end of the day it pays to live uprightly. The most trying moment out of the many difficult challenges Engr. Salifu faced in his office as the General Secretary of CAN was when the sitting President of the Federation, Gen. Matthew Aremu Olusegun Obasanjo (Rtd.), a self-professed Christian, derisively referred to CAN publicly as being under his foot and called the then Plateau State Chapter Chairman of CAN (who was standing against the injustices that were being visited upon his community by

Muslim militants) an idiot. At that material time, the president of CAN, Archbishop Peter Akinola, also happened to have come from the same state as the Nigerian president. The church was furious. Engr. Salifu's phone was ringing non-stop. Calls were coming from all over the nation. Letters were pouring into the CAN national secretariat like a torrential tropical rainstorm. People were asking what they were doing about the insult to and assault on the church. Something had to be done. Engr. Salifu went to the CAN President, who also seemed to be infuriated at the incident, and said,

> The church has been insulted, and it is the Head of State who has insulted the church. So what do we do? We now have to choose between Christ and this man; if we spare him, the church is finished. If we challenge him, he would like to show you that he is the president.

"Well, we should wait," the president replied.

"We cannot wait," protested Engr. Salifu. "I am facing pressure from our constituents."

The president told him to go and assemble all the relevant information he could and return for a meeting with his principal at a scheduled date so they could work out an appropriate response.

The next few days were filled with a flurry of activities for Engr. Salifu. He was collecting the relevant data and consulting with the national assembly leadership, as well as legal experts. He received the shock of his life when he returned for his conference with the CAN President, only to be told that the man had jetted out of the country. Engr. Salifu could hardly believe his ears and exclaimed in disgust, *"What? In this crisis? He would not even inform his secretary?"* That was the loneliest moment he had ever felt in all of his life. At that instant, his theme words flooded his mind: *"Where duty calls or danger, be never wanting there."* He was fully persuaded that he needed to act. He then called and intimated the CAN Vice President (Bishop Mike Okonkwo of The Redeem Evangelical Mission [TREM], who lives in Lagos) of what had transpired, and the latter invited him to come down to Lagos. So he flew down to Lagos with the information he had already assembled. It was there that together they crafted a rejoinder to the president's assault on and insult to the church.

The impact of their publication was immediate. The church had a sense of dignity—that it had people who could fight for it. Aso Rock was livid with rage and boiled like a volcano on Mt. Vesuvius. Word reached Engr. Salifu that there was some desire to have him extirpated. This did not bother him much because he had acted according to his conscience. He remembered the words of Martin Luther, the reformer, who said, *"It is neither right nor safe to go against conscience,"* and those of Othman Dan Fodio, *"Conscience is an open wound, only truth can heal it."* Engr. Salifu could not go against his conscience, and his wounded conscience was healed with truthful action. He was now ready for whatever may come. His conviction was:

> *I will not be the first to suffer for standing for what is right. At age 65, I need not fear anything. As long as I know that this is what is right, that is where I would stand. When I have done my part, I will tell the Lord to do his part.*

And his part, the Lord did: his servant is still alive today. The saddest part of the whole saga is that throughout those challenging days, he received no support from the then CAN president. Indeed, upon his return from his overseas trip, the CAN president summoned Engr. Salifu and for two solid hours gave him the bashing of his life—raining unprintable abuses on him. And when the archbishop lost his bid for re-election, he blamed Engr. Salifu for it, forgetting the biblical truth that you reap what you sow.

In all of this, he was not perturbed. He was no newcomer to cross-bearing for the sake of Christ and his people. He remembered what he went through because of his work both as CAN Task Force Secretary and as the CAN youth president of the northern zone. Because of their effectiveness in making Christians conscious of the dangers they were facing from unprovoked religious attacks, he (along with other Christian leaders) incurred the wrath of the Babangida administration. So when the aborted coup of Major Gideon Orkar occurred in 1990, it furnished the junta with the opportunity to unleash vendetta against him and the other Christian leaders that were perceived as the junta's enemies. He was detained for fifty-three days along with Amb. Jolly Tanko Yusuf and others: Only God rescued them from the jaws of the lion. He also recalls that toward the end of the last millennium, he was planning to return to his native Kogi State. Then, out of the blue, the 2000 Kaduna riots exploded. He found himself once more at the centre of the storm. Security agents came after him again. They picked him up, and he underwent the drudgery of interrogation all over again. To his utter surprise, it was his fellow Christian brothers who had accused him to the President of stirring up trouble in Kaduna (as if he were the one who sent Muslims on the loose, killing Christians and burning their churches). As Engr. Salifu recalls, the charlatans told the President that he (Engr. Salifu) had,

> "brought Chief Odemegwu Ojukwu [the late Ikemba of Nnewi] to come and rouse up the place. There was nothing that they were not saying. Their recommendation was that I should be shot dead if the President wanted his government to have peace. Well, at the end of the day, God saw my innocence and spared my life once again."

LAST WORDS

Looking over Engr. Salifu's lifelong struggles for the rights of Christians in this country, there are a few things that have stood him in good stead that he would readily recommend for others. First is dependence on the Lord: early in his Christian life he had learned to lean on God and to draw his strength from the Lord through daily seasons of quietness in prayer and meditation upon God's word. Second, one has to come to terms with God's purpose for one's life. Engr. Salifu points out that God has prepared each of us for specific tasks. He explains,

> *God prepares his children severally for various assignments. Only God knows what he has prepared you for; I cannot fit into that task, and he knows what he had prepared for me. So, if you go into strange areas where he has not called you, you will only be messing up your life and confusing things for others. I remember a conversation I had with an ECWA pastor friend of mine, Rev. Gordian Okezie. He said to me, "You, God called you, but you refused to come and you ran away, but he is still following you." My reply to him was, "No, I didn't refuse. He sent me to the area where I am holding fort for him. I am sure that if I were somewhere other than where he sent me, it would have been a disaster. Even this place where I am now [referring to the CAN secretariat], where I am trying to maintain sanity, if you see within a week some of the things I see, you might run away." So each of us needs to have a sense of calling; know what God has for your life, and where he wants you to be at each point in your life.*

Besides the above, Engr. Salifu is most grateful to the Lord for the wife he gave him. She has been his friend, sister, counsel, cheerleader, encouragement, and huge source of comfort in his trials. He affirms the age-old saying that marriage can make or mar a person. He encourages all those who desire to be used of God to take care of their marriages: "If your home is in turmoil, you cannot do any exploits for God."

ADDENDUM

Engr. Salifu left the services of CAN six months prior to the expiration of his tenure as General Secretary. According to him, it was his considered opinion that the campaign strategies adopted during the last presidential election of CAN were out of tune with Christian character and also devoid of virtue and godliness. In his characteristic crusading manner, he stood up against such antics. This did not go down well with the victors of that process, and made having a cordial and harmonious working relationship within the new CAN leadership impossible. The acrimonious relationships resulted in spurious and unsubstantiated allegations being levelled against him, with the desire of forcing him out of office. Seeing the handwriting clearly on the wall, Engr. Salifu decided to resign his position, rather than stay back and fight for his rights. Such fights, he thought, would not be honouring to the Lord. While many had suggested for him to seek legal redress, he preferred to leave these things in the hands of the Great Judge of all. Engr. Salifu bowed out of CAN General Secretary's office on September 9, 2011.

CHAPTER FOURTEEN

A LIGHT FOR THE SEAS

ENGINEER JOHN YKEMA

INTRODUCTION

Being now in the sunset years of my life provides me the opportunity to reflect on how God has directed me from very early years up to the present. Most of the time I was not aware of God's sovereign direction—I thought the decision to pursue a certain course was my decision, but as I reflect on my life I now acknowledge that it was and still is all in God's sovereign hands.

This chapter is divided into four parts:

1. The first dealing with my childhood and teen years,
2. The second focusing on the decision years,
3. The third relating to the weaving together the threads of family, church and vocation, and
4. The fourth focusing on the biblical impact on life in the family, church and vocation.

This is a brief sketch of the struggles and joys of my life as God has directed it and as we acknowledge his sovereign control. My prayer is that it may be helpful to others as they search for God's leading, which is mostly by what we call ordinary means: parents, family, school, friends, church, and work.

CHILDHOOD AND TEEN YEARS

I was born in 1928, the last of eight children; the oldest had just turned eighteen. Shortly after my entering the world the Great Depression of 1929 came to the United States. This caused the collapse of my father's business and put the family in survival mode. We moved into the church parsonage, since my father could no longer pay the house rent and the church could no longer afford a full-time minister. My parents agreed to take care of the parsonage and the church and also agreed to house guest ministers. So from my early years church was a normal part of my life.

Because of the Depression two of my older sisters left our small town in Minnesota and found employment in Grand Rapids, Michigan. After a couple of years they convinced my parents that it would be wise to move the entire family to Michigan, as it would provide more opportunity for employment and would be a better environment for the rest of the family. Soon after we arrived, my father found work that paid a dollar per day. We became members of a local church that also operated a Christian school in the church basement. Being of school age I was enrolled in the Christian school. The school only went from grades one to eight, but there was a Christian high school not far away, and it was decided that I should continue my education in the Christian high school.

During these early school years, I was able to find work, which was a blessing, since work was not plentiful. As events leading to World War II began heating up, work became more available for all the members of the family. This lightened the financial burden on my parents. It is interesting that most of my work was under the direction of Christian men who insisted that the work be done correctly and that one should devote himself to the job for the full day. My older brother became a mechanic, and since I respected him I also spent much time in the garage enjoying the tools and the work he would allow me to do. This introduced me to machinery, which I found very fascinating. It also afforded me the opportunity to obtain employment that permitted me to operate several types of farm machinery while on summer break from school.

As the United States entered WW II, my two brothers left for the army and left me home with our parents. My father spent time with me talking about the war and the justice of the US government to declare war to fight the evils of Hitler and Japan. He also spoke of the evils of communism, which set up the state as god, and its opposition to Christianity—even though communist Russia was our ally in the conflict against Germany. It was also during these high school years that he shared with me his love for the Bible by discussing the sermons we heard on Sunday and by reading the Bible with the family at the evening meal. Through this he shared with me the importance of knowing God and especially his sovereignty, and of our commitment to follow Christ. He would stress that all of life, including our vocation, needed to be lived for God's glory out of thankfulness for God's saving grace. As I reflect on those years I realize they were instrumental in creating in me a desire to study the Bible. Seeing my interest in the Bible and my involvement in church youth activity, my mother encouraged me to pursue the ministry. However, my interests were more in the scientific fields, and furthermore I had great difficulty with foreign languages in high school.

So as I look back over those early years, I marvel at how the Lord formed my life and prepared me for the next phase. By my parents moving to Michigan I was privileged to be reared in a community where the Christian church, the Christian school, and hard work were the norm.

THE DECISION YEARS

When I enrolled in college I selected engineering as my major. I thought I was going to focus on mechanical engineering, but I soon developed a great friendship with a young man who had been in the Navy and was pursuing electrical engineering because of his military experience. His enthusiasm for electrical engineering stirred my interest, and so I switched to electrical engineering. That decision held, and I later narrowed the field to electrical power engineering, which dealt with the generation, distribution, and utilization of electrical power. The focus was not directed on the devices as much as it was to the total electrical power system. This was the first major decision I made, though I did not realize it at the time: it set the course for the profession to which I would devote my life.

Another very important decision occurred at the same time. I was re-introduced to Marilyn, a charming young lady whom I had known in high school but who at that time did not interest me, nor did I interest her. We renewed acquaintance one Sunday evening after a hymn sing (the church fathers in Grand Rapids, Michigan, arranged for Sunday evening hymn sings for young people). A friend of mine and I saw these two young ladies waiting for a bus and we offered them a ride which they accepted. Through this church fellowship, our relationship blossomed into courtship. Our courtship lasted three years. Since I was off at college, we communicated by mail and a few phone calls. Even with that limited communication, our love for each other waxed stronger as the years progressed, and we decided to marry about the time I was ready to graduate from college. This meant life from now on would be shared with my dear wife. She would be the focus of my attention as stated in the marriage vow. I now had an additional responsibility, namely to love and cherish my wife and to be head of the family that was to follow.

The third major decision was a spiritual one. I had been raised in the church and in a Christian home; I had never known a time when Jesus Christ was not my Redeemer and Lord, so I did not have a point of decision of becoming a Christian. Recognizing this as a common situation for its young people, the church we attended had its young people affirm before the congregation their faith in God and their commitment to live for him. I took this step, although there were certainly many areas in which I needed to grow and gain a greater understanding of what it meant to be a Christian. Over time I recognized, by God's grace, that the Bible was the source of wisdom. It is not surprising that this commitment was tested in several ways. One that stands out took place in a literature course at the University of Michigan. As we were studying Puritan literature, the professor ridiculed the theology of the Puritan writers. On one occasion he stated that no one any longer believed as the Puritans did, to which I raised my hand and stated that I did. This made him laugh, and he ridiculed me in front of the class and was sure I would wise up. I left class wondering whether I was correct or the professor was correct. By God's grace I chose to accept the Scriptures as the truth and not the "wisdom" of the professor.

So during those five college years (the fifth year being necessary for an engineering degree), I made three very important decisions that directed my life from that point forward. Obviously these decisions were challenged and tested, but they did not change.

WEAVING TOGETHER THE THREADS OF FAMILY, CHURCH, AND VOCATION

As mentioned, we were married as I finished my college undergraduate work, and so it was also time to find employment. I needed to share my decision about employment with my wife, as she was part of my life and we needed to be of one mind on this matter. Two opportunities were before us. One was for me to work as a civilian engineer for the U.S. Navy, and the other was to be drafted into the Army. I did not want to be drafted into the Army, and the Navy stated that it could guarantee to keep me from being drafted—other organizations and companies stated they would try but could offer no guarantee—so the decision was easy. However, it did mean that we would move from the Midwest (Grand Rapids, Michigan), where Marilyn had lived all her life in the same house in which she was born, to Washington, DC, seven hundred miles away, not an insignificant distance in the early 1950's.

We adjusted to Washington and started a family, which was another new but wonderful experience. We soon developed friends from a local Bible-teaching church. This was of great help to us. We became active in the church and I was elected to be a deacon. After three years we decided to move to Chicago so I could pursue further education. This was another new adventure, as our income was greatly reduced, even though I was a part-time teaching assistant. After concluding my studies for an advanced degree in engineering, we moved to Philadelphia and settled into a new job, with new friends and a new church.

The family continued to grow with the arrival of three more children—what a blessing! This also meant that we needed to provide for their education so we enrolled them in a Christian school. Not only were the children enrolled in the school, but as parents we became active in the operation of the school. After a few years I was elected to the Board of Directors, which took more of my time away from the growing family. It was a challenge to keep the family as my priority, because the school could take a lot of time. Being on the Board of Directors and being chairman for several years also had its challenges, since it was necessary to ensure that all teaching was done from a biblical perspective. The school had a great headmaster, but on occasion the contracts of certain teachers had to be terminated. In addition a dispute arose on the Board requiring that one member be asked to resign. When our youngest was in middle school, Marilyn became employed in the school office.

By God's grace the family grew physically and spiritually. I found it a great pleasure to teach my children the fundamentals of the Christian faith and the importance of choosing to live for Christ. This at times required discipline. One example of teaching was to provide them with an allowance and teach them to set aside at least 10% for the Lord. We enjoyed many wonderful summer vacations—camping and experiencing different places. Marilyn and I had decided that vacations were to be a family affair so we could enjoy each other by doing things together. We also moved to a larger property as the family needs grew. This is a very brief description of the family thread that was weaving along with the church and vocation.

Church was a vital part of our lives and we became active in a small Bible-teaching church. Since the church was small, I became active on the elders' board of the church, which again took time away from the family and challenged me to remember that the family was my first responsibility. We were diligent in Sunday attendance and in this way demonstrated our desire to worship the Lord, which was beneficial in the lives of our children. It was during this time (the early 1960's) that I was challenged to read the Bible each day and to read it from beginning to end, that is, from Genesis 1 through Revelation 22, and then repeat it again and again. This practice has been continued to the present day and has been a great blessing to me. As expected, I find the Bible more exciting each time

I read it.

    I was also called upon to teach Sunday school (a Bible class) to junior high and high school kids. This was beneficial as now I needed to study and gain a greater understanding so I could teach it to others. Through the church we became closely associated with a theological seminary, and I was elected to its Board of Trustees and served on the Board for 37 years. I had the privilege of serving as chairman for about 15 of those years. This also had its challenges, since Satan continues to roar like a lion and tempt professors to go astray by becoming wise in their own eyes. These challenges are painful but also cause one to grow spiritually. I found that it teaches humility and dependence on God to give proper understanding and direction so the correct action will be taken for His glory.

    As time went on the small church of which we were members began to deviate from what we regarded as biblical norms, which necessitated our severing ties. We aligned ourselves with another church, a rather large one. The Lord called me to serve on the elders' board of that church during some of its tumultuous days. It was necessary to ask pastors to leave because of inappropriate behaviour. These struggles are time consuming. At one point my dear wife had to remind me that my first responsibility was to the family and I needed to limit my involvement in church and school so I could devote more time to her and to the children. This was good and helpful advice. This is a brief sketch of the church life and how that thread pulled on the family thread and was intertwined with it. Family and church were very closely related and impacted each other.

    My vocation or professional career started with the U.S. Navy in Washington, D.C. As an electrical engineer I was assigned to the section that dealt with the electrical power system on warships. This was great experience since it taught me the necessity of making the electrical system very reliable and easy for the sailors to operate. As new ships were being constructed we searched for ways to improve the electrical power systems. Becoming more experienced in the work, I was also given opportunities to travel, which separated me from our young family but was a growing experience regarding my career. As I became acquainted with Navy ships' electrical power systems, I decided it was prudent to enroll in school for education in nuclear energy. However, during that study I decided I really would rather focus on the complete electrical power system and thus sought means to increase my knowledge of electrical power systems. So after three years I left the Navy and, as mentioned previously, enrolled in a school in Chicago to advance my understanding of electrical power systems and obtain an advanced degree. I had a teaching assistantship and taught the younger students in a laboratory setting. This was valuable experience for me.

When that course of study was completed I was offered employment in Philadelphia with a firm called I-T-E, which produced products for electrical power distribution systems used by public utilities, the commercial industry and the Navy. I started my career with ITE by performing power system studies with a specialized computer. This utilized my graduate school education on electrical power systems. The company rented time on a special computer (network analyzer) which I operated. As time went on, since digital computers were making inroads, it lessened the need for the specialized computer. After about four years the company decided to disband the specialized computer business. I was transferred to the circuit breaker section and began learning circuit breakers and the benefit they had for electrical power systems. They monitor the power system and if a fault (short circuit or overload) occurred, the circuit breaker would interrupt the circuit to isolate the fault and allow the rest of the system to continue to operate. As I applied myself diligently to the work, I was promoted to positions of greater responsibility and was soon faced with the responsibility of managing people. This involved communicating to them what was important to accomplishing the goals of our customers and goals of the company and how their work related to it. Our company president always oriented us toward providing high-quality products for customers. These were critical for enhancing our customers' efficiency and productivity in their high precision tasks.

As I entered the management ranks, I needed additional education in accounting and business management, so I enrolled in correspondence courses and audited courses at a local university. As the responsibilities increased, they involved labour negotiations and dealing with promotions and also discharging those who did not perform according to our standards. I was given responsibility to manage a division of the company which manufactured circuit breakers. This had profit and loss responsibility and it was a time I learned about running a business. The company was so successful that several larger corporations were competitively bidding to buy it, and it was eventually purchased.

This brought additional changes and reorganization that left me without a management position. However, the new company assigned me to staff functions, so I still had employment. While these events caused me stress, they also gave me time for reflection. I wondered if the upward movement in management had come to an end because I was a failure. But I realized that by God's grace I was now able to refocus my attention on electrical power systems, and I was soon moved to the part of the organization that focused on the electrical power systems of Navy ships. As we analyzed the needs of these systems in greater depth, the Lord gave me an idea for an invention that would improve the reliability and survivability of a ship's electrical power system. The Lord also gave me insight as to how to make circuit breakers perform better and keep the system operating. The faster a fault is isolated the less damage occurs, which is very helpful for the ship to perform its functions. The new device I invented interrupted the circuit 100 times faster that the traditional circuit breakers. The weapons and communication electrical loads on Navy ships are critical. The invention was patented and I was credited with the invention. With the help of others we expanded the device so it could perform multiple functions. It became known as the **Power Node Control Center** (PNCC), which simultaneously could operate as a transfer switch, frequency converter, transformer, circuit breaker, motor controller and power conditioner. The Power Node Control Center serves as an interface between the power system and the electrical loads. It supplies the loads the power they need and also protects the power system from load transitions. As the Power Node Control Center was coming into being, the Lord opened my eyes to make a very high speed circuit breaker which was needed for the power system to preserve the system and interrupt or isolate faults in less than 400 microseconds. Again, patents were sought and granted. In total with both of these products I am listed on 8 patents. Others who contributed to the inventions are also listed. The patents, as intellectual property, are owned by my employer since the invention and development was accomplished as an employee of the company. It is interesting that the inventions were accomplished when I was nearing or beyond the traditional retirement age. The Lord has called us to subdue the earth and so I keep working to advance the electrical systems on Navy ship and make better ships for our sailors.

  This gives a brief summary of my vocational experience and its interrelation with that of the family and of the church. Any one of these threads could easily have become dominant, but based on God's teaching I put them in the order of family, church, and vocation.

THE BIBLICAL IMPACT ON FAMILY, CHURCH, AND VOCATION

BASIC PRINCIPLES

The Bible is clear that the husband and father is the head of the family. There are plenty of Bible references to this God-given mandate. One Old Testament reference is Gen 18:19 and a New Testament reference is Eph 5:21–6:8, but there are many more, such as Numbers 30. This means the father must lead the family by life and words to show that God is number one. My dear wife was a great help and taught the children that they were members of the JOY club (Jesus first, Others second, Yourself last). They had no choice if they were to live according to God's Word. The father must lead the family in worship and direct them that all tasks are to be done well, since doing all work well is part of God's command and brings praise to his name. We instructed our children to read God's Holy Word daily and to read it from cover to cover. Of course, this had to be demonstrated to them by our own actions – I read the Bible each morning and prayed for God's leading. I was blessed to have a good marriage and a good family, but I now realize more than before that the family is crucial to a good life and a good society. The destruction of the family means the destruction of society.

The church is a vital part of life, for it is the avenue for the public worship of God. Going to public worship is clearly taught in the Bible. The OT is replete with God's demands of public worship, especially from Exodus through Deuteronomy and the Psalms. The NT also exhorts the new covenant community never to neglect corporate worship; this is most clearly expressed in Hebrews 10:25. Worshiping in public as a family is beneficial to the rearing of children and the unity of the family. The children are taught to worship God regularly and be involved in activity with others who worship God. Worship of God must occupy the number one place in all of life; the family, the church, and the vocation must revolve around service to God. So personal Bible reading and prayer, good family worship, and attending a good Bible-teaching church are vital pillars of a good and productive life.

God created man so that he could give him dominion over his created world (Psalm 8:6). He then charged man to multiply, replenish, and subdue the earth (Genesis 1:26–28). In Genesis 2:5, God stated that certain of his creational activities were not yet done because man had not yet been created and man was to work the creation. In Genesis 2:15, God assigned man to work, tend, and keep the garden in which God had placed him. This was a perfect garden, and yet man was to tend and keep it. Then God gave him a helper to assist him in fulfilling this command. The task became burdensome because of man's rebellion, but it was not revoked. Genesis 3:17–19 states that the work was to be done but it would now be difficult. In Genesis 8:17–19 and Genesis 9:1, 7, God reiterates the same mandate to mankind after the flood. Psalm 19 states that the universe that God created brings praise to his name. So it is obvious that our work, our vocation, should be done for the purpose of bringing glory to God's name. 1 Corinthians 10:31 states that whether we eat or drink or whatever we do, do all to the glory of God. The calling of a Christian is to make the part of the garden in which God has called him to be beautiful so that it brings praise to God's name.

VOCATIONAL EXPERIENCE: OBSERVATIONS

Following are some observations and interactions I have experienced as I attempted to be faithful in my vocation. It is a challenge to serve as leaven—bringing godly influence—in the workplace, since each of us is being constantly tempted to serve the god of the world rather than the God who created the world. My observation is that there are many temptations to divert attention away from the calling of your vocation, but here are just a few:

1. *Elevation of making money as the chief end of business rather than service to the customer*: Making money is not wrong, but it should not be the driving force behind being in business. This temptation is evident at all levels of the business, from the corporate officer to the man on the work bench.

2. *Distortion of the truth for the supposed benefit of the business or the individual*: Producers are tempted to lie to customers regarding their ability to deliver a product when they know that it is not possible. I have fought this battle many times—won some and lost some.

3. *Dissipation*: Good behavior in the workplace is a constant challenge, and the temptation to use foul language is especially strong. At one point in my career I was labelled Deacon John due to my clean speech. On another occasion some individuals made a wager, unbeknown to me, that they could get me so upset that I would use foul language. Thankfully they lost.

4. *Slothful behaviour*: We need to be diligent workers who work hard even when the boss is not watching. We cannot take longer-than-allowed lunch breaks or come in late for work. Diligence is part of our testimony, and I can testify it is noticed.

5. *Self-aggrandizement*: Do not fret if others

get the praise for jobs well done or for new and good ideas. Many times I have seen the truth surface later. The Lord knows what you have done and he is the big Boss.

VOCATIONAL EXPERIENCE—THE CALL OF WITNESS-BEARING IN THE WORKPLACE

Those of us called to be witnesses in the market square need to live our lives so they impact the work place with biblical thoughts, actions, and ethics. God uses, in most instances, the ordinary to provide opportunities to speak of the hope within us. He tells us to always be ready to give a defence to everyone who asks us the reason for the hope that is in us, with all meekness and fear (1 Peter 2:25).

1. Language is a vital part of our behaviour. Swearing and foul language is all too common in the work place, as I previously mentioned. Avoiding the use of foul language is a witness. It is necessary to be on your guard and not copy the worldly pattern. I have had occasion in one-on-one conversations to challenge people regarding their language.

2. It is natural for people to ask you on Monday morning how your weekend was. This gives you the opportunity to share with them that you went to church and how great it was. At times this has opened the door for further conversation.

3. Early in my career I was asked by some of my fellow workers to join them on Saturday morning to play golf. After considering it, I turned down the request and related to them that I considered it more important to stay at home with my

wife and children.

4. When fellow workers are ill or in distress, you have the opportunity to tell them you will pray for them. This also at times opens up conversation about prayer and to whom we pray. This is a great time to share the hope that lies within us.
5. When you express gratitude to your fellow workers, they will notice and at times give you the opportunity to explain that the reason why we should be thankful in all things is because God is sovereign.
6. As I have reached retirement age, I have been asked why I have not retired to "enjoy life." Telling them I have not found retirement in the Bible has provided many opportunities to share with them why I still work and the real purpose for work.

VOCATIONAL EXPERIENCE— FUNDAMENTALS OF GOOD BUSINESS

During my years in business I have gathered that there are six fundamentals of good business:

1. The business must operate with honesty and integrity.
2. The business must produce a product or service that is of benefit to the customer.
3. The product or service must be of very good quality.
4. The business needs always to invest to find better ways to serve the customer.
5. The business needs to operate efficiently—this is measured by the profit.
6. To operate efficiently requires effectiveness, that its operations must be anchored

in hard work and ingenuity.

CONCLUSION

A Christian in the workplace must keep his emphasis on the command that God gave man in the beginning: to tend and care for his creation. It is an exciting task even though since the Fall thorns and thistles hinder the work or at least make it more challenging.

As Christians, we are sinful and therefore prone to accept the ways of the world, so we need constantly to be on our guard. We need to be in regular communication with our God to keep our way straight and place him first. Daily Bible reading and prayer are essential to remain focused on what God calls us to do. God did not say in vain to meditate on his Word day and night and to pray without ceasing. God's promise is that it is profitable (1 Timothy 3:16-17). We need to remind ourselves why God created man, namely, to have dominion over the wonderful world he created. Let us tend and keep it so that it brings glory to him.

POSTSCRIPT

UNIFYING THEMES AND MOTIFS

Having read through the life stories of these godly men from both sides of the Atlantic, the keen reader would see that certain themes and motifs run through all their stories, connecting them like a web. I will here draw attention to some of these themes. First and foremost, for obvious reasons, is the important role all these men's families played in moulding their lives. Almost all of them point to the significant role both of their parents played in how their lives turned out. All this buttresses the age-old saying that families are the building blocks of society: when we build strong families, we will also invariably be building strong societies. The reverse is no doubt also true: the doleful state of society reflects the forlorn condition of our families. It goes without saying, then, that if we desire a better society, we must labour to build strong families.

Second, as important as it is for the family to be strong, it is even more important that parents in a family be believers who strive to live their lives in accordance with the will of God. As seen here, those of these men who had believing parents and who also followed in the footsteps of their parents had fewer struggles in later life than they otherwise would have had. Those without Christian parents are more likely to lack the solid foundation for a stable life. This in turn would make room for them to make many mistakes that lead to disastrous ends, or at least wasted years. This is not to say that those without Christian parents have no chance for a good start in life. It only brings out the necessity for Christian parents to be measured and purposeful in their efforts to pass on their faith to their children. We live in times in which many young people look down on their Christian heritage, thinking that the ways of their parents are antiquated or dated and unfit for the (post)modern world. It is always regrettable when children despise godly parental upbringing to their own hurt. In the contemporary rat-race for the good things of life, parents also tend to be less than deliberate in their effort to pass down their faith to the next generation. This is a clear neglect of their biblical mandate: *"Did he not make them one, with a portion of the Spirit in their union? And what was the one God seeking? Godly offspring..."* (Mal 2:15 ESV). We must also say with the psalmist,

> *[T]hings that we have heard and known, that our fathers have told us. We will not hide them from their children, but tell to the coming generation the glorious deeds of the LORD, and his might, and the wonders that he has done. He established a testimony in Jacob and appointed a law in Israel, which he commanded our fathers to teach to their children, that the next generation might know them, the children yet unborn, and arise and tell them to their children, so that they should set their hope in God and not forget the works of God, but keep his commandments* (Psalm 78:3–7 ESV; cf. Deuteronomy 4:9; 6:6–9; Joel 1:3).

Third, another major godly influence of Christian parenting that we see in the lives of these men is the significant place the family altar occupied in most of their families. Several of them learned from their own parents to begin the day by seeking to discern the will of God through reading and meditation on his word, and committing their day into God's sovereign and loving hands. When they became men with their own families, they continued the same tradition. It is my sincere hope that in the spirit of Psalm 78, their own children will pass on the same legacy to their children and their children's children. As a man becomes a grandfather, he needs to draw closer to his children's families both to mentor his own children in parenting and also to support them in their parenting efforts and affirm the faith they seek to pass on to their children. There may even be children who, having grown up, may have reneged on the faith. The father may, therefore, be the appropriate (and sometimes, only) family link of faith to his grandchildren, in those circumstances. Grandparenthood must be seen in different light than just being an old man who has nothing to do and for whom no one cares, who therefore has all the time to fiddle around with children. Those who have reached that revered position need to see it as a golden opportunity the Lord has granted them, in their twilight years, to continue passing on the legacy of faith to succeeding generations, as Psalm 78 outlines.

Fourth, another intriguing aspect of this study is that all of the people represented in the book came to faith at early stages in their lives. It is well known that nearly 55% of people who are Christians come to faith before they reached 20 years of age, while nearly 90% of professing Christians accepted Christ before the age of 30. This means that the likelihood of a person over thirty years of age becoming a Christian is slim, and so parents have a huge burden to introduce their children to the gospel when they are still young and impressionable. It similarly means that Christians ought to take outreach to children and youth seriously. A number of these men testified to the impact on their lives of such ministries that reach out to youth as the FCS, SU, NIFES, and Inter-Varsity.

Unfortunately, as churches have proliferated and the founders and presidents of such ministries have sought the absolute allegiance of their members, the support these student ministries ought to have received from those who benefited from them has continued to fizzle out. Deliberate efforts must be made to renew, strengthen, and re-position these ministries for a greater impact in the twenty-first century.

Fifth, another major building block in the lives of all of these men is Christian education during their school days; almost all of these men had some form of Christian education, no matter how brief. A truly Christian mindset begins with the understanding that everything in our universe derives from and is sustained by God, and exists for his glory. John L. De Beer contends,

> The Christian gains his fullest satisfaction and attains his fullest realization by yielding himself wholeheartedly to the fulfillment of God's purpose for him. ... The function of Christian education is to enable the learner to know more adequately God Himself, God's purposes for man, the learner's own capacities and limitations, and the means by which these capacities may be utilized most fully toward the implementation of God's plan and for the glorification of His name.[8]

Put differently, while the worldly philosophy of education is anthropocentric (i.e., humanistic), a Christian education philosophy is Christo-telic (i.e., having Christ and his glory as its orientation and chief end). It therefore orients the learner toward understanding all of life as calling, which is only fulfilled if everything in life is done as unto the Lord and for his glory. This is what has governed the lives of the men whose stories are contained in this volume. In view of this, there is an urgent need to re-evaluate much that easily passes these days as Christian schools, to see if these schools really reflect an understanding of the heart of a truly Christian education, and to re-orient them towards this noble goal. More often than not one gets the feeling that amongst many a Christian school, the business side of school management trumps the missional goal. Seeing the impact of Christian education on the lives of these men, creating schools that are truly Christian, not just in name but also in their curricula, vision, and mission, should becomes a priority for the contemporary church. Quality Christian education should also not be an exclusive preserve of the wealthy, but should be accessible to even children of poor Christians and non-Christians as well.

Sixth is the impact of godly people placed by God in the paths of these men in their younger days. This point challenges us to read and re-read Jesus' parable of the Good Samaritan (Luke 10:29–36) until we come to grips with what good neighbourliness is. When God saved us, he left us here for a purpose, part of which includes being beacons of light—pointing people to the saving grace that is found in Christ Jesus. We need to step back from time to time to reflect and consider our lives, so that they may not be overrun by weeds, thorns, and thistles (i.e., the cares, riches, and pleasures of this life), and thereby remain fruitless (Luke 8:5–15). It is easy for us to become so wrapped up in our selfish desires and pursuits that we simply fail to touch others with the kindness that God's grace brings, and thereby failing to realize the very purpose of our existence.

Seventh, and closely related to the last point, is the need for us to consciously set out to live in service to others. We need to grow in our discipleship so that we will realize that our lives will attain greater significance when we begin to live for causes greater than ourselves. Our lives are petty and full of rivalry, bickering and in-fighting when all we seek is self-gratification. God has endowed each person with the capacity to serve others. We waste God's resources when we want to channel all of them in service to "Me, Myself and I." We approach greater fulfilment of our potential to the degree we give ourselves in service for the good of others. This is the story that we have read in this book in varied forms again and again.

Eighth, our world is growing ever more corrupt and depraved—much more than the the sixteenth century reformers would have conceived when they spoke of the total depravity of humanity. In times like these, a deep personal walk with God becomes a prerequisite for living above the massive decay in society. This has been the testimony of all of these men. Each of them consciously sought to maintain a personal devotional time of reading and meditation on God's word, which is God's agent for the cleansing of human lives (cf. John 15:3; 17:17; 1 Peter 1:22). It is in this light that the saintly nineteenth-century American evangelist and revivalist Dwight L. Moody said, *"The Bible will keep you from sin, or sin will keep you from the Bible."* This is true in all ages: those who desire to live in accordance with the divine purpose for God's glory must resort again and again to his revealed word to understand his will. Such daily meditation will naturally lead to times of prayer. This is the vital communication link that does exist between God and his children. Only those who strive to maintain this critical fellowship before the throne of grace are able to obtain mercy in the hour of need, as these testimonies have shown.

Nineth, undergirding all these must lie a personal passion to live a life worthy of the Lord. No amount of instruction, sermons heard, or even reading of the Bible can affect anyone's life if that person's soul has no desire to live with integrity. Again looking at these stories, we see that each of these saints of God has had a clear vision of what their lives are meant for—God's glory and that alone—and for that reason they each have had a passionate desire to be found pleasing in God's sight. We cannot live for self and God at the same time. We must daily die with Christ, so that Christ might live his life in us (Galatians 2:20; cf. John 3:30; Romans 6:4–14). Once we have taken our stand with Christ, we must make it known. We will not find this easy because the enemy will fight us: People (perhaps, even our peers) will mock us, persecute us, and deny us our rights. But when we stand steadfast and stay the course of our faith, we will prevail eventually, because in Christ we are more than conquerors (Romans 8:35–39).

Tenth, it is interesting and instructive that all of these men, though busy career men, never bought into the dichotomy between the sacred and the secular that is so prevalent among Christians nowadays. Such modernist dualism is alien to biblical faith and historic Christianity. This accounts to a large degree for the declining ethical standards in society, because this bifurcation of life (the separation of the sacred from the secular) divorces what happens on Sunday mornings from what happens Monday to Friday in the office. The lives of the brothers whose stories are contained in this volume across the board have been and will ever continue to be stars that shine to God's glory and for the edification of his church because they espoused a single ethic, whether in church, at home, or in the office. Since our lives are supposed to bring God glory and satisfaction, then, where we are becomes immaterial. Our lives, who we are, what we have, and all that is ours are supposed to be given over to God: we are to be living sacrifices (Rom 12:1). When this is done, we will be able to weather any storm, knowing that God will not abandon nor forsake us, his heritage (Psalm 94:14; Isaiah 49:15; Hebrews 13:5).

Finally, the power of a personal life vision can be seen to be the moving force behind the stories of all these men. Vision is to a life what the eyes are to a physical body. This is why the Bible says, *"Where there is no vision, the people perish"* (Prov 29:18 KJV). T. E. Lawrence, of Lawrence of Arabia fame, made a very poignant statement on vision:

> *All men dream, but not equally. Those who dream by night in the dusty recesses of their mind wake in the day to find it was vanity: but the dreamers of the day are dangerous men, for they may act their dreams with open eyes, to make it possible. This I did.*

Those who rise and make their life count in their generations and in eternity must be people who are not dreamers of the night, who dream only in the dark recesses of their minds to wake to discover it was only a dream. They must be those who are dreamers of the day, who, like Lawrence, or like Martin Luther King, Jr., act out their dreams. To this group of dreamers belong all of the men whose stories you have in your hand, like Engr. Rumberger, who has made the V-22 Osprey (a plane that takes off and lands as helicopter but flies with the speed of a turboprop aircraft) possible; or Dr. Dunn, who has given life to countless young children through organ transplantation; or Hon. Justice Ogebe, whose landmark judgments helped steer Nigeria's nascent democracy off the path of dictatorship or anarchy; or Gen. Agwai, who defied all odds, including being falsely accused of coup plotting, to rise to the pinnacle of the Nigerian military and beyond; or Dr. Kolade, whose wise decision helped his corporation avert a dangerous World Bank debt trap; or any of the other men with their unique accomplishments. These men were not born great; they rose to greatness through visionary living, coupled with hard work, dedication to duty, integrity, a holistic approach to life that views all of life as service to God and humanity, and the blessings of the God, whom they serve with all their hearts. They are just examples amongst the crowd of witnesses that God has given us, to tell us that

we too could do great things for him if we attempt great things for him.

Will you dare to stand up to be counted among the jewels of God in your generation?

ENDNOTES

1 SIM at its inception stood for **Sudan Interior Mission** due to its initial focus on the interior of sub-Saharan Africa. However, because of its contemporary intercontinental reach, the name has been changed to **Serving In Mission**.

2 These are sentences in Nigerian Pigin English, which is a common market language in much of Nigeria, but it is most common in southern Nigeria; and the most interesting dialects of it are in the Niger Delta. The first quoted speech here means something like, "Boss, when these folks give you kola nut [a bitter fruit that is chewed upon during fraternizing or socializing occasions], do not eat it. It has been poisoned." The second meanings: "Besides, the palm wine [juice extracted from the palm tree that has been fermented into an alcoholic beverage] they will serve you, do not drink it for your own good."

3 By 1986 the exchange rate was ₦2.02 for $1 (cf. http://cenbank.org/rates/ExchRateByCurrency.asp?CurrencyType=$USD accessed March 18, 2012). This means that the dollar value of the ₦11 million in dollars at the time was $5.45 million. Without even accounting for inflation, the amount of money he left for his successor at today's exchange rate of about ₦158 to $1 is ₦860.4 million.

4 In most of West Africa, beginning from the end of November to March, a northeasterly trade wind, flowing from the high pressure centre north of Africa pass over the Sahara Desert toward the low pressure centre in Gulf of Guinea, packs large amounts of dust particles in its wake. This produces hazy atmospheric conditions, low visibility, low humidity, lower temperatures, and a lot of dust. This is what is called the Harmattan season.

5 The Dutch Reformed Church Mission (DRCM) was the mission, within the Sudan United Mission (SUM),

that founded the predominant Protestant denomination in Tivland, the NKST Church. In the pre-independence and early post-independence days, the churches and schools established by this mission agency were called DRCM churches or schools, just like the Anglican churches and schools were called CMS, and those of the Roman Catholic institutions were called RCM. The DRCM missionaries, who first laboured amongst the Tiv people, beginning from 1911, came from South Africa. It was the rise of an indigenous government in the run up to independence that led to the expulsion of the South African missionaries on account of the apartheid system in their home country. They were subsequently replaced by the Christian Reformed Church Mission (CRCM) of the United States of America.

6 The cleanup of the banking sector to avert a total melt down of the sector and of course the economy as well, which was done by Dr. Sanisu (the CBN governor), that Engr. Izuogu spoke of took place between 2010 and 2011.

7 HRH. Engr. Dr. Harrison Bungon (FNSE) at the time was also a lecturer at the Kaduna Polytechnic. He presently is the Agwatyap (Paramount Chief) of the Kafaf people in Kaduna state.

8 John L. De Beer, "An Overview of Christian Education," in *Toward a Philosophy of Christian Education* by John De Beer and Cornelius Jaarsma (Grand Rapids: National Union of Christian Schools, 1953; reproduced in electronic form by Calvin College, 2000; available at: http://www.calvin.edu/academic/education/news/publications/monoweb/debeer~1.htm, accessed December 21, 2012).

CONTACT THE AUTHOR

tushima.cephas@gmail.com

www.ingramcontent.com/pod-product-compliance
Lightning Source LLC
LaVergne TN
LVHW051543070426
835507LV00021B/2387